British English

Carolyn Wright with
Caroline Nixon &
Michael Tomlinson

Shaftesbury Road, Cambridge CB2 8EA, United Kingdom

One Liberty Plaza, 20th Floor, New York, NY 10006, USA

477 Williamstown Road, Port Melbourne, VIC 3207, Australia

314–321, 3rd Floor, Plot 3, Splendor Forum, Jasola District Centre, New Delhi – 110025, India

103 Penang Road, #05–06/07, Visioncrest Commercial, Singapore 238467

Cambridge University Press & Assessment is a department of the University of Cambridge.

We share the University's mission to contribute to society through the pursuit of education, learning and research at the highest international levels of excellence.

www.cambridge.org
Information on this title: www.cambridge.org/9781108895552

First published 2008
Second edition 2014
Updated second edition 2017
Third edition 2023

20 19 18 17 16 15 14 13 12 11 10 9 8 7 6 5 4 3 2 1

Printed in Malaysia by Vivar Printing

A catalogue record for this publication is available from the British Library

ISBN 978-1-108-89555-2 Teacher's Book with Digital Pack

Additional resources for this publication at www.cambridge.org/kidsboxng

Contents

Language summary

	Key vocabulary	Key language	Sounds and spelling
Hello! page 4	**Character names:** *Simon, Stella, Suzy* **Numbers:** *1–20* **Colours:** *black, blue, green, grey, orange, pink, purple, red, white, yellow* **Toys:** *bike, camera, computer, doll, game, helicopter, kite, lorry, monster, train*	**Introductions:** *Hello. What's your name? My name's … How old are you? I'm … What's … called? She's/He's called …* **Present continuous** (not with future reference) **Prepositions of place:** *next to, on, in front of, under, between, behind*	*i–e* – ride *y* – fly *ay* – play *ai* – paint *ei* – eight *a–e* – late *ey* – grey
1 Family matters page 10	**Family:** *aunt, uncle, daughter, son, granddaughter, grandson, parents, grandparents* **Appearance:** *beard, clever, curly hair, fair hair, straight hair, moustache, naughty, quiet*	Possessive 's **Present continuous** (not with future reference) **Present simple:** *Yes, I do. / No, I don't.* **Verb + infinitive:** *want to do* **Verb + *ing*:** *like / love / enjoy doing*	*er* – dinner
Maths: how big is your family? page 16			
2 Home sweet home page 18	**Numbers:** *21–100* **The home:** *balcony, basement, downstairs, flat, lift, stairs, upstairs* **The world around us:** *city, town, village*	*What's your address? It's …* **Present continuous** (not with future reference) **Present simple:** *need/needs, have got / has got*	*ee* – sheep
Geography: how are our homes unique? page 24			
Review: units 1 and 2 page 26			
3 A day in the life page 28	**Daily routines:** *catch the bus, do homework, get dressed, get undressed, get up, go to bed/ school, have a shower, put on, seven o'clock, take off, wake up, wash* **Days of the week:** *Monday, Tuesday, Wednesday, Thursday, Friday, Saturday, Sunday*	**Present simple** (for routines) *How often …? I always …* **Adverbs:** *always, sometimes, never, every day*	/iz/ – dances /z/ – plays /s/ – eats
Science: what do astronauts do in space? page 34			
4 In the city page 36	**Places:** *bank, bus station, car park, cinema, hospital, library, market, shop, sports centre, supermarket, swimming pool*	*Where's the …? It's …* **Prepositions of place:** *opposite* Infinitive of purpose *Must* for obligation	*ere* – where *ear* – bear *air* – hair
Geography: where do we go shopping? page 42			
Review: units 3 and 4 page 44			

Welcome to Kid's Box New Generation

Kid's Box New Generation is a new and enhanced edition of the trusted course that has inspired thousands of teachers and a whole generation of pupils all over the world to teach and learn English.

Kid's Box New Generation represents the ideal combination of contemporary, research-backed methodology with learner-friendly content. Our course characters will take your pupils on an English-language learning journey, with lessons on values, such as giving and sharing and helping our world, and CLIL lessons about maths, science, geography, and music, all the while developing the language they need to succeed in the Cambridge English Qualifications for young learners.

Kid's Box New Generation takes a blended approach to learning English and includes a wide variety of print and digital components:

- The **Pupil's Book with eBook** features all the Class Videos and embedded Class Audio.
- The **Activity Book with Digital Pack** includes Practice Extra, our suite of online practice activities, as well as the Class Audio and a downloadable Learner Resource Bank.
- The **Teacher's Book with Digital Pack** includes a host of resources, such as Presentation Plus, Test Generator and an extensive Teacher Resource Bank.

The digital components are delivered through our new-generation learning environment Cambridge One.

Hi! We're Stella, Simon, Meera and Lenny. We'll take your pupils on a learning journey!

I'm Lock. Your pupils will practise sounds and spelling with me!

The Kid's Box World sections will help your pupils with maths, science, technology, geography, sport, music and art!

We're Lock and Key. Through our stories, your pupils will have fun and learn.

We asked teachers from around the world to tell us what they like about *Kid's Box*, as well as what they would like to see in *Kid's Box New Generation*.

Course characters and design

"From the start, pupils seem to identify with the characters and the topics."

So, Stella and Simon, Suzy and their family and friends are back again to continue inspiring learners. Although the same course characters are back, the artwork and page design have been completely updated.

Resources

"What I would highlight most about Kid's Box is the quality of the material that complements the book: the audio, flashcards and Activity Book."

There are now even more resources available. See pages 10 and 11 of this introduction for a full overview of the course components.

Language focus

"The grammar topics are exactly what we want to teach our pupils."

The language focus of each lesson is clearly indicated both in the Teacher's Book, as it was previously, and now at the bottom of each page in the Pupil's Book.

Enhanced Teacher's Book

From the outset, our aim has been to provide even more support to teachers through the new and enhanced Teacher's Book. This ranges from how to structure a lesson to different ways of providing extra support and challenges to pupils. Each page clearly specifies the objectives, target language and materials needed. Digital Classroom components and Extra Resources for each lesson are indicated at the end of each page.

Audio and video

"The large number of audio recordings that the book offers seems to me a very useful resource that multiplies the percentage of what learners will absorb."

Kid's Box New Generation continues to offer lots of audio material, as well as even more video content, including videos for all *Sounds and spelling* and CLIL pages. We have also recreated the story and song animations in a contemporary style.

Unit walkthrough

Songs

Practise and extend the unit vocabulary and language. Song animations and karaoke versions are available in Presentation Plus and Practice Extra on Cambridge One.

Presentation

Introduces the unit topic and the key vocabulary through the Star family and friends.

Key language

Presented in a fun and engaging way.

2 Home sweet home

upstairs
stairs
downstairs
basement
A house in the village
lift
balcony
A flat in the town

1 Look, think and answer. Listen and check.
1 What buildings can you see?
2 What's in the room under the house?
3 Where's the flat?
4 Has the flat got a garden?

2 Describe your house or flat. Then write.
My house is in the village. It has got a kitchen downstairs.
My house is in the city. It has got a balcony.

3 Listen and say the letter.
A basement
Letter d.

18 Vocabulary: the home and the world around us

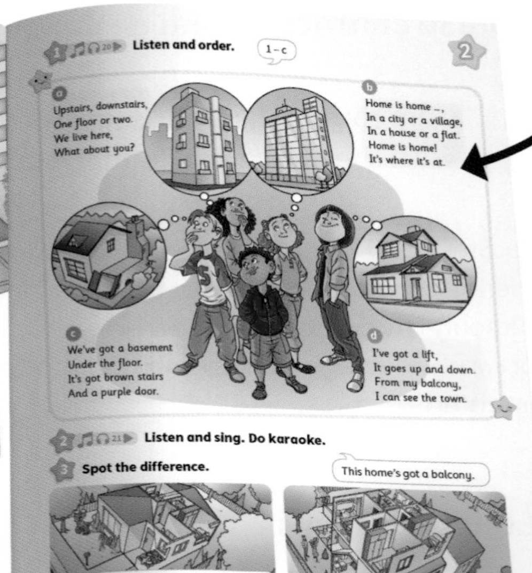
1 Listen and order. 1 – c

a
Upstairs, downstairs,
One floor or two.
We live here,
What about you?

b
Home is home ...,
In a city or a village,
In a house or a flat.
Home is home!
It's where it's at.

c
We've got a basement
Under the floor.
It's got brown stairs
And a purple door.

d
I've got a lift,
It goes up and down.
From my balcony,
I can see the town.

2 Listen and sing. Do karaoke.

3 Spot the difference.
This home's got a balcony.
This home hasn't got a balcony.

Language: have got / has got 19

Chant

Encourages pupils to listen, point to and repeat the vocabulary in context.

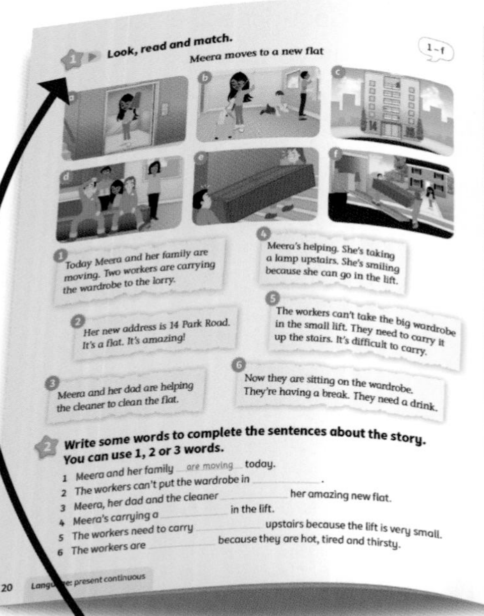
1 Look, read and match. 1 – f
Meera moves to a new flat

1 Today Meera and her family are moving. Two workers are carrying the wardrobe to the lorry.
2 Her new address is 14 Park Road. It's a flat. It's amazing!
3 Meera and her dad are helping the cleaner to clean the flat.
4 Meera's helping. She's taking a lamp upstairs. She's smiling because she can go in the lift.
5 The workers can't take the big wardrobe in the small lift. They need to carry it up the stairs. It's difficult to carry.
6 Now they are sitting on the wardrobe. They're having a break. They need a drink.

2 Write some words to complete the sentences about the story. You can use 1, 2 or 3 words.
1 Meera and her family are moving today.
2 The workers can't put the wardrobe in ______.
3 Meera, her dad and the cleaner ______ her amazing new flat.
4 Meera's carrying a ______ in the lift.
5 The workers need to carry ______ upstairs because the lift is very small.
6 The workers are ______ because they are hot, tired and thirsty.

20 Language: present continuous

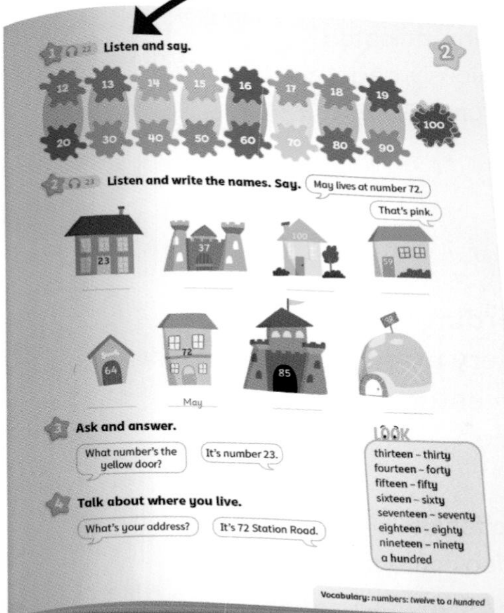
1 Listen and say.
12 13 14 15 16 17 18 19
20 30 40 50 60 70 80 90 100

2 Listen and write the names. Say.
May lives at number 72.
That's pink.
May

3 Ask and answer.
What number's the yellow door?
It's number 23.

4 Talk about where you live.
What's your address?
It's 72 Station Road.

LOOK
thirteen – thirty
fourteen – forty
fifteen – fifty
sixteen – sixty
seventeen – seventy
eighteen – eighty
nineteen – ninety
a hundred

Vocabulary: numbers: twelve to a hundred 21

Values

The course characters explore the Cambridge Life Competencies Framework and universal values.

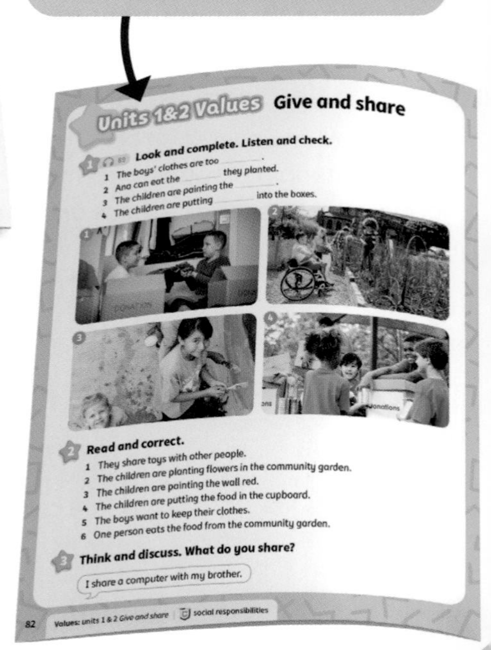
Units 1&2 Values Give and share

1 Look and complete. Listen and check.
1 The boys' clothes are too ______.
2 Ana can eat the ______ they planted.
3 The children are painting the ______.
4 The children are putting ______ into the boxes.

2 Read and correct.
1 They share toys with other people.
2 The children are planting flowers in the community garden.
3 The children are painting the wall red.
4 The children are putting the food in the cupboard.
5 The boys want to keep their clothes.
6 One person eats the food from the community garden.

3 Think and discuss. What do you share?
I share a computer with my brother.

82 Values: units 1 & 2 Give and share | social responsibilities

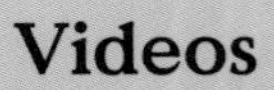

Videos

A wide variety of content presents and reviews key vocabulary and language. This page includes an introductory video with the Star family and friends.

Sounds and spelling

Pupils practise pronunciation and spelling with Lock in a step-by-step video lesson.

Kid's Box World

Learn about maths, art, science, geography and sports with new audio and video.

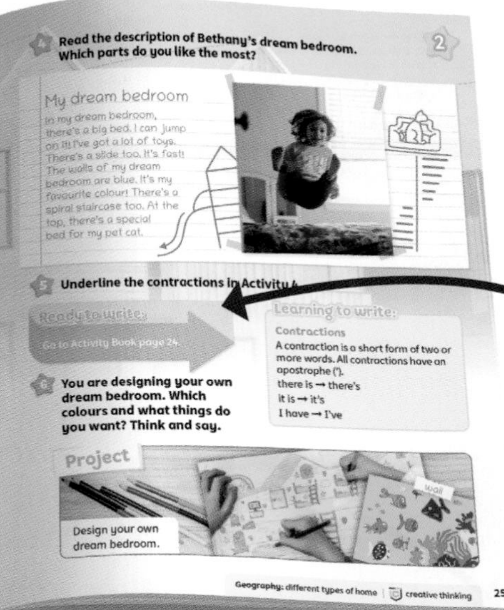

Story

New video animations recycle and reinforce the vocabulary and language from the unit.

Ready to write

Guides pupils through the writing process and helps them to write a variety of text types.

Review

Revise the language and vocabulary covered in the preceding two units through Cambridge exam-style questions and games.

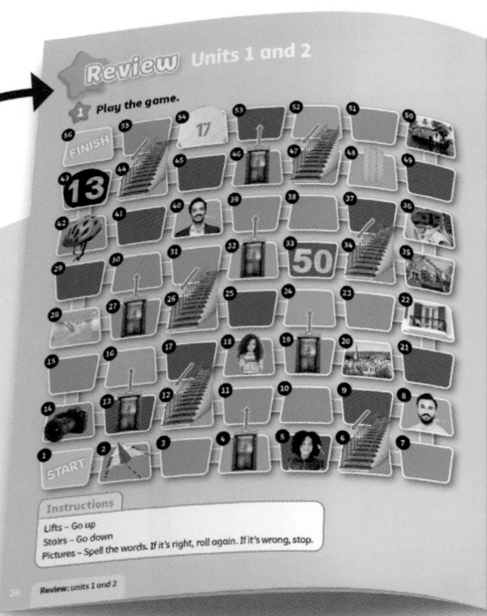

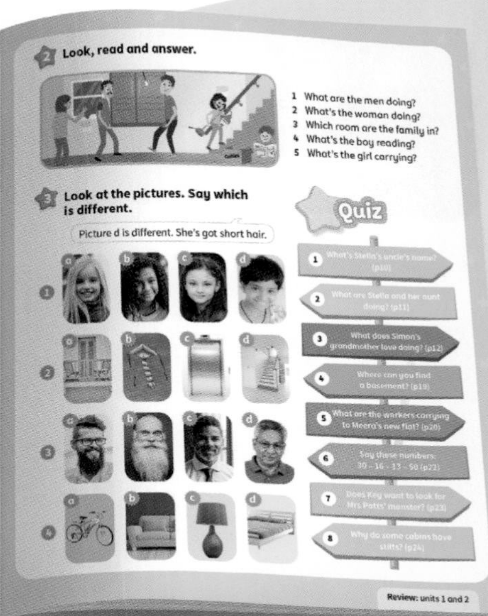

Kid's Box New Generation for Learners

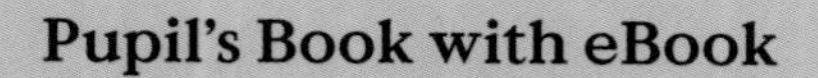

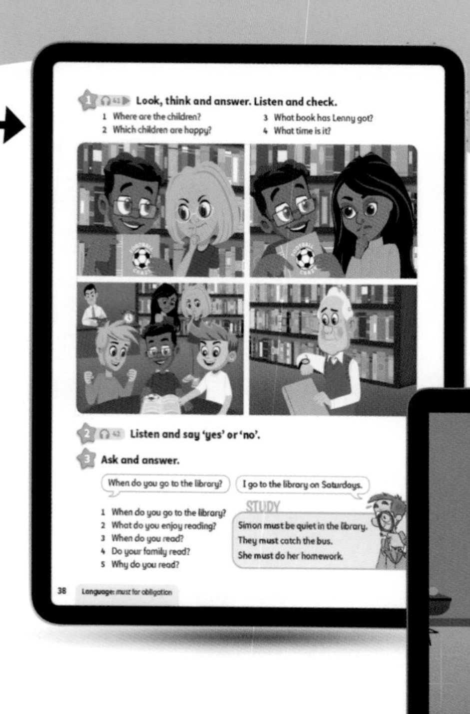

1 Look, think and answer. Listen and check.

1 Where are the children?
2 Which children are happy?
3 What book has Lenny got?
4 What time is it?

2 Listen and say 'yes' or 'no'.

3 Ask and answer.

When do you go to the library?
I go to the library on Saturdays.

1 When do you go to the library?
2 What do you enjoy reading?
3 When do you read?
4 Do your family read?
5 Why do you read?

STUDY
Simon must be quiet in the library.
They must catch the bus.
She must do her homework.

38 Language: *must* for obligation

Pupil's Book with eBook

Learners can listen to all the audio and watch all the videos from the course in their eBook.

Activity Book with Digital Pack

The Activity Book practises the target language and vocabulary from the Pupil's Book and includes games and puzzles to add enjoyment of vocabulary practice.

Accessing the Digital Pack via the code inside the front cover, learners have a further chance to practise the language and exams skills online. Practice Extra includes a selection of activities and games designed to reinforce the language in each unit.

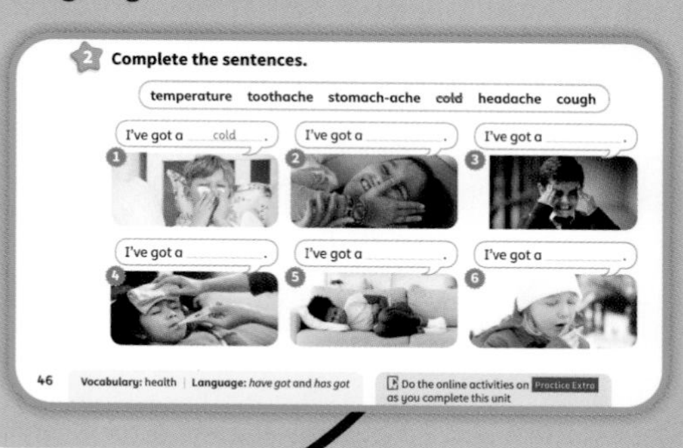

2 Complete the sentences.

temperature toothache stomach-ache cold headache cough

1 I've got a cold.
2 I've got a ....
3 I've got a ....
4 I've got a ....
5 I've got a ....
6 I've got a ....

46 Vocabulary: health Language: *have got* and *has got* Do the online activities on Practice Extra as you complete this unit

Kid's Box New Generation for Teachers

Teacher's Book with Digital Pack

The interleaved Teacher's Book makes your lesson planning and teaching experience as straightforward as possible. Lessons are structured logically and provide instructions for warmers, presentation, activities and class games, groupwork and pairwork, and ending lessons. You can find what's in the Digital Pack for each unit by looking at the end of each unit for links.

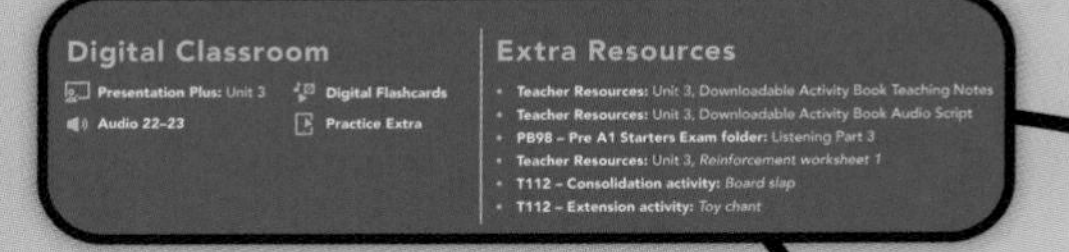

Presentation Plus

The software includes interactive activities from the Pupil's Books and Activity Books and all the course videos.

Teacher Resources

All the Audio, worksheets and additional photocopiable activities to supplement your classes.

The Digital Pack includes:

- Presentation Plus
- Practice Extra
- Class Audio
- Class Video
- Digital Flashcards
- Teacher Resource Bank
- Test Generator

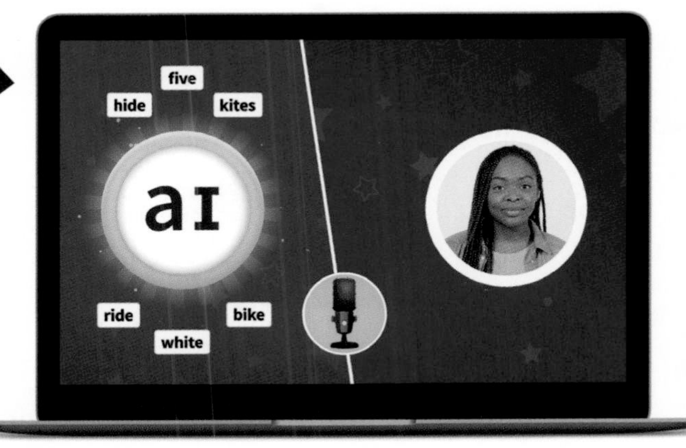

Flashcards and Posters

Flashcards are a fun way to help learners practise the unit vocabulary. See the Teacher's Book for suggestions on how to use them in class.

There are 8 colourful posters which focus on key language from the Pupil's Book, providing teachers with an eye-catching, engaging resource for language practice.

Cambridge English Qualifications and Kid's Box New Generation

Cambridge English Qualifications

Cambridge English's three exams for young learners, Pre A1 Starters, A1 Movers and A2 Flyers, are the first steps in a language learner's journey. Learners between the ages of six and 12 can take these exams to start learning English in a positive and practical way. The exams are fun, colourful and activity based, motivating children to learn. They help pupils develop the skills needed for everyday life and build their confidence step by step.

Each exam focuses on a level of the Common European Framework of Reference (CEFR), helping learners improve their speaking, writing, reading and listening skills.

> "95% of teachers and school leaders agree that preparing for Cambridge English Qualifications improves their learners' English."

*The Cambridge English Qualifications School Survey**

Kid's Box New Generation

The *Kid's Box New Generation* syllabus is built around the Cambridge Engish exams for young learners, which means your pupils will be well prepared for any exams they take. We break down exam preparation into small steps and make pupils aware of the progress they are making towards their end goal.

Pupil's Book

Each unit of the Pupil's Book prepares learners for their exam by practising the vocabulary and language they see on the exam. The *Exam folder* at the back of the book, helps familiarise pupils with the level and task types in the exam. Warmer activities in the Teacher's Book help introduce the language learners need to know before each task.

Many *Review* activities are based on the Listening, Speaking and Reading and Writing exam tasks.

Exam folder

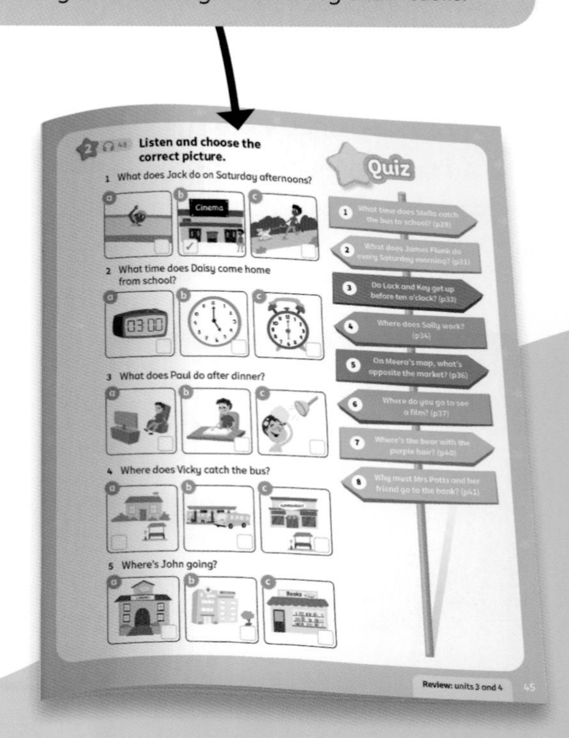

*Cambridge English Qualifications Schools Survey asked teachers and school leaders their views about the impact Cambridge English Qualifications have on learning and teaching. It received a total of 5,789 responses from 109 countries.

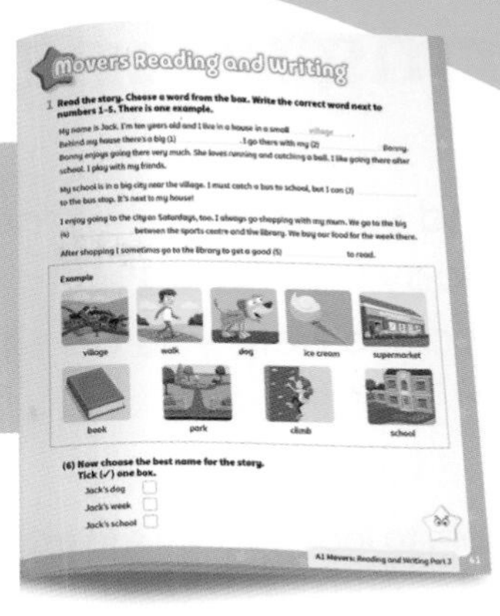

Activity Book

In the Activity Book there is one task per unit that familiarises pupils with the format of the exam tasks.

From the Teacher's Book

EXAM SKILLS

- Marking sentences with ticks and crosses to indicate whether sentences are true or false.
- Reading a sentence and looking at the corresponding picture carefully to check they match.

EXAM TIPS

- Pupils' ticks and crosses must be clear.
- Pupils should run their finger to the side of each sentence to find the key word. They should then keep one finger on the key word, and place another on the picture to check they match up correctly.

Teacher's Book

There are also useful Exam skills and Exam tips in the Teacher's Book. See page 14 of this introduction for more tips on preparing young learners for exams.

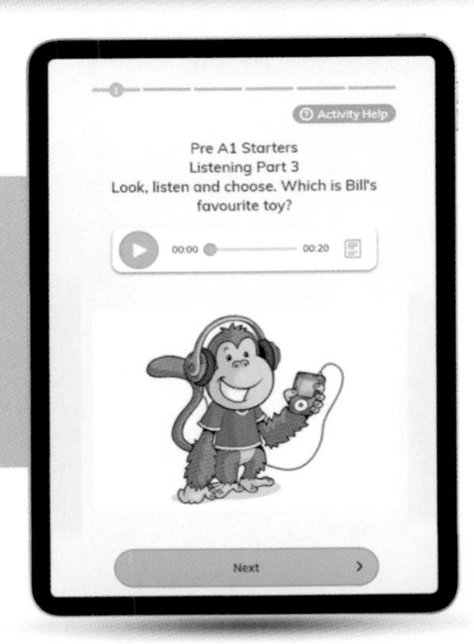

Practice Extra

Practice Extra features one exam preparation activity per unit. This allows pupils to practise target language and exam techniques while working on their own.

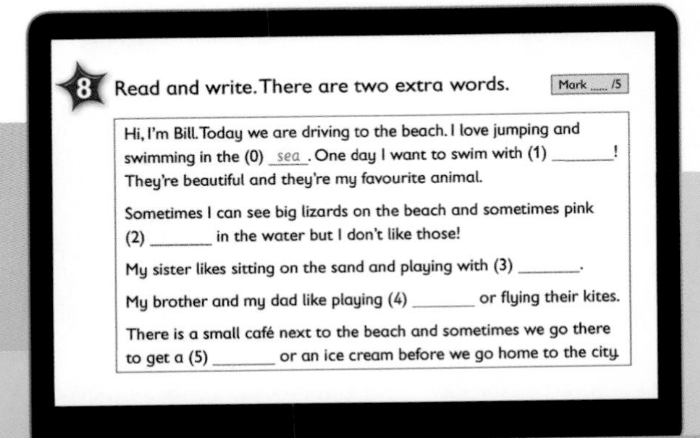

8 Read and write. There are two extra words. Mark ..... /5

Hi, I'm Bill. Today we are driving to the beach. I love jumping and swimming in the (0) sea . One day I want to swim with (1) _______! They're beautiful and they're my favourite animal.

Sometimes I can see big lizards on the beach and sometimes pink (2) _______ in the water but I don't like those!

My sister likes sitting on the sand and playing with (3) _______.

My brother and my dad like playing (4) _______ or flying their kites.

There is a small café next to the beach and sometimes we go there to get a (5) _______ or an ice cream before we go home to the city.

Test Generator

The Test Generator includes even more exam tasks as well as a full practice test at the end of level 3.

Preparing young learners for exams

Motivating and supporting learners as they approach exam day and on exam day itself are key to their success. Here is some practical advice to help you do this.

Look back and reflect

Allow time for pupils to look back on the exam tasks they have completed and the progress they are making. The *Exam folder* (on pages 88–95 of the *Kid's Box New Generation* Pupil's Book) provides a useful record of progress for learners to reference. See pages 12–13 of this introduction for more information on where exam-style activities can be found in the Pupil's Book, Activity Book, Practice Extra and Test Generator.

Practise exam tasks in class

Practising exam tasks in class gives pupils a chance to show what they know and what they can do, as well as an opportunity to practise the exam strategies you have taught them. Doing a full mock exam also helps to make pupils aware of the tasks they have to do and the time they have to complete the exam.

On exam day

In your last lesson before the exam, remind learners of anything they need to bring and of the structure and length of the exam. Communicate with parents to share information and work with them to help relax and reassure learners. Make sure that everyone knows what time the exam will start and how long it will last! When pupils arrive, smile and do your best to put them at ease. Remind them that they have prepared well for the exam.

After the exam

Praise learners for completing the exam. Allow them time to reflect and share how they felt about the experience. Ask learners questions and encourage them to ask questions, too. Try to build up a positive attitude towards examination. This positive outlook is invaluable to learners' long-term academic success.

The Cambridge Life Competencies Framework

Kid's Box New Generation is aligned to the Cambridge Life Competencies Framework. The Framework outlines six key areas of competency that are important for both personal and educational development: creative thinking, critical thinking, learning to learn, communication, collaboration and social responsibilities.

Developing these competencies not only helps pupils to learn, but also to communicate and collaborate in the classroom and the world outside.

Competencies combine knowledge, skill and attitudes:

- **Knowledge** is what you need to know to do something well.
- **Skill** refers to the level of mastery or fluency when you apply a competency.
- **Attitudes** involve mindset and a willingness to develop and use competencies.

For more information on the Cambridge Life Competencies Framework, visit our dedicated webpage. The webpage features downloadable competency-specific and learning stage-specific booklets, which help you to introduce these skills to you learners.

CLIL and Values pages

The CLIL and Values pages which follow every second unit specifically develop the Cambridge Life Competencies. The competency being developed is flagged at the bottom of each page.

Through CLIL, pupils learn useful knowledge and skills for maths, geography, art, science and sports, while engaging with topics critically and creatively. The projects on these pages encourage pupils to use and develop useful skills, such as planning and presenting.

The Values pages help pupils to appreciate cultural diversity, respect differences and develop human values. He also encourages pupils to understand the importance of respecting and protecting our natural environment.

Ready to write

These practical sections walk pupils through the stages of the writing process, from planning to review. The model texts from various genres give pupils a reference point to support them in structuring their writing.

Inclusive classes

One in every 10 learners is likely to exhibit signs of specific learning difficulties (SpLDs). These pages outline some strategies for supporting all learners in order to create an inclusive environment in which everyone can thrive.

Supporting all learners

As we all know, every learner is unique. SpLD learners often have strengths, such as holistic thinking, and problem-solving and visuospatial skills. Individual strengths should be recognised and used to each learner's benefit.

Many of the following suggestions are beneficial for SpLD learners, and for all learners in your classes.

Raise self-esteem and self-confidence

Regular praise and acknowledgement of learners' work and effort are crucial. Setting short-term, achievable goals and rewarding learners for reaching them are great ways of boosting self-confidence and self-esteem.

Create an inclusive environment

- If possible, speak with learners and their parents to establish what adjustments and assistance they might find useful.
- Assess progress regularly and make adjustments to learning goals and instructional methods.
- Assess learning outcomes fairly: focus on more than tests of spelling and vocabulary knowledge as these are areas that some learners with SpLDs find challenging.

Practical tips

- Make allowances for learners with SpLDs who work more slowly and need extra time to complete tasks.
- Give learners extended time and additional breaks to complete assessment tasks.
- Give learners the opportunity to work (or participate) in a variety of group and pair activities, in roles based on their strengths.
- Organise peer support for learners.

Language skills

When **reading**, some learners may:

- read more slowly and less accurately.
- misread words which can result in misunderstanding.

When **listening**, some learners may:

- find it challenging to listen to longer texts and remember specific information.
- find it difficult to distinguish between similar sounds in English or sounds that are different from the sound system of their first language.

When **writing**, some learners may:

- find it particularly hard to spell in English.
- have difficulties organising ideas.
- find handwriting challenging.
- make more grammatical errors.
- be less skilled at reviewing their work.

When **speaking**, some learners may:

- find it challenging to express their ideas coherently.
- struggle to retrieve words quickly from memory under the pressure of oral communication.
- have difficulty paying attention to accuracy and content at the same time, when either speaking or writing.

Support programmes and strategies

These can be applied in regular classroom teaching and are beneficial for all learners.

Phonological awareness-raising

These programmes support learners in developing phonological processing skills, which are the key foundations of reading and spelling. Learners are explicitly taught how to manipulate sounds and syllables.

Reading comprehension enhancement

A key element of these programmes is the development of learners' vocabulary knowledge. This involves explicit vocabulary teaching, for example:

- pre-teaching key words before reading a text
- providing glossaries with reading texts
- doing practice activities using the target vocabulary
- teaching techniques that help with memorising new words.

Reading comprehension strategies

Teachers can use a variety of strategies, such as: setting reading goals; previewing the text and predicting what the text will be about; verifying and revising these predictions; drawing inferences based on the text and background knowledge; and monitoring comprehension.

Learner preferences

Research and experience show that pupils have different needs when it comes to learning English. There will probably be a mixture of levels in your classroom, with some learners needing more support or perhaps more time to complete an activity.

Extra support and challenges

The Teacher's Book is full of suggestions on how to give learners extra support. There are also extra challenges for pushing stronger learners further. The *Extra support* and *Extra challenge* features are highlighted in yellow in the Teacher's Book to make them easy to spot.

Extra support Pupils can write key words from their lines in their notebooks.

Extra challenge The groups can change some words from the story, e.g. *ugly*, *walk*, *talk*, *fly*.

Catering for diversity

Classes also display differences in the way they like to learn. Some pupils are quieter and might prefer sitting down and reading. Others may enjoy more action and movement. All pupils need to have opportunities to practise and revise new language and vocabulary. *Kid's Box New Generation* features a variety of activities and skills work, so all pupils will find things to enjoy and help them learn.

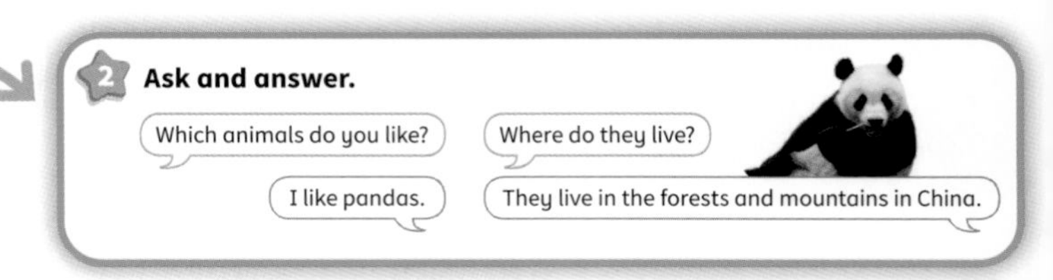

Recyling and reinforcing

Vocabulary and language are reinforced and recycled: pupils have multiple opportunities to put them into practice through songs, chants and games, as well as through traditional activities. This approach also helps improve memory and retention as content is presented and practised in different modes and contexts.

See pages 16–17 of this introduction for information and advice on creating an inclusive classroom environment.

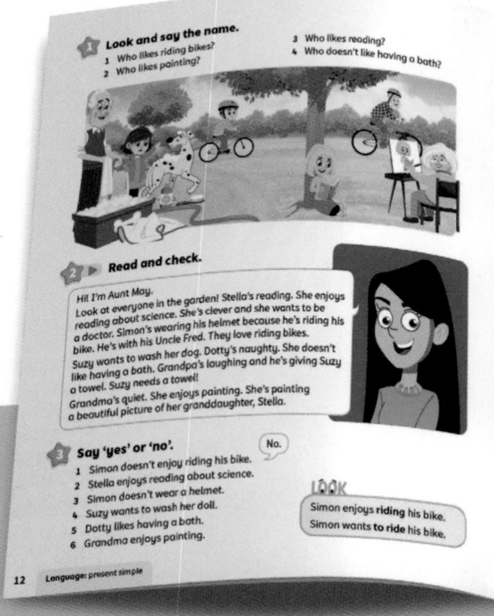

1 Look and say the name.

1 Who likes riding bikes?
2 Who likes painting?
3 Who likes reading?
4 Who doesn't like having a bath?

2 Read and check.

Hi! I'm Aunt May.
Look at everyone in the garden! Stella's reading. She enjoys reading about science. She's clever and she wants to be a doctor. Simon's wearing his helmet because he's riding his bike. He's with his Uncle Fred. They love riding bikes.
Suzy wants to wash her dog. Dotty's naughty. She doesn't like having a bath. Grandpa's laughing and he's giving Suzy a towel. Suzy needs a towel!
Grandma's quiet. She enjoys painting. She's painting a beautiful picture of her granddaughter, Stella.

3 Say 'yes' or 'no'.

No.

1 Simon doesn't enjoy riding his bike.
2 Stella enjoys reading about science.
3 Simon doesn't wear a helmet.
4 Suzy wants to wash her doll.
5 Dotty likes having a bath.
6 Grandma enjoys painting.

LOOK

Simon enjoys **riding** his bike.
Simon wants **to ride** his bike.

12 Language: present simple

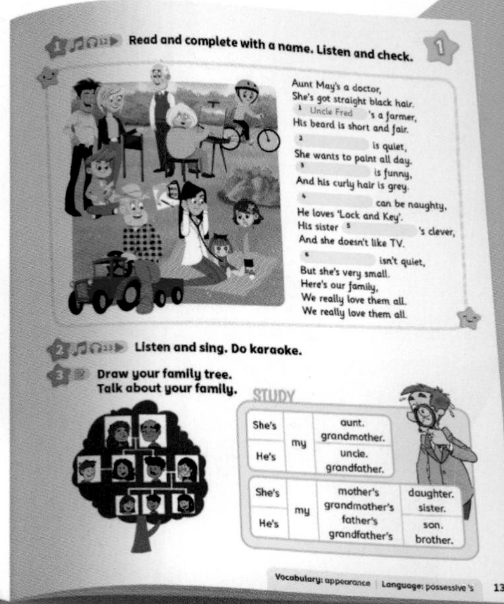

1 Read and complete with a name. Listen and check.

Aunt May's a doctor,
She's got straight black hair.
1 Uncle Fred 's a farmer,
His beard is short and fair.
2 ______ is quiet,
She wants to paint all day.
3 ______ is funny,
And his curly hair is grey.
4 ______ can be naughty,
He loves 'Lock and Key'.
His sister 5 ______ 's clever,
And she doesn't like TV.
6 ______ isn't quiet,
But she's very small.
Here's our family,
We really love them all.
We really love them all.

2 Listen and sing. Do karaoke.

3 Draw your family tree. Talk about your family.

STUDY

She's	my	aunt. grandmother.
He's		uncle. grandfather.

She's	my	mother's grandmother's	daughter. sister.
He's		father's grandfather's	son. brother.

Vocabulary: appearance | Language: possessive 's 13

Kid's Box New Generation Online Teacher Training on Cambridge One

We live in an ever-changing world with disruptions to teaching becoming more and more frequent. We have worked hard to provide support for these new challenges by updating the teaching scenarios in the enhanced Teacher's Book.

These updated scenarios include:

- in-person classes with emergency remote teaching plans, if needed
- in-person classes with social distancing and measures such as mask wearing
- 'simultaneous teaching', i.e. classes that alternate between in-person and remote learning
- a permanent mix of in-person and remote classes
- remote teaching as the norm.

In addition, we've developed an online training course for teachers on our learning environment, Cambridge One.

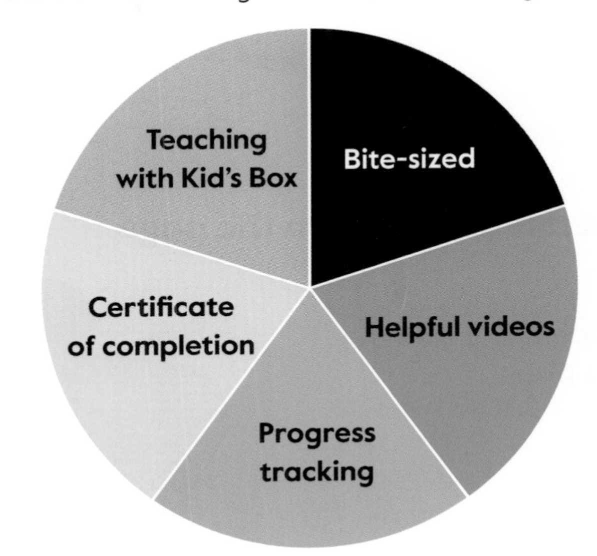

A final word

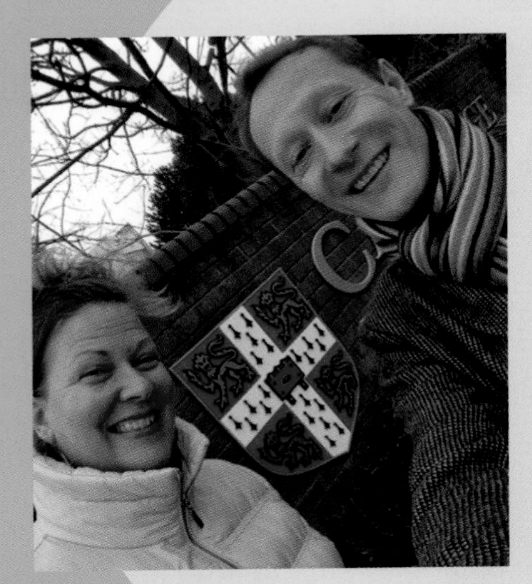

Dear teachers,

We are honoured and excited to be presenting *Kid's Box New Generation.*

We are deeply grateful to all the schools and teachers worldwide who have continued to put their faith in the efficiency of our teaching method throughout the years – this new version is for you. We hope you have as much fun teaching it as we've had writing it.

Caroline Nixon and Michael Tomlinson

The classic course for a New Generation

Classroom language

Lenny, Stella, Simon and Meera have shared some useful phrases and expressions for use in different teaching contexts. Whatever the scenario, always start each class by smiling and saying hello to everyone.

When teaching from the page

Open your books at page ...

Look at the picture.

Listen and point.

Listen and repeat / say / answer.

Work in pairs / groups.

What do you remember about ... ?

Ask and answer.

Sing the song.

Do the actions.

Say the chant.

Have you got a pen / pencil / coloured pencils?

Close your books.

Put your hand up if you know the answer.

When teaching online

Turn on / off your camera.

Mute / Unmute your microphone.

Look at the screen.

Put up your hands.

Type (your answer) into the chat.

It's your turn.

It's at the top / at the bottom / on the left / on the right of the screen.

Other useful language

Quietly, please.

One at a time, please.

Much better.

Well done!

I'm very pleased with you today.

Thank you. Goodbye.

See you next class!

1 2 Read and say the name. Listen and check.

a Hello. I'm nine. I've got a brother and a sister. This is my favourite computer game. It's called 'Brainbox'.

b Hello. I'm five. I've got a big dog. She's black and white and she's called Dotty.

c Hi. I'm eight. I like reading comics. My favourite comic's called 'Lock and Key'.

2 Ask and answer. Write.

What's your name? My name's …

1 What's your name?
2 How old are you?
3 Have you got a brother or a sister?
4 What's your favourite toy called?

My name's Zak. I'm nine.

LOOK

My favourite comic's **called** 'Lock and Key'.

Starter Unit Hello!
Pupil's Book p.4

Objectives

To review understanding and give personal information.

Target language

- **Key language:** character names, *Hello, What's your name? My name's …, How old are you? I'm (eight). What's … called? She's/He's called …*
- **Additional language:** *Have you got …? I've got (a brother / a dog). I like (reading), comic*
- **Revision:** family, pets, numbers, adjectives, colours, toys, *favourite*

Warmer

- Greet the class by saying, e.g. *Hello, everyone. My name's …* Ask a pupil *What's your name?* The pupil responds *My name's …* Invite two pupils to the front. They greet each other using the model:
  A: *Hello.*
  B: *Hello.*
  A: *My name's … What's your name?*
  B: *My name's …*
- Pupils stand up and walk around the class. Clap your hands. They make pairs and do the dialogue. Repeat.

Presentation

- Use prompts to elicit/review language. Say, e.g. *Age. What's the question?* Elicit the question from a pupil (*How old are you?*) and the answer from another (*I'm …*). Practise the question and answer, using open pairs. Use other prompts, e.g. *pet, brothers and sisters*, to elicit other personal questions (*Have you got a pet? Have you got brothers or sisters?*) and responses (*No, I haven't. / Yes, I've got …*). Use other prompts if appropriate to review questions about favourite toys, games, clothes, etc.

PB4. ACTIVITY 1

Read and say the name. Listen and check.

- Show Activity 1 on the whiteboard. Focus pupils on the picture. Elicit/Say who the characters are. If pupils studied *Kid's Box 1* and/or *Kid's Box 2*, briefly elicit what they remember about the Star family. Elicit what they can see in the picture.
- Say *Open your Pupil's Books at page 4, please.* Focus pupils on the speech bubbles. They read and match, and then check in pairs. Do not confirm answers at this stage.
- Tell pupils to listen carefully. Play the **Audio**. Pupils listen and check. Check with the class. Ask volunteers to read the texts in the speech bubbles aloud. Elicit other information about the characters. Ask questions to check understanding of *called*, e.g. *What's your favourite toy called? Have you got a pet? What's it called?*
- Focus pupils on the *Look* Box. Read the sentence aloud for pupils to repeat. Elicit other sentences using *called*.

Key: a Stella, **b** Suzy, **c** Simon

2

a **Stella:** Hello, I'm Stella. I'm nine. I've got a brother and a sister. This is my favourite computer game. It's called 'Brainbox'.
b **Suzy:** Hello, I'm Suzy. I'm five. I've got a big dog. She's black and white and she's called Dotty.
c **Simon:** Hi, I'm Simon. I'm eight. I like reading comics. My favourite comic's called *Lock and Key*.

PB4. ACTIVITY 2

Ask and answer. Write.

- Focus pupils on the *Look* Box. Read aloud the sentence for them to repeat it after you.
- Focus pupils on Activity 2. Pupils work in pairs and take turns to ask and answer about themselves using the question prompts. Check using open pairs. Pupils then write their answers in their notebooks.

Extra support Invite volunteers to ask you the questions first.

AB4. Answer key, see page T96

Ending the lesson

- Play a memory game about the characters in the book, and about the pupils, if they had time to read their sentences aloud from Activity Book Activity 2. Say, e.g. *Her dog's called Dotty.* (Suzy). *He likes reading comics.* (Simon).
- Say *Goodbye, everyone.* Pupils respond *Goodbye, teacher.*

Digital Classroom

 **Presentation Plus:** Unit 0

 **Digital Flashcards**

Audio 2

 **Practice Extra**

Extra Resources

- **Teacher Resources:** Unit 0, Downloadable Activity Book Teaching Notes
- **Teacher Resources:** Unit 0, *Reinforcement worksheet 1*
- **T104 – Extension activity:** *What's it called?*
- **T104 – Consolidation activity:** *Who's who?*

Objectives

To use colours and numbers to talk about toys.

Target language

- **Key language:** colours: *blue, pink, black, red, yellow, green, orange, white, grey, purple, brown,* toys: *helicopter, helmet, computer, kite, game, lorry, camera, train, bike, monster,* numbers: 11 (*eleven*) to 20 (*twenty*), prepositions of place
- **Additional language:** *playroom, cupboard, shelf,* the alphabet
- **Revision:** greetings, *Can you spell …? How do you spell …?*

Warmer

- Invite five pupils to come to the front. Make sure their names begin with different letters of the alphabet. Ask them to stand in alphabetical order. Help if necessary. Pupils then say their names for the class to check. Repeat.
- Invite several pupils to spell out their names as you write them on the board. If pupils know it, sing the Alphabet song from *Kid's Box 1* page 6.

PB5. ACTIVITY 1

Listen and say the number and the colour.

- Show Activity 1 on the whiteboard. Review the colours by pointing to objects around the room and eliciting the colour. Review numbers 11 to 20.
- Say *Open your Pupil's Books at page 5, please.* Ask a pupil to read the instructions aloud (*Listen and say the number and the colour*). Play the example in the **Audio**. Check pupils know what to do. Play the rest of the **Audio**. Pupils whisper the number and the colour to their partner.
- Play the **Audio** again. Pause after each one and elicit the answer. Check spelling by asking, e.g. *How do you spell (doll)?* Check comprehension of the toy vocabulary.

Key: Helmet. That's number eighteen and it's pink and green.
Bike. That's number seventeen and it's purple.
Train. That's number twelve and it's grey.
Monster. That's number fourteen and it's purple.
Game. That's number nineteen and it's green.
Computer. That's number fifteen and it's black.
Kite. That's number eleven and it's yellow and red.
Camera. That's number twenty and it's black.
Lorry. That's number sixteen and it's red.
Helicopter. That's number thirteen and it's blue.

3

H-E-L-M-E-T, B-I-K-E, T-R-A-I-N, M-O-N-S-T-E-R, G-A-M-E, C-O-M-P-U-T-E-R, K-I-T-E, C-A-M-E-R-A, L-O-R-R-Y, H-E-L-I-C-O-P-T-E-R

PB5. ACTIVITY 2

Play the game.

- Focus pupils on Activity 2. Demonstrate the game, using open pairs. One pupil spells out one of the toys, e.g. *H-E-L-M-E-T;* another answers, e.g. *Helmet. That's number 18 and it's pink and green.*
- Repeat to check pupils know how to respond.
- Pupils play the game in pairs. They take turns to spell out a toy, and say the toy, the number and the colour.

PB5. ACTIVITY 3

Read and answer.

- Review prepositions of place: *on, under, next to, in front of, behind, between.*
- Pupils work in pairs and take turns to read a sentence aloud and answer. They continue the activity, creating other sentences about the picture for the other toys. Check using open pairs.

Key: **2** camera, **3** lorry, **4** helicopter, **5** game, **6** kite

AB5. Answer key, see page T96

Ending the lesson

- Say *I can see something and it's (red) and it begins with (b).* Pupils take turns to guess (e.g. bag). The pupil who guesses correctly is the caller. Encourage pupils to say different colours and objects in the room. They must be things they can see in the room.

Digital Classroom

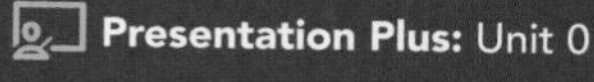

Practice Extra

Extra Resources

- **Teacher Resources:** Unit 0, Downloadable Activity Book Teaching Notes
- **Teacher Resources:** Unit 0, Downloadable Activity Book Audio Script
- **Teacher Resources:** Unit 0, *Reinforcement worksheet 2*
- **T104 – Consolidation activity 1:** *Find the number*
- **T104 – Consolidation activity 2:** *Spell it*

1 Listen and say the number and the colour.

H-E-L-M-E-T

Helmet. That's number 18 and it's pink and green.

2 Play the game.

B-I-K-E

Bike. That's number 17 and it's purple.

3 Read and answer.

Computer.

1 It's on the table, next to the books.
2 It's on the box, next to the ball.
3 It's on the floor, in front of the train.
4 It's under the table.
5 It's on the floor, between the helicopter and the monster.
6 It's behind the bike.

1 Read and match the names.

Meera – c

2 Listen. Who is it?

She's drinking orange juice.

That's Meera.

3 Answer the questions.

1 What's Stella doing? She's reading.
2 What's Alex doing?
3 What's Lenny eating?
4 What's Suzy doing?
5 What's Meera drinking?
6 What's Simon doing?
7 What's Alex kicking?
8 What's Stella reading?

STUDY

What**'s** Suzy doing?	What **is** Suzy doing?
She**'s** jumping.	She **is** jumping.

Objectives

To talk about actions children are doing.

Target language

- **Key language:** character names, present continuous: *He's/She's (eating an apple). What's he/she (reading)?*
- **Additional language:** *playground*
- **Revision:** actions: *jumping, reading, sitting, drinking, talking, eating, playing, kicking, doing, showing,* nouns: *book, orange juice, apple, bag, football, baseball*

Warmer

- Review the action verbs using mime. Mime an action, e.g. drinking. Pupils guess. Invite a pupil to come to the front and whisper an action to him/her. The pupil mimes and the class guesses. Repeat to review the other actions for the lesson.

PB6. ACTIVITY 1

Read and match the names.

- Show Activity 1 on the whiteboard. Use the picture to review/introduce the characters. Write the names on the board if necessary. Check pupils know which are girls' names and which are boys' names. Elicit where the children are (playground).
- Say *Open your Pupil's Books at page 6, please.* Check pupils know what to do. Pupils read silently. They match the names with the children in the picture. They check in pairs. Check with the class.
- Answer any questions about vocabulary.
- Watch the ▶ Video and answer the questions in the ▶ Video.

Key: Lenny – b, Alex – a

PB6. ACTIVITY 2

Listen. Who is it?

- Focus pupils on the instructions in Activity 2. Check pupils know what to do. Remind them to whisper the name to their partner the first time they listen. Play the first sentence and point to the example answer. Play the rest of the Audio. Pupils listen and whisper/point.
- Play the Audio again. Check with the class.

Key: That's Suzy. That's Lenny. That's Simon. That's Stella. That's Alex.

4

She's drinking orange juice.
She's jumping.
He's eating an apple.
He's showing Lenny his new school bag.
She's reading a book.
He's playing football.

PB6. ACTIVITY 3

Answer the questions.

- Focus pupils on the *Study* Box. Read each question and answer for pupils to repeat. Elicit what the differences are between the two questions and answers (contraction) and when we use one or the other (spoken/written). Pupils can respond in L1 if they can't explain in English.
- Focus pupils on Activity 3. Pupils work in pairs. They take turns to ask and answer the questions orally about the picture. Elicit the first question and answer from a pair to make sure pupils are using the contraction. Check using open pairs.
- Pupils write the answers to the questions in their notebooks.

Key: **2** He's playing football. **3** He's eating an apple. **4** She's jumping. **5** She's drinking orange juice. **6** He's showing Lenny his new school bag. **7** He's kicking a football. **8** She's reading a book.

AB6. Answer key, see page T96

Ending the lesson

- Play a game of Simon says. Pupils stand up. Say, e.g. *Simon says ride a bike.* Pupils mime riding a bike. Say, e.g. *Play baseball.* Pupils don't mime. Continue with other activities to review language from the lesson.

Digital Classroom

Audio 4

Practice Extra

Extra Resources

- **Teacher Resources:** Unit 0, Downloadable Activity Book Teaching Notes
- **AB86 and PB86 – Grammar reference 0**
- **T104 – Consolidation activity:** *Making patterns*
- **T104 – Extension activity:** *Jumbled questions*

Objectives

To practise talking about possessions using *have got* and to sing a song.

Target language

- **Key language:** present continuous, toys
- **Additional language:** *have/has got: I've/He's/She's/We've got*, contracted *'s, photograph*, names
- **Revision:** *bounce*, adjectives, *cousin, and, street, garden, park, taking, camera*

Warmer

- Write these adjectives on the board at random: *big, small, fat, thin, new, old, long, short, young*. First ask pupils to pair the adjectives. Give an example (*big–small*). Elicit the others from pupils and check they understand how *old* can match with both *young* and *new*. Elicit an example sentence from pupils for each word to make the meaning clear.

Song

PB7. ACTIVITY 1

Listen and say the name.

- Show Activity 1 on the whiteboard. Elicit what they can see (a street with children doing things). Elicit some of the things the children are doing. Check understanding of *street, house, garden*. Say the children's names for pupils to repeat, as these are new.
- Say *Open your Pupil's Books at page 7, please*. Ask a pupil to read the instruction aloud (*Listen and say the name*) and check pupils understand what to do.
- Play the first part of the **Audio** (*I've got an old bike and I'm riding it*). Put your finger to your lips to stop pupils calling out. They point to the character and silently check with their partner. Elicit the answer from a pupil (Fred). Play the rest of the **Audio**. Remind pupils to be silent. They point to the character in their books each time to show their partner. Play the **Audio** again. This time pause after each section and elicit the name from different pupils.
- Encourage pupils to say *Everyone!* for the line *We've got toys!*
- Review the structure by asking, e.g. *Tell me about Anna.* Prompt pupils to answer *She's got a new ball and it's bouncing*. Repeat for the other characters. Listen for correct use of the structure and of *'s*.
- **Note:** Pupils need to change the verb to third person for Fred and Yasmin.

Key: Fred, Max, Vicky, everyone, Yasmin, Paul, Anna, everyone

5

As in Pupil's Book

PB7. ACTIVITY 2

Listen and sing. Do karaoke.

- Focus pupils on Activity 2. Pupils stand up. Play the **Audio** again in short sections. Pupils repeat section by section. Pupils repeat verse by verse and then sing the whole **Song**. Divide the class into six groups. Each group is one of the children. Sing the **Song** again. The groups sing their section and then everyone sings the last line of each verse together.

5

As in Pupil's Book

- Say *Do karaoke*. Pupils listen to the karaoke version. They sing the **Song** as a class.

6

Karaoke version of the song

PB7. ACTIVITY 3

Read and complete.

- Read the first sentence aloud. Pupils point to the relevant part of the picture. Ask pupils to look at the picture and complete the sentences. They check in pairs. Check with the class.

Key: **2** riding, **3** flying, **4** driving, **5** bouncing, **6** walking

AB7. Answer key, see page T96

Ending the lesson

- Sing the **Song** from the Pupil's Book, dividing the class into the same six groups as before. Do a 'hands up' before you start, to check which group are which character and which part they're going to sing. Say, e.g. *I've got an old bike and I'm riding it. Who's that?* Pupils respond *Fred*. The 'Fred' group put their hands up. Sing the **Song** with the class.

Digital Classroom

Presentation Plus: Unit 0
Audio 5–6
Digital Flashcards
Practice Extra

Extra Resources

- **Teacher Resources:** Unit 0, Downloadable Activity Book Teaching Notes
- **Teacher Resources:** Unit 0, *Song worksheet*
- **T104 – Consolidation activity:** *Magic pocket*
- **T104 – Extension activity:** *Put them in order*

1 5 Listen and say the name.

2 6 Listen and sing. Do karaoke.

3 Read and complete.

1 Yasmin's holding a fat doll.
2 Fred's __________ an old bike.
3 Max is __________ a big kite.
4 Vicky's __________ a small car.
5 Anna's __________ a new ball.
6 Paul's __________ with a robot.

Language: present continuous

Lock's sounds and spelling

1 7 **Watch the video. Watch again and practise.**

2 **Find the sounds and draw a circle or a triangle. Say.**

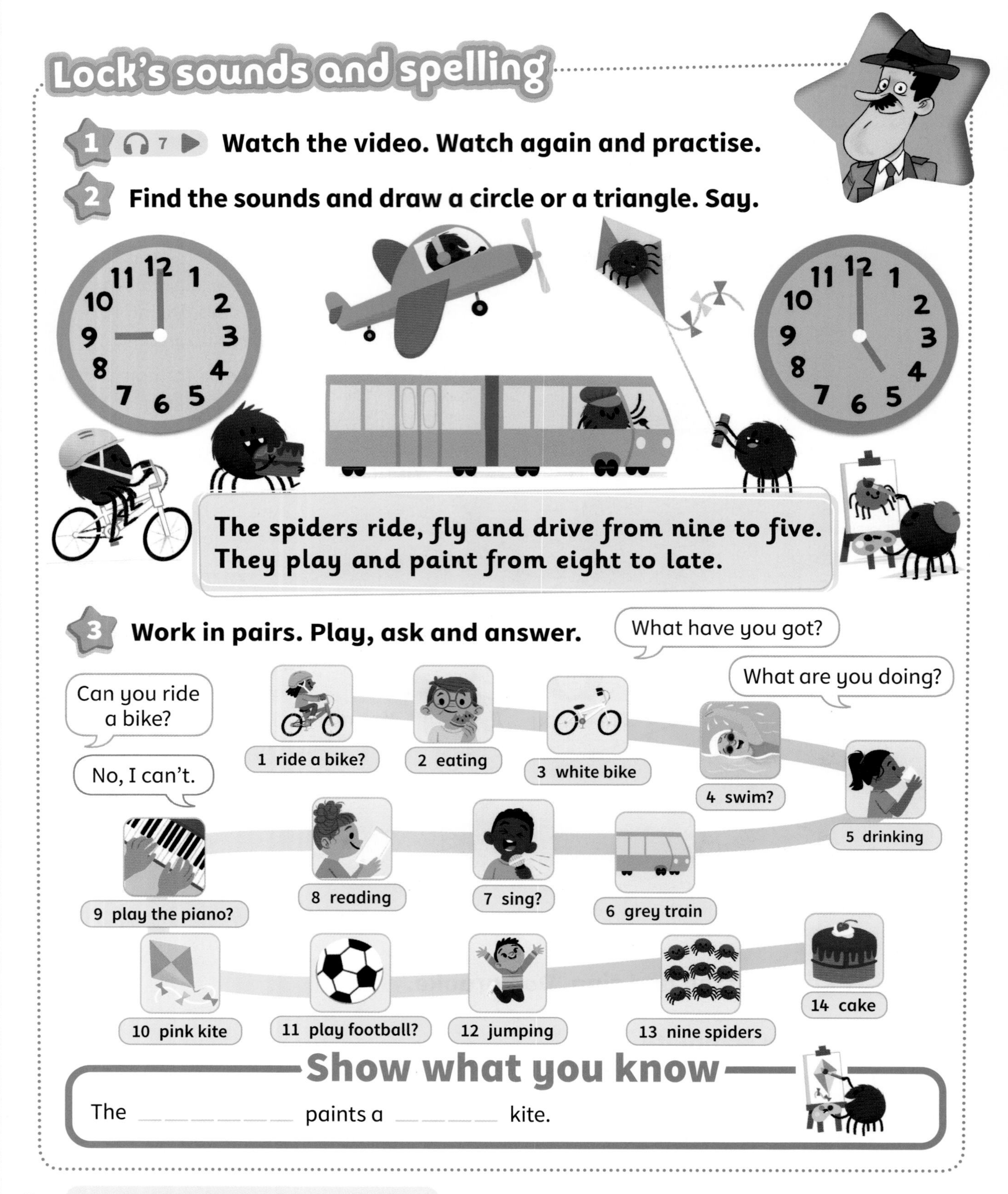

3 **Work in pairs. Play, ask and answer.**

Show what you know

The __________ paints a ________ kite.

Objectives

To recognise and practise sounds /aɪ/ and /eɪ/ in text and notice spelling patterns.

Target language

- **Key language:** sounds /aɪ/ (*spider, ride, drive, nine, five*) and /eɪ/ (*they, play, paint, eight, late*)
- **Revision:** *Can you (ride a bike)? Yes, I can. / No, I can't.* present continuous, *I've got (a white bike).*

Warmer

- Mime actions from the unit, e.g. *eating, drinking, jumping*, and write them on the board.
- Elicit more actions and add them to the board. In small groups, pupils select an activity each and create a tableau freeze of everyone in the group. Ask each group to come to the front and show their tableau. Ask *What's (Sara) doing?* The rest of the class guess and say *She's (jumping).*
- Alternatively, with large classes or little space, pupils can create their tableau freeze in pairs to show another pair at their table.

Presentation

PB8. ACTIVITY 1

Watch the video. Watch again and practise.

- Focus pupils on Activity 1. Draw two clocks on the board, one showing nine o'clock and the other showing five o'clock. Ask pupils what they do between those two times. Pupils discuss in pairs and then feed back to the class.
- Watch the ▶ Video and ask pupils what the spiders do between nine and five, to elicit *ride, fly* and *drive*. Ask pupils what other time is mentioned to elicit *from eight to late*.
- Ask pupils what else they remember from the ▶ Video. Write any words with /aɪ/ and /eɪ/ sounds on the board, without focusing on the sounds yet.

🔊▶ 7

Voice: /ai/ /ai/ /ei/ /ei/
Lock: What can you see, Key?
Voice: ride /ai/ fly /ai/ drive /ai/ nine /ai/ five /ai/
Lock: The spiders ride, fly and drive from nine to five.
Key: The spiders ride, fly and drive from nine to five.
Voice: /ei/ play /ei/ paint /ei/ eight /ei/ late
Lock: They play and paint from eight to late.
Key: They play and paint from eight to late.
Lock & Voice: The spiders ride, fly and drive from nine to five. They play and paint from eight to late.
Lock: Come on, everyone. One, two, three … let's say it with Key!
Lock, Key & Voice: The spiders ride, fly and drive from nine to five. They play and paint from eight to late.
Lock: I say – well done, Key!

PB8. ACTIVITY 2

Find the sounds and draw a circle or a triangle. Say.

- Focus pupils on Activity 2. Point to the picture and elicit what pupils can see.
- Say *Open your Pupil's Books at page 8, please.* Pupils say and circle the words with /aɪ/. Then they say and draw a triangle around the words with /eɪ/.

Extra support Pupils work in pairs and say the words together.

- Ask pupils to tell you the words and write them on the board in random order. Point to a word and pupils say the corresponding sound and either clap or stomp.

Key: Circle: spiders, ride, fly, drive, nine, five;
Triangle: They, play, paint, eight, late

PB8. ACTIVITY 3

Work in pairs. Play, ask and answer.

- Focus pupils on the game board in Activity 3. For the first picture, elicit the question *Can you ride a bike?* For the second picture, elicit the sentence *He's eating*. For the third picture, elicit *I've got a white bike*. Demonstrate how to play by rolling a dice, moving to the correct square and using the prompt to say a sentence or ask a question.
- Put pupils into pairs. Give each pair a dice and two counters. Pupils play together, asking, answering and saying as they move around the board.

AB8. Answer key, see page T96

Ending the lesson

- Call out words from the unit. Pupils clap if the word has the /aɪ/ sound, stamp if it has the /eɪ/ sound, or do nothing if it has neither sound.

Show what you know

- Focus on the *Show what you know* Box. Pupils complete the sentence with the missing words and practise saying it.

Key: spider, grey

Digital Classroom

Presentation Plus: Unit 0
Digital Flashcards
Audio 7
Practice Extra

Extra Resources

- **Teacher Resources:** Unit 0, Downloadable Activity Book Teaching Notes
- **T104–5 – Extension activity:** *Sound cards*

Objectives

To read a story and review language from the unit.

Target language

- **Key language:** language from the unit
- **Additional language:** *fur, Sorry, we can't answer the phone at the moment. Please leave a message. We've got work to do.*
- **Revision:** *Lock and Key, Please help me. Can I help you? No problem.*

Warmer

- Play a guessing game to review vocabulary. Say, e.g. *I'm thinking of an animal. It's big and grey. It's got four legs and a long nose. It's got a tail.* Pupils take turns to guess (elephant). Repeat for other known animals to review adjectives and body parts.

Story

PB9.

Watch the video.

- Say *Open your Pupil's Books at page 9, please.* Elicit what they can see (part of a comic / comic strip) and the title (*Lock and Key*). Elicit/Teach *detective agency* and the names of the detectives (Lock and Key). Explain the meaning of *lock* and *key* in L1. Set the pre-watching questions: *Who answers the phone? Who is Clarence? What's the problem?* Watch the ▶ Video. Pupils answer the questions and check in pairs. Check with the class (Key; a cat; Clarence is lost).
- Watch the ▶ Video with the class. Pupils listen and repeat. Give pupils the option of watching it twice if they need to. They answer the questions and check in pairs. Encourage them to say it with intonation and feeling.
- Check comprehension by pointing to the pictures on the whiteboard, pointing to each picture in turn and asking, e.g. *What's this?* (an answerphone). *Who's talking on the phone? Is it Lock?* (it's the cat's owner). *What's happening?* (Key is falling over). *What does he say?* (Argh! Oops!). *Is Clarence a small cat?* (no, he's a big fat cat). *What colour's his fur?* (white). Check understanding of *fur* and elicit other animals which have fur. Ask *What's in the detective box?* (brush, magnifying glass, salt).

Extra support When eliciting the answers, write key words on the board and leave them up to support pupils with Activity 1.

- Ask pupils who their favourite cartoon/TV detectives are.

🔊 ▶ 8

Answer phone: Hello. This is the Lock and Key Detective Agency. Sorry we can't answer the phone at the moment. Please leave a message.
Voice on phone: Please help me! I'm in the house next to your agency. I can't find Clarence!
Key: Argh! Oops! Hello, hello. This is Key. Can I help you?
Voice on phone: Oh! Please find Clarence. He's a big fat cat. He's got long white fur and blue eyes. He hasn't got a tail.
Lock: Get the Detective Box, Key. We've got work to do!
Lock: Come on, Key. What are we looking for?
Key: We're looking for a big white cat, Lock. No problem!

PB9. ACTIVITY 1

Describe the pictures in pairs.

- Ask a pupil to read the instructions aloud. Give pupils time to describe each picture in pairs. Monitor and help with language as necessary. Check answers as a class.

AB9. Answer key, see page T96

Ending the lesson

- Ask pupils which chant/song they'd like to do again from the unit. Do it together to end the lesson.

Digital Classroom

Presentation Plus: Unit 0

Audio 8

Digital Flashcards

Practice Extra

Extra Resources

- **Teacher Resources:** Unit 0, Downloadable Activity Book Teaching Notes
- **Teacher Resources:** Unit 0, Downloadable Activity Book Audio Script
- **Teacher Resources:** Unit 0, *Extension worksheet 2*
- **Teacher Resources:** Unit 0, *Video, Suzy's room*
- **T105 – Extension activity:** *Role play*
- **T105 – Consolidation activity:** *Spelling race*

1 Describe the pictures in pairs.

1 Family matters

Look, think and answer. Listen and check.

1 Is Stella at school?
2 Who's on the poster?
3 Has Stella got a brother?
4 How many sisters has she got?

2 Ask and answer.

1 Who's Stella's uncle? — Uncle Fred.
2 Who's Suzy's aunt?
3 Who are Simon's grandparents?
4 Who are Mrs Star's daughters?
5 Who's Mr Star's son?
6 Who's Grandpa Star's grandson?

LOOK

Who's Stella**'s** uncle?
Who's Suzy**'s** aunt?

Choose and describe. Write.

My aunt is tall. She's got black hair.

Objectives

To interpret a family tree and talk about family relationships.

Target language

- **Key language:** family: *aunt, uncle, daughter, son, granddaughter, grandson, grandparents, parents,* possessive *'s*
- **Additional language:** Star family characters, *then*
- **Revision:** family, toys, transport, *I'm/She's/He's …, my, your, their, That's right, Let's …*

Materials

- **Flashcards:** family (13–20)
- **Warmer:** Pictures of people from magazines
- **Ending the lesson:** Three pieces of paper: *'s* written on one, *'s* written on another, *is* written on another. Use one colour for *'s* and *is*, and another colour for the other *'s* (possessive)

Warmer

- Draw a simple family tree on the board. Include a mother, a father, grandparents (two sets), a sister and a brother. Name each person, e.g. *Jane*, and attach a magazine picture or draw a picture. Say *This is my family. This is my mother*, etc.
- Check understanding, e.g. point to a grandfather and ask *Is this my father?* Pupils respond, e.g. *No, it's your grandfather.* Use other questions, e.g. *Who's this? Who's (Jim)?*

Presentation

- Extend the family tree on the board to include aunts, uncles and more grandchildren. Use the tree and the flashcards to elicit/teach the new vocabulary: *aunt, uncle, daughter, son, granddaughter, grandson, grandparents, parents.* Add pictures to the tree on the board.
- Check understanding, e.g. ask *Who's my aunt? Who's (Jim)'s grandson?* Write *A family tree* on the board.

PB10. ACTIVITY 1

Look, think and answer. Listen and check.

- Show Activity 1 on the whiteboard. Elicit what they can see (a family tree).
- Say *Open your Pupil's Books at page 10, please.* Ask pupils to read the activity instruction aloud and to read the four questions. Pupils study the picture to find the answers and compare their predictions in pairs.
- Play the Audio. Pupils listen for the answers. They check in pairs. Play the Audio again. Check with the class.

Key: **1** Yes, she's at school. **2** Her family is on the poster (grandparents, parents, aunt and uncle, brother and sister). **3** Yes, she's got a brother. **4** She's got one sister.

9

Stella: Hi, everyone. This is my project. Here's my family tree.
These are my parents, Mr and Mrs Star.
And look, here are Grandma and Grandpa Star.
They're my grandparents and they've got two children: a son and a daughter.
Their son's my dad and their daughter's my Aunt May. I've got one aunt and one uncle: Aunt May and Uncle Fred. Aunt May's my dad's sister. Uncle Fred's my mum's brother.
Grandma and Grandpa Star have got three grandchildren: one grandson, Simon, and two granddaughters, Suzy and me.

PB10. ACTIVITY 2

Ask and answer.

- Focus pupils on the *Look* Box. Read each question for pupils to repeat after you.
- Tell pupils to look at Activity 2. Choose two pupils to read the first question and example answer. Point to Stella's uncle on the family tree. Point to Aunt May on the family tree and elicit her name. Pupils ask and answer questions 2–6 in pairs.

Extra challenge Pupils write two more questions. Then they ask and answer their questions in pairs.

Key: **2** Aunt May, **3** Grandma and Grandpa Star, **4** Suzy and Stella, **5** Simon, **6** Simon

PB10. ACTIVITY 3

Choose and describe. Write.

- Focus pupils on Activity 3. Ask a pupil to read the example in the speech bubble. Write *tall* and *black hair* on the board. Elicit other words and phrases pupils know to describe people and write them on the board. Give a short description of someone in your family using some of the brainstormed words, e.g. *My brother is short. He's got blue eyes.*
- Pupils choose a family member and describe them in pairs. Then they write a short description in their notebooks. Tell them to leave space in their notebooks to add to the description later in the unit when they've learnt more language for talking about people.

Practice

AB10. Answer key, see page T96

Ending the lesson

- Write *Suzy Stella sister* on the board. Hold up the three pieces of paper with *'s, 's* and *is*. Pupils volunteer to put the word in the right place to make a sentence.
- Repeat with other sentences, e.g. *Who (is) Mr Star('s) dad?*

Digital Classroom

Presentation Plus: Unit 1
Audio 9
Digital Flashcards
Practice Extra

Extra Resources

- **Teacher Resources:** Unit 1, Downloadable Activity Book Teaching Notes
- **Teacher Resources:** Unit 1, Downloadable Activity Book Audio Script
- **T105 – Extension activity:** *Family game*
- **T105 – Consolidation activity:** *True or false*

Unit 1 Family matters
Pupil's Book p.11

Objectives
To have more practice talking about family relationships.

Target language
- **Key language:** present continuous for present actions, *children, grandparents, good at*
- **Additional language:** *chess*
- **Revision:** family, contracted *'s*, actions, *Who's (Stella's aunt)?*

Materials
- **Flashcards:** family (13–20)
- **Warmer:** Eight cards, each with a different action: painting a picture, playing football, reading a book, taking a photo, playing a game, sleeping, playing baseball, driving a car

Warmer
- Review the family words using the flashcards. Show each flashcard in turn and elicit the words. Show the flashcards again in a different order. Pupils chorus the words. Show individual flashcards to different pupils. They say the words.
- Mime, e.g. painting a picture. Pupils guess the action, e.g. *painting a picture*. Pupils come up in turn and take one of the cards. They read it (silently) and mime the action. The pupil asks *What am I doing?* The class guess.

PB11. ACTIVITY 1

Listen and say the letter.
- Show Activity 1 on the whiteboard. Elicit who they can see in the picture. Elicit some of the actions.
- Say *Open your Pupil's Books at page 11, please.* Invite a pupil to read the instruction aloud. Check pupils know what to do. Play the **Audio**. Pupils listen and say the correct letters. They check in pairs. Check with the class by asking, e.g. *What's Grandma Star doing?* Ask some questions in the plural form, e.g. *What are Simon and his Uncle Fred doing? What are Stella and her Aunt May doing? What are Suzy and her mother doing?*

Key: **a** (Simon), **b** (Mrs Star), **c** (Stella), **d** (Grandma Star)

10

He's taking a photo of his son.
He's playing football with his uncle.
She's reading a book to her daughter.
She's playing a game with her aunt.
She's painting a picture of her granddaughter.

PB11. ACTIVITY 2

Listen and complete.
- Invite a pupil to read the instruction aloud. Play the first one as an example. Pupils put their hands up. They don't shout out. When all hands are up, elicit the word. Play the rest of the **Audio**. Pupils whisper the word to their partner each time. Play the **Audio** again. Check with the class. Check for correct pronunciation.

Key: granddaughter, uncle, daughter, son, aunt

11

Suzy's sitting next to her [beep].
Grandma Star's painting a picture of her [beep].
Simon's playing football with his [beep].
Mrs Star's reading a book to her [beep].
Grandpa Star's taking a photo of his [beep].
Stella's playing a game with her [beep].

PB11. ACTIVITY 3

Ask and answer.
- Focus pupils on Activity 3. Ask two more confident pupils to read the example question and answer. Elicit the other questions from the class, reminding them to use the prompts in the *Study* Box.
- In pairs, pupils take turns to ask and answer about the people and actions in the picture.

Extra support Pupils can work in pairs to formulate their questions first.

- Monitor pairs as they work. Check as a class.

AB11. Answer key, see page T96

Ending the lesson
- Draw eight steps going from a boat into the sea. Draw a stick figure on the top step. Draw a big shark's mouth in the sea. Choose one of the family words and write it as dashes on the board, e.g. _ _ _ _ _ _ (to represent *parent*). Pupils take turns to guess a letter. Write the letter in the word if it's in the word. If not, write it in the corner of the board and move the stick figure down one step. Continue until pupils guess or the figure is eaten by the shark. Clean the board and repeat with a different word.

Digital Classroom

Presentation Plus: Unit 1

Digital Flashcards

Audio 10–11

Practice Extra

Extra Resources
- **Teacher Resources:** Unit 1, Downloadable Activity Book Teaching Notes
- **Teacher Resources:** Unit 1, *Reinforcement worksheet 1*
- **T105 – Consolidation activity:** *Questions and answers*
- **T105 – Extension activity:** *Chant*

Listen and say the letter.

He's taking a photo of his son.

Letter e.

2 11 **Listen and complete.**

Suzy's sitting next to her …

… mum.

Ask and answer.

Who's playing a game with her aunt?

Stella!

STUDY

He**'s** tak**ing** a photo.

She**'s** paint**ing**.

They**'re** read**ing**.

Look and say the name.

1 Who likes riding bikes?
2 Who likes painting?
3 Who likes reading?
4 Who doesn't like having a bath?

Read and check.

Hi! I'm Aunt May.

Look at everyone in the garden! Stella's reading. She enjoys reading about science. She's clever and she wants to be a doctor. Simon's wearing his helmet because he's riding his bike. He's with his Uncle Fred. They love riding bikes.

Suzy wants to wash her dog. Dotty's naughty. She doesn't like having a bath. Grandpa's laughing and he's giving Suzy a towel. Suzy needs a towel!

Grandma's quiet. She enjoys painting. She's painting a beautiful picture of her granddaughter, Stella.

Say 'yes' or 'no'.

No.

1 Simon doesn't enjoy riding his bike.
2 Stella enjoys reading about science.
3 Simon doesn't wear a helmet.
4 Suzy wants to wash her doll.
5 Dotty likes having a bath.
6 Grandma enjoys painting.

LOOK

Simon enjoys **riding** his bike.
Simon wants **to ride** his bike.

Objectives

To talk about preferences, using *like, love, enjoy, want.*

Target language

- **Key language:** present simple, *like, love, enjoy* + *-ing* / nouns, *want* + infinitive, *science, doctor, naughty, quiet, towel, clever, read about, catch, helmet*
- **Additional language:** *because, and, need*
- **Revision:** present continuous, family, shopping, action verbs

Materials

- **Flashcards:** family (13–20)
- Photocopiable 1, one copy of the survey for each pupil

Warmer

- Draw a simple family tree on the board (beginning with a brother and a sister at the bottom) to review the family vocabulary. Stick the family flashcards on the tree to be the members of the family. Point to, e.g. the grandparents and say *These are the children's …* Pupils respond *grandparents*. Repeat for *parents*, *uncle* and *aunt*. Say statements about the family tree which are false, for pupils to correct, e.g. (Name) *and* (name) *are the children's parents* (no – they're their grandparents). Pupils correct. Invite pupils to come to the board and do the same.

PB12. ACTIVITY 1

Look and say the name.

- Show Activity 1 on the whiteboard. Elicit some of the people and things they can see in the picture. Elicit where the people are (in the garden).
- Say *Open your Pupil's Books at page 12, please.* Ask a pupil to read the activity instruction aloud and others to take turns to read the four questions. Pupils study the picture to find the answers and compare their predictions in pairs.

PB12. ACTIVITY 2

Read and check.

- Focus pupils on the text. They take turns to read it aloud around the class to check/find the answers to Activity 1. Check answers with the class.
- Watch the ▶ Video and answer the questions in the ▶ Video.

Key: **1** Simon and Uncle Fred, **2** Grandma Star, **3** Stella, **4** Dotty

PB12. ACTIVITY 3

Say 'yes' or 'no'.

- Focus pupils on the *Look* Box. Say the sentences. Pupils repeat. Point out the difference in the *-ing* and *to* forms. Elicit/Explain that these depend on the verb (*enjoy* or *want*). Ask pupils to find and underline an example of a phrase with *love* in the text (*They love riding bikes*). Point out that the verb after *love* is also in the *-ing* form. Elicit another verb which uses *-ing* in the text (*like*).
- Ask pupils to look at Activity 3. Do the first one as an example. Pupils work individually and decide if the rest of the statements are true or false. They check in pairs. They take turns to read the statement and to say *yes* or *no*. Check with the class in the same way.

Extra challenge Ask pupils to correct the sentences which are not true.

Key: **2** Yes, **3** No, **4** No, **5** No, **6** Yes

- Use Photocopiable 1 from the Teacher Resources.

AB12. Answer key, see page T96

Ending the lesson

- Pupils close their books. Say *Can you remember? Who's clever in the story? Why?* Repeat for *naughty, quiet, beautiful.* After the class has talked about the words, let pupils look again at the picture in the Pupil's Book and at the words in the text.
- Ask pupils to bring photos of their family members to the next class.

Digital Classroom

Presentation Plus: Unit 1

Practice Extra

Extra Resources

- **Teacher Resources:** Unit 1, Downloadable Activity Book Teaching Notes
- **Teacher Resources:** Unit 1, *Reinforcement worksheet 2*
- **AB86 and PB86 – Grammar reference 1**
- **T105 – Consolidation activity:** *Catch and say*

Objectives

To describe family members and to sing a song.

Target language

- **Key language:** *beard, curly, fair, straight, hair, farmer, funny*
- **Revision:** adjectives, colours, *have got, doctor, love, like* + noun

Materials

- **Presentation:** Five magazine pictures to show people with the following: curly hair, straight hair, a moustache, a dark beard, a fair beard
- Photos of pupils' family members

Warmer

- Play a game of Simon says to review body parts. Pupils stand up. Say, e.g. *Simon says touch your head.* Pupils touch their head. Say, e.g. *Touch your nose.* Pupils don't touch their nose. Continue. Include these words: *hair, arm, leg, face, eye, ear.*

Presentation

- Place the five magazine pictures on the board. Point to one of the pictures. Elicit/Teach the description for each one, e.g. *She's got curly hair.* Place the pictures in different parts of the room. Point to them in turn to elicit the correct sentence. Personalise the activity by asking *Who's got straight hair?* (pupils with straight hair put up their hands) and *Who's got curly hair?* (pupils with curly hair put up their hands).
- Place the pictures on the board. Elicit each sentence again and write it under the picture.
- Say each of the new words in turn (*beard, straight, curly, hair*). Teach a mime for each one, e.g. stroking chin for *beard*, twirling index fingers next to head for *curly hair*. Repeat the words at random. Pupils mime the action. Mime the actions and elicit the words from pupils. Pupils continue in pairs.

Song

PB13. ACTIVITY 1

Read and complete with a name. Listen and check.

- Show Activity 1 on the whiteboard. Focus pupils on the picture and elicit who they can see and what they're doing.
- Say *Open your Pupil's Books at page 13, please.* Ask a pupil to read the instructions aloud. Check understanding. Play the **Audio**. Pupils listen and point / whisper the names to their partner. Pairs check with pairs. Check with the class.
- Play the **Audio** again. Pupils follow the text in their books. Pause after each section for pupils to point to / identify the correct person in the picture.

Key: **2** Grandma Star, **3** Grandpa Star, **4** Simon, **5** Stella, **6** Suzy

12

As in Pupil's Book

PB13. ACTIVITY 2

Listen and sing. Do karaoke.

- Pupils stand up. Play the **Audio** again, verse by verse. Pupils join in. Sing the **Song** again with pupils until they are confident with the words. Invite seven pupils to come to the front. Each pupil is one of the characters in the **Song** (Aunt May, etc.). Encourage them to act the part. The other pupils sing the **Song** and when they sing about, e.g. Aunt May, 'Aunt May' mimes being a doctor. Repeat with seven different pupils in role.

12

As in Pupil's Book

- Say *Do karaoke.* Pupils listen to the karaoke version and stand up and sing the **Song** as a class.

13

Karaoke version of the song

PB13. ACTIVITY 3

Draw your family tree. Talk about your family.

- **Note:** If you have pupils who would find this activity upsetting, adapt it to an imaginary family tree.
- Focus pupils on Activity 3. Invite different pupils to read a sentence of the instruction. Say *First, draw your family tree. Draw it in your notebooks.* Remind pupils who to include and to write the names, e.g. *Uncle Charlie / Mum.* If pupils have brought in photos of their family members, they can add them to the family tree. Alternatively, they can draw pictures. In pairs, they take turns to talk about their family tree.

Extra challenge In small groups, each person tells the group something they've learnt about their partner's family.

AB13. Answer key, see page T96

Ending the lesson

- Sing a song, play a game or read a story, depending on which activity came out as the favourite in the survey.

Digital Classroom

- **Presentation Plus:** Unit 1
- **Audio 12–13**
- **Digital Flashcards**
- **Practice Extra**

Extra Resources

- **Teacher Resources:** Unit 1, Downloadable Activity Book Teaching Notes
- **Teacher Resources:** Unit 1, *Extension worksheet 1*
- **Teacher Resources:** Unit 1, *Song worksheet*
- **T105 – Consolidation activity:** *Spelling game*

Read and complete with a name. Listen and check.

Aunt May's a doctor,
She's got straight black hair.
1 Uncle Fred 's a farmer,
His beard is short and fair.
2 ________ is quiet,
She wants to paint all day.
3 ________ is funny,
And his curly hair is grey.
4 ________ can be naughty,
He loves 'Lock and Key'.
His sister 5 ________ 's clever,
And she doesn't like TV.
6 ________ isn't quiet,
But she's very small.
Here's our family,
We really love them all.
We really love them all.

2 Listen and sing. Do karaoke.

Draw your family tree. Talk about your family.

STUDY

She's	my	aunt. grandmother.
He's		uncle. grandfather.

She's	my	mother's grandmother's father's grandfather's	daughter. sister.
He's			son. brother.

Lock's sounds and spelling

1 14 **Watch the video. Watch again and practise.**

2 **Find and underline the *er* sounds.**

Bread, butter, burgers – what's for dinner?
Father, mother, brother and sister love making dinner.

3 **Work in pairs. Describe and say 'yes' or 'no'.**

The mother is holding a flower.

No, the mother is eating a burger.

Show what you know

What's for __________ ? It's a __________ .

Objectives

To recognise and practise the sound /ə/ in words ending in *-er* in familiar context vocabulary.

Target language

- **Key language:** the sound /ə/ (*brother, sister, mother, father, burger, butter, dinner*)
- **Revision:** *love, like, enjoy +ing* / verbs

Warmer

- Mime actions to elicit *watching, wearing, eating, drinking, riding, playing, listening* and write them on the left-hand side of the whiteboard. Ask pairs to think of one thing for each verb, e.g. *a film, a coat, a burger*, and write the answers on the right-hand side of the whiteboard.
- Write *Do you like …?* and ask pupils to use a verb/action from the left side of the board and match it with a phrase from the right side of the board.
- Put pupils into groups of four to create, ask and answer questions.

Presentation

- Write *fath_ _* and elicit the last two letters (*er*). Elicit a few more examples of words which end in *-er* (e.g. *mother, sister, brother, dinner*).
- Play a game. Pupils listen carefully while you say some words in English. If the word ends in *-er*, they do a thumbs up sign. If the word doesn't end in *-er*, they do a thumbs down.

PB14. ACTIVITY 1

Watch the video. Watch again and practise.

- Show Activity 1 on the whiteboard. Ask pupils what they can see in the picture and what they are doing. Play the ▶ **Video**. Ask pupils what they were doing in the ▶ **Video** to elicit *making dinner*. Ask pupils who was making dinner, to elicit *mother, father, brother* and *sister*. Ask pupils how they feel about making dinner.
- Watch the ▶ **Video** again. Make a fist with your hand and punch out the rhythm of the sentences across from right to left, facing your pupils. On the *-er* ending /ə/ sound, raise your fist up, to highlight the sound. Ask pupils to punch out along with you and notice the *-er* ending /ə/ sound.

Extra challenge Divide the class into group A and group B. Group A say the sentences together and group B only say the /ə/ sound in the correct places in the sentences. Swap groups.

▶ 14

Voice & Key: /ə/ /ə/
Lock: What can you see, Key?
Voice: burgers /ə/ butter /ə/ dinner /ə/
Lock & Key: Bread, butter, burgers – what's for dinner?
Voice: father /ə/ mother /ə/ brother /ə/ sister /ə/ dinner /ə/
Lock & Key: Father, mother, brother and sister love making dinner.
Lock & Voice: Bread, butter, burgers – what's for dinner? Father, mother, brother and sister love making dinner.
Lock: Come on, everybody. One, two, three … let's say it with Key!
Voice, Lock & Key: Bread, butter, burgers – what's for dinner? Father, mother, brother and sister love making dinner.
Lock: I say, well done, Key!

PB14. ACTIVITY 2

Find and underline the *er* sounds.

- Pupils underline the words ending in the /ə/ sound in the rhyme in the blue box. Say the rhyme together in chorus.

Key: butter, burgers, dinner, father, mother, brother, sister, dinner

---

PB14. ACTIVITY 3

Work in pairs. Describe and say 'yes' or 'no'.

- Look at the picture together and ask pupils what they can see. Say *Look, the mother is holding a flower.* Ask pupils to find the mother and tell you if your sentence is true by saying *yes* or *no*. Invite pupils to correct your sentence (*No, the mother is eating a burger*). Divide pupils into pairs and tell them to create true or false sentences for each other.

Extra support Elicit more examples and write some on the board as a point of reference and extra support.

Show what you know

- Focus on the *Show what you know* Box. Pupils complete the sentence with the missing words and practise saying it.

Key: dinner, burger

AB14. Answer key, see pages T96–7

Ending the lesson

- Elicit words for people and animals ending in *-er* and write them on the board (*mother, father, brother, sister, tiger, baker, butcher, spider, farmer*).
- Say *Thicker, thinner, stir and simmer*. Invite a pupil to suggest a person/animal word for the next line. Say the new rhyme together, e.g. *Teacher loves making dinner!*
- Repeat the activity with other pupils.

Digital Classroom

Presentation Plus: Unit 1
Digital Flashcards
Audio 14
Practice Extra

Extra Resources

- **Teacher Resources:** Unit 1, Downloadable Activity Book Teaching Notes
- **T105 – Consolidation activity:** *Plate mingle*
- **T105 – Extension activity:** *Stop!*

Objectives

To watch and read a story and review language from the unit.

Target language

- **Key language:** language from the unit, *pet, thief, dirty, jacket, detective agency*
- **Additional language:** *We can find him. episode*
- **Revision:** language from the story, *No problem, Lock and Key, look, park, Let's ..., agency*

Warmer

- Write prompts from the first episode of the story on the board, e.g. *Please help me! Please find Clarence. Get the Detective Box.* Elicit the story so far from pupils in the present tense. Ask other questions, e.g. *What are the names of the detectives? Are they good at their jobs? Are Lock and Key using a laptop?*

Story

PB15.

Watch the video.

- Show Activity 1 on the whiteboard. Tell pupils that this is the next episode of the story. Elicit/Teach *pet thief*. Set the pre-listening questions and write them on the board: *Who's the man on the screen? Is the pet thief in the park?*

Extra support Before watching, show the page on the whiteboard and elicit who and what pupils can see in each picture, and where they are.

- Watch the ▶ Video with the class. Give pupils the option of watching it twice if they need to. They answer the questions and check in pairs. Check with the class (the pet thief; no, it's a lady).
- Say *Open your Pupil's Books at page 15, please.* Play the Audio. Pupils listen and repeat. Encourage them to say it with intonation and feeling.
- Check comprehension by pointing to each picture in turn on the whiteboard and asking, e.g. *What's this?* (a picture of the pet thief). *Has he got curly brown hair?* (no, he's got straight black hair). *Is he wearing a hat?* (yes). *What does Lock say?* (*Let's look in the park*). *What's the lady wearing?* (a dirty hat and an old jacket). *Is the cat called Clarence?* (yes, it is).

▶ 15

Lock: Hmmm, that's the pet thief. He's got straight black hair, a black beard and a moustache.
Key: Yes, and he's wearing a big dirty hat and an old jacket. We can find him, no problem!
Key: Where are you going, Lock?
Lock: I want to find that pet thief. Let's look in the park.
Lock: Look! There's the pet thief ... and he's got Clarence!
Key: Yes, I can see his dirty hat and old jacket. Let's get him!
Mrs Potts: There you are Clarence! Naughty cat!
Mrs Potts: What are you doing? Give me my cat! Who are you?
Key: I'm Mr Key, from Lock and Key Detective Agency. We're looking for the pet thief.
Mrs Potts: I'm not a pet thief!
Lock: That's right, Key. She hasn't got a beard or a moustache. Give her the cat.
Key: No problem, Lock.

PB15. ACTIVITY 1

Are Lock and Key good detectives? Why? Why not?

- Ask pupils if Lock and Key are good detectives. If pupils answer *yes*, look quizzical and ask *Why?* If pupils answer *no*, ask *Why not?* Give pupils time to discuss their answers in pairs before sharing ideas with the class. If pupils answer in L1, help them rephrase their ideas in English.

AB15. Answer key, see page T97

Ending the lesson

- Write *Lock, Key* and *Mrs Potts* on the board. Say phrases from the Unit 1 episode of *Lock and Key*, e.g. *We can find him, no problem!* and *I'm not a pet thief!* If you can, put on voices to represent the characters when you say the lines. Encourage pupils to say whose line it is.

Digital Classroom

Presentation Plus: Unit 1

Audio 15
Digital Flashcards
Practice Extra

Extra Resources

- **Teacher Resources:** Unit 1, Downloadable Activity Book Teaching Notes
- **Teacher Resources:** Unit 1, Downloadable Activity Book Audio Script
- **Teacher Resources:** Unit 1, *Extension worksheet 2*
- **Teacher Resources:** Unit 1, *Video, Suzy's room* or *The living room*
- **T105 – Extension activity:** *Role play*
- **T105 – Consolidation activity:** *Guess who*

1 **Are Lock and Key good detectives? Why? Why not?**

How big is your family?

1 16 **Listen and read. How many cousins has Sofia got? How many have you got?**

My name's Sofia. This is my family. There are 11 people in my family.
That's me in the middle with my dad, my mum, my brother Felipe, and Baby Elias.

On the left, you can see Uncle Victor, Grandma and Aunt Fernanda.
On the right, you can see my adult cousins Raquel and Raul, and Raul's wife, Alicia.

2 Use Sofia's poster to answer the questions.

1 How many adults are there? ___8___
2 How many children are there? ______
3 Uncle Victor is 183 cm tall. Grandma is 163 cm tall. What's the difference? ______ cm
4 How many fingers and toes have Felipe, Sofia and Elias got in total? ______ fingers and toes
5 How many feet are there in the family? ______ feet
6 Sofia's family are going to a restaurant. Four people can sit at each table. How many tables do they need? ______ tables

3 When do you use maths in real life? Think and say.

I count my coloured pencils.

I share sweets with my friends.

DID YOU KNOW...?
Counting is the oldest form of maths. Humans have been counting for 35,000 years!

Unit 1 Family matters
Pupil's Book p.16

Objectives
To talk about numbers and the people in families.

Target language
- **Key language:** language from the unit
- **Additional language:** *aunt, centre, count, cousins, foot, left, moustache, right, share, uncle, wife*
- **Revision:** *brother, dad, family, friends, long, mum, old, people, tall*

Materials
- Rulers or measuring tape

Warmer
- Review numbers with the class. Challenge pupils to count in tens (*ten, twenty, thirty, forty, …*), twos (*two, four, six, eight, …*) and fives (*five, ten, fifteen, twenty, …*).
- You are now ready to watch the ▶ Video.

PB16.

How big is your family?
- Tell pupils that they're going to learn more about numbers in this lesson.
- Watch the ▶ Video and answer the questions in the ▶ Video.

PB16. ACTIVITY 1

Listen and read. How many cousins has Sofia got? How many have you got?
- Show Activity 1 on the whiteboard. Ask pupils to look at the family in the picture. Point out Sofia in the centre of the photo. Ask *Who do you think these other people are?* (Sofia's family).
- Say *Open your Pupil's Books at page 16, please.* Play the Audio while pupils follow along in their books.
- Ask a pupil to read the first question in the rubric. Pupils read the text again to find the answer to the first question.
- Ask a pupil to read the second question in the rubric. Pupils answer the question in small groups. Elicit answers from a few volunteers.

Extra support Write *on the left, on the right* and *in the centre,* on the left, right and centre of the board, respectively. Tell pupils to underline these phrases in the text and highlight how Sofia uses them to describe the photo.

Key: Sofia has two cousins, Raquel and Raul.

16

Sofia: My name's Sofia. This is my family. There are eleven people in my family. That's me in the middle with my dad, my mum, my brother Felipe, and baby Elias. On the left, you can see Uncle Victor, Grandma and Aunt Fernanda. On the right, you can see my adult cousins Raquel and Raul, and Raul's wife, Alicia.
Sofia: How old am I?
Boy: Eight years old.
Sofia: How tall is Uncle Victor?
Boy: 183 cm.
Sofia: How tall is Grandma?
Boy: 163 cm.
Sofia: How old is Felipe?
Boy: Seven years old.
Sofia: How long is Dad's moustache?
Boy: 5 cm.
Sofia: How long is baby Elias's foot?
Boy: 6 cm.
Sofia: How long is Mum's foot?
Boy: 24 cm.

PB16. ACTIVITY 2

Use Sofia's poster to answer the questions.
- Ask pupils to circle the numbers in the text. If possible, give pupils rulers or measuring tape to look at.
- Ask a pupil to read the first question out loud. Elicit the answer. Put pupils into pairs to answer the remaining questions. Monitor and, if necessary, help pupils.
- Check answers as a class. Encourage pupils to say where in the text they found the answers. If time, use Extension activity (T105–6): *Measure the teacher.*

Key: 2 3, 3 20, 4 60, 5 22, 6 3

PB16. ACTIVITY 3

When do you use maths in real life? Think and say.
- Ask the question. Volunteers read the example answers. Groups discuss ways people use maths in real life.

Did you know …?
- Invite a volunteer to read the information in the box out loud. Ask pupils if this fact surprises them. Encourage pupils to close their eyes and imagine life 35,000 years ago.
- Give some context to the time period by showing a picture of the cave paintings at Lascaux.
- Ask *What type of things do you think people in this time period counted?* Accept reasonable answers.

AB16. Answer key, see page T97

Ending the lesson
- Say simple riddles for pupils to guess the family member, e.g. *She's my cousin's mum.* (Your aunt!)

Digital Classroom

- **Presentation Plus:** Unit 1
- **Audio 16**
- **Digital Flashcards**
- **Practice Extra**

Extra Resources
- **Teacher Resources:** Unit 1, Downloadable Activity Book Teaching Notes
- **T105–6 – Extension activity:** *Measure the teacher*

Objectives

To guess and measure the size of things.

Target language

- **Additional language:** *divided by, equals, greater than, less than, minus, plus, times, wide, Get ready*
- **Revision:** *book, hair, hand, foot, long, old, tall*

Materials

- **Warmer:** Flyswatter or rolled-up newspaper
- White paper (one sheet per pupil)
- Photos of pupils' families (optional)

Warmer

- Write *14* and *40* on the board. Say both numbers and point out that they sound similar. Invite a pair of volunteers to the board and give each a flyswatter or a rolled-up newspaper. Say one of the two numbers. The first volunteer to hit the correct number with the flyswatter or newspaper wins a point. Play again with new volunteers and different similar numbers, such as *18* and *80*.

PB17. ACTIVITY 4

Look at the chart. Listen and write the symbol.

- Show Activity 4 on the whiteboard. Ask pupils to look at the chart. Point out the maths symbols. Ask pupils if any of these symbols are familiar.
- Direct pupils' attention to the words in the chart. Explain that these are the words that we use for the symbols.
- Say *Open your Pupil's Books at page 17, please.* Play the Audio while pupils follow along with the maths sentences. Tell them to listen for the symbol in each problem. Pupils don't need to write the first time they listen.
- Play the Audio again. Pupils listen and write the symbols.
- Check by asking volunteers to read the maths sentences out loud.

Key: b ÷, c <, d +, e –, f x

17

a Fifteen is greater than twelve.
b Six divided by two equals three.
c Sixteen is less than nineteen.
d Ten plus ten equals twenty.
e Twenty-five minus eight equals seventeen.
f Three times two equals six.

Project

- Remember to download your project notes from *Cambridge One.*

Extra support Draw the > and < symbols on the board and show which side we write the bigger number and the smaller number in each case.

PB17. ACTIVITY 5

Guess and measure. Complete the table.

- Show Activity 5 on the whiteboard. Read out the questions and headings in the table. Tell pupils to guess the measurements and complete the first column.
- Ask pupils to compare their guesses with their classmates. Ask *Are any of your guesses and measurements the same?*
- Tell pupils to measure themselves and the objects and write the measurements in the table. They compare their answers with a partner.

PB17. ACTIVITY 6

Survey and measure your classmates. Complete the table in your notebook. Make greater/less than sentences.

- Explain to pupils that they are going to survey and measure their classmates. Put them into small groups and tell them to ask and measure to complete the table in their notebooks.
- Draw pupils' attention to the last part of the instruction. Write *12 > 11* on the board. Invite a volunteer to read it out loud: *Twelve is greater than eleven.* Invite a volunteer to read the example sentences in the book out loud.
- Pupils take turns making other greater/less than sentences with their classmates' measurements.

AB17. Answer key, see page T97

Ending the lesson

- Ask pupils which chant/song they'd like to do again from the unit. Do it together to end the lesson.

Digital Classroom

Presentation Plus: Unit 1
Audio 17
Digital Flashcards
Practice Extra

Extra Resources

- **Teacher Resources:** Unit 1, Downloadable Activity Book Teaching Notes
- **Teacher Resources:** Unit 1, Downloadable Activity Book Audio Script
- **Teacher Resources:** Unit 1, *Project notes*
- **PB88–95 – A1 Movers Exam folder**
- **T106 – Extension activity 1:** *Creating maths sentences*
- **T106 – Extension activity 2:** *Word train*

4 Look at the chart. Listen and write the symbol.

	Maths function	Symbol	Words
a 15 ___>___ 12	Addition	+	plus
b 6 ______ 2 = 3	Subtraction	-	minus
c 16 ______ 19	Multiplication	x	times
d 10 ______ 10 = 20	Division	÷	divided by
e 25 ______ 8 = 17		=	equals
f 3 ______ 2 = 6		>	is greater than
		<	is less than

5 Guess and measure. Complete the table.

	Guess!	Measure!
How tall am I?	______ cm	______ cm
How long is my foot?	______ cm	______ cm
How wide is my hand?	______ cm	______ cm
How wide is my English book?	______ cm	______ cm
How long is my hair?	______ cm	______ cm

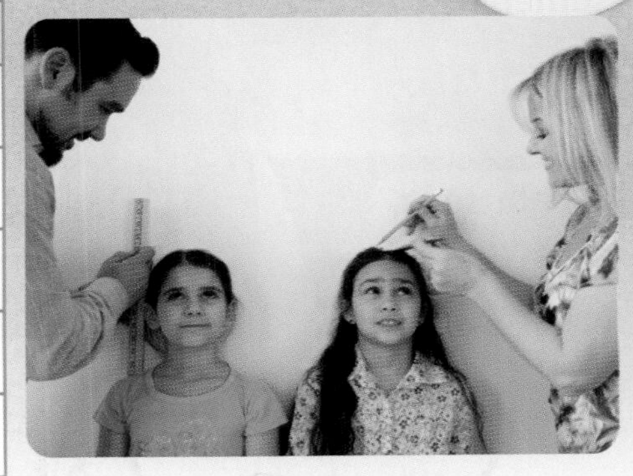

6 Survey and measure your classmates. Complete the table in your notebook. Make greater/less than sentences.

Name	Age	How tall ...?

Jackie is 12. Megan is 11.

12 is greater than 11. 12 > 11.

Ready to write:

Go to Activity Book page 16.

Project

Make a family numbers poster.

1 18 Look, think and answer. Listen and check.

1 What buildings can you see?
2 What's in the room under the house?
3 Where's the flat?
4 Has the flat got a garden?

2 Describe your house or flat. Then write.

My house is in the village. It has got a kitchen downstairs.

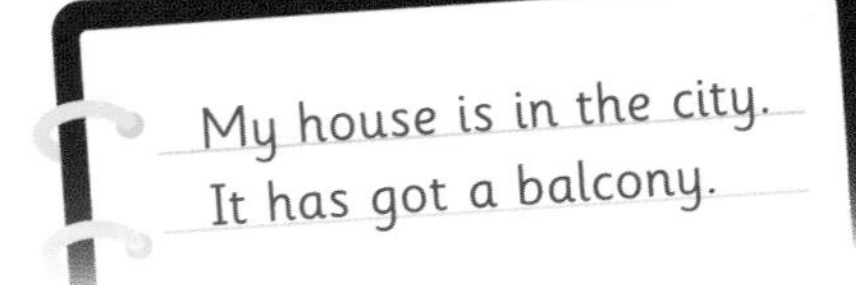

3 19 Listen and say the letter.

A basement

a 
b 
c 
d 
e 
f 
g 

Unit 2 Home sweet home
Pupil's Book p.18

Objectives
To talk about different places to live.

Target language
- **Key language:** *city, town, village, balcony, basement, downstairs, flat, lift, stairs, upstairs*
- **Additional language:** *home sweet home, crossword, across, down*
- **Revision:** *like + -ing, live, walk, come, door, house, quiet, trees, lots of / a lot of, present simple, have got, can/can't, Who lives in a flat?*

Materials
- **Flashcards:** home (26–34)

Warmer
- Stick the flashcards city, town and village on the board and teach or elicit the words.
- Elicit/Discuss the difference between a city, a town and a village. Elicit if your school is in a town, a city, a village and/or the country. Ask, e.g. *Do you like living in the country?* Elicit where different pupils live (a flat, a house, etc.). Pupils say, e.g. *I live in a house.* Ask, e.g. *Do you like living in a house?*
- **Note:** A town is bigger than a village, but usually smaller than a city.

Presentation
- Draw simple pictures of a block of flats and a house. Using the drawings and the home flashcards, elicit/teach *lift, stairs, downstairs, upstairs, basement, balcony.*

PB18. ACTIVITY 1

Look, think and answer. Listen and check.
- Show Activity 1 on the whiteboard. Focus pupils on the pictures and elicit what/who they can see.
- Say *Open your Pupil's Books at page 18, please.* Ask a pupil to read the activity instruction aloud and others to take turns to read the four questions. Pupils discuss their answers/predictions in pairs, looking for clues in the pictures.
- Play the **Audio**. Pupils listen for the answers. They check in pairs. Play the **Audio** again. Check with the class. Elicit complete sentences for the answers.

Key: **1** I can see a house and a flat. **2** There are boxes and old toys. **3** It's in the town. **4** No, it hasn't.

18

Meera: We've got a new flat. We're moving from our house in the country to a flat in the town.
Alex: Do you like living in the country?
Meera: I love the country. At the moment I live in a small village. It's quiet and there are a lot of trees.
Lenny: Has your house got a basement under the floor?
Meera: Yes, it's full of boxes and old toys.
Alex: And what about your new flat?
Meera: Well, it hasn't got a basement or a garden, but it's got a beautiful balcony for my plants.
Lenny: Cool. What else?
Meera: The house in the village has got stairs to go up and down, but the flat in the city is different. There are five floors so we go upstairs and downstairs in a lift!
Lenny: Wow! I want to live in a flat!

PB18. ACTIVITY 2

Describe your house or flat. Then write.
- Ask pupils questions, e.g. *Where's your house? Has your house got a garden? Has your flat got a balcony?*
- In pairs, pupils describe their house or flat. Encourage pupils to ask their partner follow-up questions.
- Pupils write a short description of their house or flat.

Extra support Write some useful language on the board, e.g. *My house/flat is in … It has got …*

PB18. ACTIVITY 3

Listen and say the letter.
- Focus pupils on Activity 3. Elicit some of the things they can see in the pictures, e.g. *town, lift, upstairs.* Play the **Audio**. Pupils whisper the letter to their partner or point to the picture. Play the **Audio** again. Pause after each one and check with the class.

Key: b, g, a, c, e, f

19

a basement, a village, a lift, upstairs, a balcony, a town, downstairs

AB18. Answer key, see page T97

Ending the lesson
- In pairs, pupils say *One, two, three,* then both say a word from the lesson together. If it's the same, e.g. *balcony,* they say *Snap.*

Digital Classroom

Presentation Plus: Unit 2
Audio 18–19
Digital Flashcards
Practice Extra

Extra Resources
- **Teacher Resources:** Unit 2, Downloadable Activity Book Teaching Notes
- **Teacher Resources:** Unit 2, *Reinforcement worksheet 1*
- **T106 – Consolidation activity 1:** *Chain game*
- **T106 – Consolidation activity 2:** *Match the word*

Objectives

To talk and write about their homes and sing a song.

Target language

- **Key language:** *flats*
- **Additional language:** *What about you? where it's at, here, same, different, order*
- **Revision:** house and home, colours, *have got*, present simple, *can, under, in, up, down*

Materials

- **Flashcards:** home (26–34)

Warmer

- Use the home flashcards to review the vocabulary from the previous lesson. Show each flashcard and elicit the word. Pupils repeat. Show a flashcard and say the wrong word. Pupils correct you. Repeat. Ask questions to check comprehension, e.g. *What's the room under the house?* (basement). *Which is bigger, a village or a city?* (a city).

Song

PB19. ACTIVITY 1

Listen and order.

- Show Activity 1 on the whiteboard. Elicit some of the things pupils can see in the pictures. Supply *block of flats*.
- Say *Open your Pupil's Books at page 19, please.* Direct pupils to the activity instruction and check understanding of *order*. Play the **Audio**. Pupils listen and place a sharpener or eraser on each verse as they hear it. Elicit the order (point to the example answer in the speech bubble first).

Key: **2** b, **3** d, **4** a

20

As in Pupil's Book

PB19. ACTIVITY 2

Listen and sing. Do karaoke.

- Play the **Audio** again line by line for pupils to repeat. Check understanding by asking, e.g. *Who's got a purple door? What goes up and down?* Introduce mimes for pupils to do while they repeat. Play the **Audio** again verse by verse and then right through for pupils to join in. They sing and mime.

20

As in Pupil's Book

- Say *Do karaoke*. Pupils listen to the karaoke version and stand up and sing the **Song** as a class.
- Divide the class into three groups. Each group sings and mimes a verse and everyone joins in with the chorus. Swap roles and pupils repeat.

21

Karaoke version of the song

PB19. ACTIVITY 3

Spot the difference.

- Ask pupils what they can see in the two pictures. Ask *What's different?* Invite a volunteer to read the text in the example speech bubble. Ask pupils to point to the balcony in the picture.
- In pairs, pupils take turns to find differences between the two pictures and tell their partner. Check answers as a class.

Extra support When checking answers, invite volunteers to circle each difference on the whiteboard.

Key: This home hasn't got stairs. This home's got stairs.
This home's got a small garden. This home's got a big garden.
This home hasn't got an upstairs. This home's got an upstairs.
This home's got a green door. This home's got a red door.
This home hasn't got a basement. This home's got a basement.

AB19. Answer key, see page T97

Ending the lesson

- Pupils sing the Pupil's Book **Song** again and mime the actions.

Digital Classroom

Presentation Plus: Unit 2
Audio 20–21
Digital Flashcards
Practice Extra

Extra Resources

- **Teacher Resources:** Unit 2, Downloadable Activity Book Teaching Notes
- **Teacher Resources:** Unit 2, *Song worksheet*
- **AB86 and PB86 – Grammar reference 2**
- **T106 – Consolidation activity:** *Letter chant*
- **T106 – Extension activity:** *My house/flat*

1 Listen and order.

1 – c

a

Upstairs, downstairs,
One floor or two.
We live here,
What about you?

b

Home is home …,
In a city or a village,
In a house or a flat.
Home is home!
It's where it's at.

c

We've got a basement
Under the floor.
It's got brown stairs
And a purple door.

d

I've got a lift,
It goes up and down.
From my balcony,
I can see the town.

2 Listen and sing. Do karaoke.

3 Spot the difference.

This home's got a balcony.

This home hasn't got a balcony.

Look, read and match.

1 – f

Meera moves to a new flat

1. Today Meera and her family are moving. Two workers are carrying the wardrobe to the lorry.

2. Her new address is 14 Park Road. It's a flat. It's amazing!

3. Meera and her dad are helping the cleaner to clean the flat.

4. Meera's helping. She's taking a lamp upstairs. She's smiling because she can go in the lift.

5. The workers can't take the big wardrobe in the small lift. They need to carry it up the stairs. It's difficult to carry.

6. Now they are sitting on the wardrobe. They're having a break. They need a drink.

Write some words to complete the sentences about the story. You can use 1, 2 or 3 words.

1 Meera and her family <u>are moving</u> today.
2 The workers can't put the wardrobe in ____________ .
3 Meera, her dad and the cleaner ____________ her amazing new flat.
4 Meera's carrying a ____________ in the lift.
5 The workers need to carry ____________ upstairs because the lift is very small.
6 The workers are ____________ because they are hot, tired and thirsty.

 Language: present continuous

Objectives

To read and answer questions about a story and talk about needs.

Target language

- **Key language:** present continuous, *need, address, move house, amazing*
- **Additional language:** *difficult to carry, have a break, wardrobe*
- **Revision:** *sofa, lamp, lorry, smile, sit, drink, flat,* action verbs

Materials

- **Flashcards:** home (26–34)

Warmer

- Review the home words using the flashcards. Write six of the words as anagrams on the board (e.g. *ftil* (lift), *ylbaonc* (balcony), *glilvea* (village), *trpssuai* (upstairs), *mbneseat* (basement), *wntsarsoid* (downstairs)). Pupils work in pairs. They race to unscramble the words and write them correctly. Check by asking one pair to spell a word out and another to write it on the board. Tell pupils to look at the building in picture c. Ask *What's the name of the road? What's Meera's new address? How many balconies can you see?*

Presentation

- Personalise use of *need* with the class. Say, e.g. *I need to sit down.* Elicit reasons from the class, e.g. *You're tired. You're ill.* Repeat with other sentences, e.g. *I need a drink. I need to go to bed. I need to open the window. I need a sandwich. I need to go upstairs.*
- Choose a confident pupil, say a reason and elicit a sentence with *need* (e.g. say *You're thirsty* for the pupil to respond *I need a drink*). Repeat with different pupils (e.g. *You're tired. – I need to have a rest. You're hungry. – I need a sandwich. You're ill. – I need to go to bed. You're late. – I need to say sorry. You're cold. – I need to put on my coat.*)

PB20. ACTIVITY 1

Look, read and match.

- Show Activity 1 on the whiteboard. Focus pupils on the pictures and elicit/teach *moving house/flat* and find out if any pupils have moved recently. Elicit who is in the pictures (Meera, a man and a woman, Meera's mother and father) and what they are carrying (the man and woman – a sofa, Meera – a lamp).
- Say *Open your Pupil's Books at page 20, please.* Direct them to the activity instruction and check understanding. Point out the example answer (1–f). Tell pupils to underline any words they don't know as they do the activity. Pupils work individually. They check in pairs. Check with the class.
- Pupils take turns to read the text aloud (in the correct order) around the class. Check understanding, e.g. *Are the men happy in picture b? Why? / Why not? Is Meera moving to the country? What's her new address?*
- In groups of four, pupils look at each other's underlined words. If any pupils know what the word is, they explain it to their friends. Elicit the words the groups don't know. Write them on the board and ask pupils to guess/suggest what they mean. Confirm/Tell the class.
- Watch the ▶ **Video** and answer the questions in the ▶ **Video**.

Key: 2 c, 3 b, 4 a, 5 e, 6 d

PB20. ACTIVITY 2

Write some words to complete the sentences about the story. You can use 1, 2 or 3 words.

- Focus pupils on Activity 2. Direct them to the activity instruction and the example and check understanding. Tell them to look back at the story in Activity 1. Pupils work individually and write the answers in their notebooks. They check in pairs and then pairs check with other pairs. Check with the class. Discuss any questions pupils found difficult.

Extra support Monitor and, if pupils are struggling to find some of the answers, help them decide which section of the text will give them the answer.

Key: 2 the lift, 3 are cleaning, 4 lamp, 5 the wardrobe, 6 having a break

AB20. Answer key, see page T97

Ending the lesson

- With books closed, read out the questions below about the story in the Pupil's Book. Pupils work in pairs and discuss each answer. Make sure they don't look at their books. They write down their ideas. Check answers with the class. Pupils correct their answers. See if any pairs got all the answers right. *1 Is Meera moving to a house or a flat?* (a flat). *2 What colour is Meera's jacket?* (purple). *3 What's Meera's new address?* (14 Park Road). *4 How many people are at Meera's flat in picture d?* (five). *5 How many people are carrying the wardrobe?* (two). *6 What colour is the wardrobe?* (brown). *7 Has 14 Park Road got a lift?* (yes, it has). *8 What's Meera carrying upstairs?* (a lamp). *9 What colour is the lamp?* (red). *10 Who is carrying the glasses of water at the end of the story, Meera or Meera's dad?* (Meera's dad).

Digital Classroom

Presentation Plus: Unit 2

Practice Extra

Digital Flashcards

Extra Resources

- **Teacher Resources:** Unit 2, Downloadable Activity Book Teaching Notes
- **T106 – Consolidation activity 1:** *Meera says ...*
- **T106 – Consolidation activity 2:** *Word lines*

Unit 2 Home sweet home
Pupil's Book p.21

Objectives

To use numbers up to 100 and review colours and location.

Target language

- **Key language:** numbers 21–100, colours, *address, above, below, between, next to, at*
- **Additional language:** *true, false*
- **Revision:** house and home, numbers 1–20, *What colour's ...? What number's ...?*

Materials

- Photocopiable 2, one for each pupil

Warmer

- Invite ten pupils to come to the front. Whisper a number between 11 and 20 to each pupil. They quickly line up in the correct order and then say their numbers in turn for the class to check. Repeat. Pupils can also say their numbers in reverse order (20–11) for the class to check.

PB21. ACTIVITY 1

Listen and say.

- Show Activity 1 on the whiteboard. Focus pupils on the picture and elicit what they can see (numbers).
- Say *Open your Pupil's Books at page 21, please.* Direct pupils to the activity instruction and check understanding. Play the Audio. Pupils listen and repeat. Write the numbers on the board to highlight the pattern and the differences in pronunciation (word stress falling on the second and then the first syllable), e.g. *six**teen**/**six**ty*. Practise the chant with the class, quickly, loudly, softly, etc. Listen for correct pronunciation.

Extra challenge Pupils write four numbers from Activity 1. Play Bingo by calling out the numbers at random.

22

12, 20, 13, 30, 14, 40, 15, 50, 16, 60, 17, 70, 18, 80, 19, 90, a hundred!

PB21. ACTIVITY 2

Listen and write the names. Say.

- Give pupils three minutes to write down all the colours they can remember. Check with the class and elicit the colours onto a mind map on the board.
- Focus pupils on Activity 2. Direct pupils to the activity instructions and check understanding. Play the **Audio.** Pupils listen and check with their partner. Play the **Audio** again if necessary. Check with the class.

Key: 23 – Jack (purple), 37 – Sally (grey), 100 – Daisy (yellow), 59 – Vicky (orange), 64 – Peter (purple), 85 – Mary (grey), 98 – Tom (white)

23

May lives at number seventy-two.
Tom lives at number ninety-eight.
Jack lives at number twenty-three.
Daisy lives at number a hundred.
Peter lives at number sixty-four.
Mary lives at number eighty-five.
Sally lives at number thirty-seven.
Vicky lives at number fifty-nine.

PB21. ACTIVITY 3

Ask and answer.

- Focus pupils on Activity 3. Ask two pupils to read out the dialogue in the speech bubbles. Practise two or three more questions and answers in open pairs. Focus pupils on the *Look* Box and on the parts of the words in bold. Elicit a pair, e.g. *thir**teen** – **thir**ty* and check pronunciation. Focus on the long and short vowel sounds and where the word stress falls. Repeat for the other words. In closed pairs, pupils take turns to ask and answer about the pictures.

PB21. ACTIVITY 4

Talk about where you live.

- Focus pupils on the speech bubbles. Check understanding of *address*. Practise in open pairs, eliciting other questions, e.g. *What colour's your door?* Pupils work in groups of four and take turns to ask and answer about where they live.
- Use Photocopiable 2 from the Teacher Resources.

AB21. Answer key, see page T97

Ending the lesson

- Play a guessing game. Say, e.g. *I can see something in the classroom. It's white and it's below the window.* (shelf). Repeat for other objects in the classroom to review colours and location. More confident pupils can take turns to be the callers.

Digital Classroom

Presentation Plus: Unit 2
Audio 22–23
Digital Flashcards
Practice Extra

Extra Resources

- **Teacher Resources:** Unit 2, Downloadable Activity Book Teaching Notes
- **Teacher Resources:** Unit 2, *Reinforcement worksheet 2*
- **T106 – Consolidation activity:** *Whisper and write*

1 Listen and say.

2 Listen and write the names. Say.

May lives at number 72.

That's pink.

May

3 Ask and answer.

What number's the yellow door?

It's number 23.

4 Talk about where you live.

What's your address?

It's 72 Station Road.

LOOK

thirt**een** – thirty
fourt**een** – forty
fift**een** – fifty
sixt**een** – sixty
sevent**een** – seventy
eight**een** – eighty
ninet**een** – ninety
a **hun**dred

Vocabulary: numbers: *twelve* to *a hundred*

Lock's sounds and spelling

1 24 Watch the video. Watch again and practise.

2 Look and find. Read and underline the sounds.

See the street where we meet.

Bees at number three and sheep at number thirteen.

Green trees in between.

3 Work in pairs. Write and say. Listen and complete.

The house is number 13. My number 13 is blue.

13 14 15 30 40 50

Show what you know

There are ________ bees in the ______.

Objectives

To recognise and practise the long /iː/ sound in context and with familiar vocabulary, noticing *ee* spelling patterns.

Target language

- **Key language:** the vowel sound /iː/ (*thirteen*)
- **Additional language:** *in between, meet*
- **Revision:** *village, city, street, bees, sheep, trees*

Materials

- **Flashcards:** village (34), city (32)

Warmer

- Draw a simple house on the board. Ask pupils to name the parts of the house and elicit *upstairs, downstairs, basement, stairs, lift, balcony*. Label those on the house. Describe a part of the house for pupils to guess, e.g. *You walk up or down the …* (stairs). *You are outside on the …* (balcony). Divide pupils into groups of four to describe and guess.

Presentation

PB22. ACTIVITY 1

Watch the video. Watch again and practise.

- Ask pupils *What animals live in this street?* Watch the ▶ **Video**. Pupils answer *Bees and sheep.*
- Ask *What house number do the bees live at?* and *What house number do the sheep live at?* Pupils watch the ▶ **Video** again and check (3 and 13).

24

Voice & Key: /iː/ /iː/
Lock: What can you see, Key?
Voice: see /iː/ street /iː/ meet /iː/
Lock & Key: See the street where we meet.
Voice: bees /iː/ three /iː/ sheep /iː/ thirteen /iː/
Lock & Key: Bees at number three and sheep at number thirteen.
Voice: /iː/ trees /iː/ between
Lock & Key: Green trees in between.
Lock & Voice: See the street where we meet.
Bees at number three and sheep at number thirteen. Green trees in between.
Lock: Come on, everybody. One, two, three … let's say it with Key!
Voice, Lock & Key: See the street where we meet. Bees at number three and sheep at number thirteen. Green trees in between.
Lock: I say – well done, Key!

- Ask pupils to hold up a pencil. As you say the /iː/ sound in *thirteen*, move the pencil in a straight line across from left to right, to represent a long sound.
- Move the pencil across and pupils say the corresponding sound /iː/. Repeat a few times.

PB22. ACTIVITY 2

Look and find. Read and underline the sounds.

- Show Activity 2 on the whiteboard. Point to the picture and elicit the words *bees* and *sheep*. Say the sentences for pupils, and together move your pencils across on the /iː/ sounds. Put pupils into pairs and ask them to say the sentences and move their pencils on the sounds. Ask pupils to look at the sentences and underline the letters for the /iː/ sound. Check together (ee).

PB22. ACTIVITY 3

Work in pairs. Write and say. Listen and complete.

- Look at the two streets in Activity 3 and the numbers in the word box. Say the numbers together. Tell pupils to work alone and write the numbers they want on the houses in the picture on the left. Put pupils into pairs A and B. A describes their street numbers and B listens and writes the numbers they hear in the street on the right. Pairs swap roles. Once pairs have finished, they look and check.

Extra support Before doing the activity, review and write up the phrases needed: *My first house is number … My number 14 house is blue … My next house is … What number/colour …?*

Show what you know

- Focus on the *Show what you know* Box. Pupils complete the sentence with the missing words and practise saying it.

Key: twenty, trees

AB22. Answer key, see page T97

Ending the lesson

- Pupils stand in a line. Say words with or without the /iː/ sound. If the word doesn't have the /iː/ sound, pupils jump to the left. If it has the /iː/ sound, they jump to the right.
- Invite volunteers to be the caller.

Digital Classroom

Presentation Plus: Unit 2

Digital Flashcards
Audio 24

Practice Extra

Extra Resources

- **Teacher Resources:** Unit 2, Downloadable Activity Book Teaching Notes
- **T106 – Consolidation activity:** *Street number sums*
- **T106 – Extension activity:** *ee and y words*

Objectives

To watch and read a story and review language from the unit.

Target language

- **Key language:** language from the unit, *lovely, torch*
- **Additional language:** *There you are, episode*
- **Revision:** language from the story, descriptions, adjectives, *monster*

Materials

- **Warmer:** Six sentences (some true, some false) about the story so far, written on a large piece of paper.

Warmer

- Display the large piece of paper with sentences about the story, e.g. *Clarence is a dog.* (false). *Lock and Key are detectives.* (true). *Clarence hasn't got a tail.* (true). *Lock and Key are good at their jobs.* (false). *The pet thief has got a black beard.* (true). *The pet thief is in the garden.* (false). In pairs, pupils read the sentences and decide if they are true or false. They don't look back at the story. Check the answers with the class, eliciting the corrections for the false sentences to build up the story so far.

Story

PB23.

Watch the video.

- Say *Open your Pupil's Books at page 23, please.* Ask pupils who they can see in the pictures and where they are. Tell pupils they are going to watch a ▶ **Video** of the story. Set the pre-watching questions: *What's in the basement? What does Mrs Potts think? What is it?*

Extra support Use the pictures to guide pupils to predict the story.

- Watch the ▶ **Video** with the class. Give pupils the option of watching it twice if they need to. They answer the questions and check in pairs. Check with the class (a monster; the cat).
- Focus on page 23 again. Play the **Audio**. Pupils listen and repeat. Encourage them to say it with intonation and feeling.
- Check comprehension by asking, e.g. *Is Mrs Potts' house new?* (no, it's old). *Has it got a basement?* (yes). Elicit what Lock is holding on his way down the stairs (a torch).

▶ 25

Lock: Lovely house, Mrs Potts. It's very old.
Mrs Potts: I think it's got a monster.
Mrs Potts: It lives under the stairs in the basement. It comes upstairs at night.
Lock: Oh, I don't think so, Mrs Potts. There are no monsters.
Mrs Potts: Can you go downstairs and look in the basement for me?
Lock: Of course we can
Key: Er, yes … No problem, Mrs Potts.
Key: I'm not happy about this, Lock. I don't like it.
Cat: YOWL!
Lock: Aagghhh!
Key: It's a monster!
Mrs Potts: There you are, Clarence. You naughty cat!
Key: The house hasn't got a monster, Mrs Potts.
Lock: No, it's got a cat … called Clarence.

PB23. ACTIVITY 1

What does Mrs Potts think about the monster? Say two things.

- Ask a pupil to read the question aloud. Give pupils time to talk about it in pairs. They can reread the story if necessary. Check answers as a class (it's in the basement under the stairs; it comes upstairs at night).

Extra challenge To elicit negative sentences, ask *What does Lock think about the monster?* (e.g. He thinks there are no monsters in the basement. He thinks it doesn't live under the stairs. He thinks it doesn't come upstairs at night.)

AB23. Answer key, see page T97

Ending the lesson

- Say true and false sentences about today's episode of Lock and Key, e.g. *Lock and Key are at Mrs Potts' house.* (true). *Mrs Potts thinks there's a monster in the wardrobe.* (false). *Lock and Key go downstairs to the basement.* (true). *Lock and Key find a monster in the basement.* (false). If the sentence is true, pupils put their hands on their heads. If the sentence is false, they cross their arms in front of their chests.

Digital Classroom

Presentation Plus: Unit 2
Digital Flashcards
Audio 25
Practice Extra

Extra Resources

- **Teacher Resources:** Unit 2, Downloadable Activity Book Teaching Notes
- **Teacher Resources:** Unit 2, *Extension worksheet 2*
- **Teacher Resources:** Unit 2, *Video, Suzy's room*
- **T106 – Extension activity 1:** *Read and draw*
- **T106 – Extension activity 2:** *Role play*

1 **What does Mrs Potts think about the monster? Say two things.**

How are our homes unique?

1 26 **Listen and read. Which is your favourite home? Why?**

1 These **cabins** in Norway are on **stilts**, so they don't get wet.

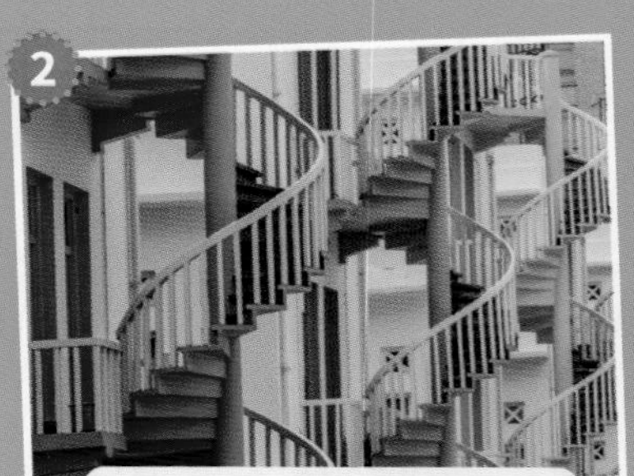

2 These **flats** in Singapore have got colourful **spiral staircases**.

3 This **cave home** is in Turkey. It's very old!

4 Can you imagine living on a traditional Indian **houseboat**? This house can float!

5 This **tree house** in the USA has got a **rope bridge**.

2 **Write the words from Activity 1 to complete the chart.**

Types of homes	Features
cabin	

3 **What are the advantages and disadvantages of the homes in Activity 1? Think and say.**

It's in a city with shops and transport.

It's very cold / hot.

DIDYOUKNOW...?

Some cave homes are more than 2,000 years old!

Objectives

To compare and contrast living in different types of homes.

Target language

- **Key language:** language from the unit
- **Additional language:** *cabin, cave, float, home, houseboat, rope bridge, spiral staircase, stilts, tree house*
- **Revision:** *city, cold, colourful, flat, hot, house, old, traditional*

Warmer

- Show the pictures from Pupil's Book page 24 Activity 1. Give pupils 30 seconds to try to remember as much as they can about the different pictures. Then close the page on the whiteboard.
- Invite volunteers to say things they remember from the pictures, e.g. *the sea*. Confirm correct statements. After eliciting suggestions, show the pictures again for pupils to check.
- You are now ready to watch the ▶ Video.

PB24

How are our homes unique?

- Tell pupils that they're going to learn more about different types of homes in this lesson.
- Watch the ▶ Video and answer the questions in the ▶ Video.

PB24 ACTIVITY 1

Listen and read. Which is your favourite home? Why?

- Say *Open your Pupil's Books at page 24, please.* Focus pupils on Activity 1. Ask *What places does the text mention?* Pupils scan the text for the answers (Norway, Singapore, Turkey, India, the USA).
- Ask a pupil to read the activity instruction and questions aloud. Play the 🔊 Audio while pupils follow along in their books. Pupils discuss their answers to the questions in pairs. Then discuss as a class. Encourage pupils to explain their answers.

Extra support Put pupils into pairs. Ask *What is unusual about each house?* Allow pupils to discuss answers in their pairs. Then invite volunteers to share their ideas.

🔊 26

1 **Boy:** These cabins in Norway are on stilts, so they don't get wet.
2 **Girl:** These flats in Singapore have got colourful spiral staircases.
3 **Boy:** This cave home is in Turkey. It's very old.
4 **Girl:** Can you imagine living on a traditional Indian houseboat? This house can float.
5 **Boy:** This tree house in the USA has got a rope bridge.

PB24 ACTIVITY 2

Write the words from Activity 1 to complete the chart.

- Focus pupils' attention on the headings in the chart. Elicit one type of home from Activity 1 and tell pupils to write it in the first column. Pupils work in pairs to write the other types of homes.
- Focus pupils' attention on the second column. Elicit a feature, or characteristic, of one of the homes in Activity 1, e.g. *stilts*. Tell pupils to write this and the other features in the second column.
- Monitor pupils' progress. Check answers as a class.

Key: Types of homes: (cabin), flat, cave home, houseboat, tree house; Features: stilts, spiral staircase, rope bridge

PB24 ACTIVITY 3

What are the advantages and disadvantages of the homes in Activity 1? Think and say.

- Focus on Activity 3 and ask a pupil to read the instructions aloud. Remind pupils that advantages are good or positive, and disadvantages are bad or negative. Ask volunteers to read the examples out loud, and then ask which of the homes those comments might be referring to.
- Put pupils into small groups to discuss other advantages and disadvantages.
- Encourage volunteers to share their ideas with the class.

Did you know …?

- Invite a volunteer to read the information in the box out loud. Ask pupils if this fact surprises them. Ask pupils if they would like to live in a cave home. Encourage them to explain their answers.

AB24. **Answer key, see page T97**

Ending the lesson

- Ask pupils about their homes. Ask *Is there anything interesting or unusual about your home?* Give an example, e.g. *My home has big windows. I have a lot of plants because of the sunlight.*
- Put pupils into pairs to talk about their homes.

Digital Classroom

Presentation Plus: Unit 2
Digital Flashcards
Audio 26
Practice Extra

Extra Resources

- **Teacher Resources:** Unit 2, Downloadable Activity Book Teaching Notes
- **T106 – Consolidation activity:** *Describe and guess*
- **T106 – Extension activity:** *Draw and guess*

Objectives
To write a description of their dream bedroom.

Target language
- **Key language:** language from the unit
- **Additional language:** *pet cat, top, bed, bedroom, slide, toys, walls*
- **Revision:** *big, favourite, jump, many, spiral staircase*

Warmer
- Explain that you're going to write a word in the air for pupils to guess. Turn to face away from the class and trace the word *houseboat* in the air with your finger. Repeat if necessary. Pupils call out the word. Play again with a different home or home feature.

PB25 ACTIVITY 4

Read the description of Bethany's dream bedroom. Which parts do you like the most?
- Ask pupils to look at the picture and the description. Ask *What does the picture show? What do you think the text will say?*
- Ask a pupil to read the instruction and question aloud. Give pupils time to read the text. Help with vocabulary if needed, but encourage pupils to use context to understand any unfamiliar words.
- Pupils answer the question in pairs. Invite volunteers to share their opinions with the class.

Extra support Tell pupils to circle each instance of the word *it* in Bethany's description. Ask what each *it* refers to in each case (the bed, the slide, blue). Put pupils into pairs. Ask *What do you like about your bedroom at home? What don't you like?* Ask volunteers to share their ideas with the class.

PB25 ACTIVITY 5

Underline the contractions in Activity 4.
- Point out the examples of contractions in the box. Explain that a contraction is a short form of two or more words. Draw an apostrophe on the board and say *All contractions have got an apostrophe. People use contractions to speak quickly and naturally.*
- Tell pupils to underline the contractions in Activity 4. They check in pairs. Monitor the activity and check answers as a class.

Key: Pupils underline: there's, I've, There's, It's, It's, There's, there's

Project
- Remember to download your project notes from *Cambridge One*.

Extra challenge Brainstorm other contractions pupils know and write them on the board, e.g. *you are / you're*.

PB25 ACTIVITY 6

You are designing your own dream bedroom. Which colours and what things do you want? Think and say.
- Explain to pupils that they are going to discuss their own ideas for a dream bedroom. Ask a pupil to read out the instructions aloud. Put pupils into pairs to answer the question and discuss their ideas.
- Monitor pupils' progress and help with vocabulary if needed.

AB25. Answer key, see pages T97–98

Ending the lesson
- Ask pupils which chant/song they'd like to do again from the unit. Do it together to end the lesson.

Digital Classroom

Presentation Plus: Unit 2

Practice Extra
Digital Flashcards

Extra Resources
- **Teacher Resources:** Unit 2, Downloadable Activity Book Teaching Notes
- **Teacher Resources:** Unit 2, *Project notes*
- **PB88–95 – A1 Movers Exam folder**
- **T107 – Consolidation activity:** *Chain game*

4 Read the description of Bethany's dream bedroom. Which parts do you like the most?

My dream bedroom

In my dream bedroom, there's a big bed. I can jump on it! I've got a lot of toys. There's a slide too. It's fast! The walls of my dream bedroom are blue. It's my favourite colour! There's a spiral staircase too. At the top, there's a special bed for my pet cat.

5 Underline the contractions in Activity 4.

Ready to write:

Go to Activity Book page 24.

Learning to write:

Contractions

A contraction is a short form of two or more words. All contractions have an apostrophe (').

there is → there's

it is → it's

I have → I've

6 You are designing your own dream bedroom. Which colours and what things do you want? Think and say.

Project

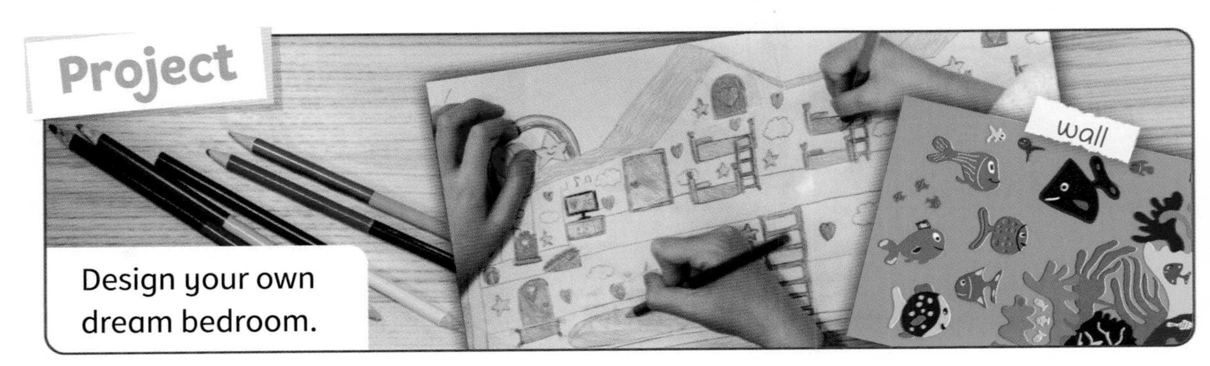

Design your own dream bedroom.

Geography: different types of home | creative thinking

Review Units 1 and 2

1 Play the game.

Instructions

Lifts – Go up
Stairs – Go down
Pictures – Spell the words. If it's right, roll again. If it's wrong, stop.

Objectives

To review language from Units 1 and 2 and play a game.

Target language

- **Key language:** vocabulary and language from Units 1 and 2
- **Additional language:** procedural language: *It's my/your/his/her turn. Pass the dice, please. I'm/You're/He's/She's (yellow). I've/You've/He's/She's finished/won. That's wrong/right. If it's right, roll again. If it's wrong, stop. Wanted!*
- **Revision:** character names, present continuous, *have got, play the game*

Materials

- Dice and four different coloured counters
- **Warmer:** Eight to ten pictures of people from magazines, a short description of the person in each picture

Warmer

- Stick the pictures cut from magazines on the board. The pictures should feature young and old people, beards, curly hair, fair hair, straight hair, long/short hair, moustache, different coloured eyes (if visible), glasses. Write a letter (a, b, c, d, etc.) under each one. Read out your descriptions one by one. Read each one twice. They shouldn't be in the same order as the pictures. Pupils listen and write the letter corresponding to the picture in their notebooks. They check in pairs. Check with the class.

PB26. ACTIVITY 1

Play the game.

- Show Activity 1 on the whiteboard. Elicit what pupils can see (a game). Say *Yes, you're going to play a game.* Quickly review the home/house vocabulary.
- Say *Open your Pupil's Books at page 26, please.* Say, e.g. *Can you find a kite?* Point to it. Do the same for *balcony, village, basement, stairs, lift*, etc.
- Demonstrate the game using four pupils, before handing out the dice and counters to the rest of the class. Pupils take turns to throw the dice and move. When they land on a picture, they spell the word. If it's correct, they roll again. If not, they stop. If they land on a lift, they go up; if stairs, they go down. Pupils say the numbers aloud as they move (for practice).
- Direct pupils to the instructions on the Pupil's Book page. Make groups of four. Pupils clear their desks and place one book in the centre. Hand out a dice and four different coloured counters to each group. Pupils throw the dice to see who starts (the one with the highest number). Play moves up the board. The first pupil in each group to finish is the winner.
- If time, pupils can play the game again.

Extra support Allow pupils to work in pairs and help each other.

AB26. **Answer key, see page T98**

Ending the lesson

- On the board, draw a house with ten stairs going down into a swamp. Draw a big crocodile in the swamp. Draw a stick figure at the top of the stairs. Write a word from Units 1 or 2 as dashes, one for each letter in the word. Pupils take turns to guess a letter. Write correct letters in the word and write incorrect letters on the right of the board. For each incorrect guess, move the stick figure one step down. Continue until pupils guess or the figure is eaten. Clean the board and repeat with a different word.

Digital Classroom

Presentation Plus: Unit 2

Practice Extra

Digital Flashcards

Extra Resources

- **Teacher Resources:** Unit 2, Downloadable Activity Book Teaching Notes
- **Teacher Resources:** Unit 2, Downloadable Activity Book Audio Script
- **T107 – Consolidation activity:** *Sing a song*

Review Units 1 and 2
Pupil's Book p.27

Objectives
To review language from Units 1 and 2 and talk about pictures.

Target language
- **Key language:** vocabulary and language from Units 1 and 2, *armchair*
- **Additional language:** *This picture is different.*
- **Revision:** descriptions, food, clothes, toys, family, present continuous

Warmer
- Describe someone in the class without giving their name, referring to hair, eyes, clothes, e.g. *This pupil's got short, dark hair. This pupil …* The class guesses who it is. Repeat.

PB27. ACTIVITY 2

Look, read and answer.
- Show Activity 2 on the whiteboard. Elicit what pupils can see (people in a house doing different things). Elicit some of the things they are doing.
- Say *Open your Pupil's Books at page 27, please.* Pupils work in pairs to complete the activity.

Key: **1** They are carrying a cupboard. **2** She's cleaning the window. **3** They're in the basement. **4** He's reading a comic. **5** She's carrying a lamp.

PB27. ACTIVITY 3

Look at the pictures. Say which is different.
- Focus pupils on Activity 3 and on the first row of pictures. Elicit what each one is and which one is different (go through the example answer, but accept other options, as long as pupils can explain them – there may be more than one possible answer).
- Direct pupils to the activity instructions to remind them this is a speaking activity. In pairs, they look at the rows of pictures and decide which ones are different. Check with the class and discuss.

Key: **2** Picture b is different. It's a toy. **3** Picture d is different. The man hasn't got a moustache. **4** Picture a is different. It's a toy.

PB27.

Quiz
- Say *Now let's read and remember.* Explain/Elicit the meaning of *quiz*. Focus pupils on the questions. Pupils look back through Units 1 and 2 and find the answers to the questions. They discuss them in groups of four. Check with the class.

Extra challenge Tell pupils to try to answer the questions from memory before looking back in their books.

- Pupils write two more questions of their own to help them remember the language and/or vocabulary from the units. They write the questions in their notebooks. Pupils close their Pupil's Books. Volunteers ask the class one of their revision questions.

Key: **1** Uncle Fred. **2** They're playing a game. **3** She loves painting. **4** You can find a basement under a house. **5** A wardrobe. **6** thirty, sixteen, thirteen, fifty, **7** No, he doesn't. **8** So they don't get wet.

AB27. **Answer key, see page T98**

Ending the lesson
- Ask pupils which lessons, topics and/or activities were their favourites.

Digital Classroom

Presentation Plus: Unit 2

Practice Extra
Digital Flashcards

Extra Resources
- **Teacher Resources:** Unit 2, Downloadable Activity Book Teaching Notes
- **T107 – Consolidation activity :** *Play a game*

2 Look, read and answer.

1 What are the men doing?
2 What's the woman doing?
3 Which room are the family in?
4 What's the boy reading?
5 What's the girl carrying?

3 Look at the pictures. Say which is different.

Picture d is different. She's got short hair.

1 a  b  c  d  

2 a b c d  

3 a  b  c  d 

4 a  b  c  d 

Quiz

1 What's Stella's uncle's name? (p10)

2 What are Stella and her aunt doing? (p11)

3 What does Simon's grandmother love doing? (p12)

4 Where can you find a basement? (p19)

5 What are the workers carrying to Meera's new flat? (p20)

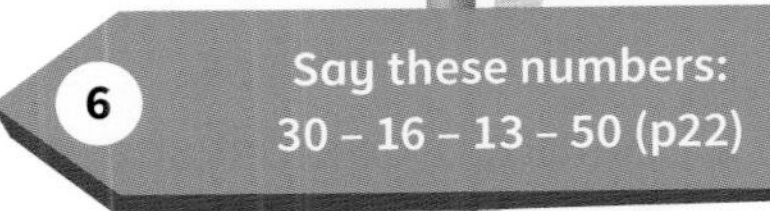

6 Say these numbers: 30 – 16 – 13 – 50 (p22)

7 Does Key want to look for Mrs Potts' monster? (p23)

8 Why do some cabins have stilts? (p24)

3 A day in the life

1 27 Listen and say the letter. Match.

catch the bus ☐ do homework ☐ get dressed ☐ get undressed ☐
get up ☐ go to bed ☐ have a shower ☐ put on ☐
wake up a take off ☐ wash ☐

2 Read and complete.

1 Stella wakes up at seven o'clock every day.
2 Before breakfast she ______________ .
3 Then she gets dressed and puts on her ______________ and leggings.
4 After school Stella does her ______________ .
5 She washes her ______________ before dinner.
6 She ______________ and takes off her T-shirt and leggings.
7 Stella goes to bed ______________ nine o'clock.

3 28 Listen and do the actions.

LOOK

She wakes up at **seven o'clock**.

At **eight o'clock** she catches the bus.

Objectives

To read about daily routines and times.

Target language

- **Key language:** present simple for routines: statements and questions, *catch the bus, do homework, get dressed, get undressed, get up, put on, take off, wash, go to bed, go to school, have a shower, wake up, have breakfast/lunch/ dinner, every day*
- **Additional language:** *a day in the life, first, then*
- **Revision:** character names, descriptions, house and home, clothes, homework, present continuous

Materials

- **Flashcards:** daily routine (44–51)

Warmer

- Say, e.g. *Pupils with white socks, stand up. Pupils who like fish, put your hands on your head. Pupils with straight hair, sit down.* Continue, using, e.g. *like / don't like computer games, reading, TV, sleeping; with curly hair, dark hair, fair hair; turn around, point to the board, point to the window.*

Presentation

- Review/Elicit the daily routine words using the flashcards.
- Mime the following story: *wake up, get up, have a shower, get dressed, put on, take off, wash, get undressed, go to bed.*
- Repeat each action from the story. Elicit the words. Mime the story again. Pupils say the words as you mime the actions.

PB28. ACTIVITY 1

Listen and say the letter. Match.

- Say *Open your Pupil's Books at page 28, please.* Focus on Stella. Say, e.g. *get dressed.* Pupils point. Say *Stella does these things every day.* Direct pupils to the activity instruction and check understanding. Play the Audio. Pupils whisper the answer to their partner. Play the Audio again. Pause to elicit the letters.
- Pupils match the words and phrases in the box with the pictures a–i. They write the letters in the boxes. Note that pictures h and i each relate to two phrases. Check answers as a class. Elicit sentences using: *First, Then* and the present simple.

Key: catch the bus c, do homework f, get dressed h, get undressed i, get up g, go to bed d, have a shower e, put on h, take off i, wash b

27

Stella wakes up at seven o'clock every day.
Stella gets up.
Stella has a shower.
Then Stella gets dressed. She puts on her leggings and her T-shirt.
Stella catches the bus to school.
Stella does her homework.
Before dinner, Stella washes her hands.
Stella gets undressed. She takes off her leggings and her T-shirt.
Stella goes to bed at nine o'clock.

Presentation

PB28. ACTIVITY 2

Read and complete.

- Focus pupils on the clocks in three of the pictures in Activity 1. Elicit/Teach the times. Draw six or seven clocks showing different times on the board. Ask *What's the time?*
- Focus pupils on Activity 2 and the *Look* Box. Remind them to use *at* for times. Practise pronunciation of *o'clock*. Ask volunteers to read the example sentence and draw pupils' attention to the verb ending *s*. Pupils complete the sentences with the correct form of the verbs. They check in pairs. Monitor and help. Check with the class.

Extra challenge Pupils use the sentences in Activity 2 to talk about the differences between Stella's day and their own day.

Key: 2 has a shower, **3** T-shirt, **4** homework, **5** hands, **6** gets undressed, **7** at

PB28. ACTIVITY 3

Listen and do the actions.

- Review the actions from your mime story in the Presentation. Focus pupils on the activity instruction and check understanding. Pupils stand up. Play the Audio. Pupils listen and do the actions. Repeat.
- **Note:** Pupils can adapt the actions if they wish.

28

Have breakfast. Go to bed. Have lunch. Put on your jacket. Take off your shoes. Wake up. Have a shower. Put on your T-shirt. Get up. Wash your hands. Have dinner. Catch the bus.

AB28. Answer key, see page T98

Ending the lesson

- Draw ten clocks on the board with different times. Write a letter (a–j) under each one. Pupils draw a 2 × 2 Bingo square and write different letters in the squares corresponding to the clocks. Call out the times in random order. Pupils cross out the letters if they correspond to times called. The first to cross out all four shouts *Bingo!* Check by eliciting the times.

Digital Classroom

Presentation Plus: Unit 3

Digital Flashcards

Audio 27–28

Practice Extra

Extra Resources

- **Teacher Resources:** Unit 3, Downloadable Activity Book Teaching Notes
- **Teacher Resources:** Unit 3, *Reinforcement worksheet 1*
- **T107 – Extension activity:** *Clocks*
- **T107 – Consolidation activity:** *Mime*

Objectives

To have further practice talking about routines and times and to sing a song.

Target language

- **Key language:** present simple for daily routines: questions, long and short answers, *before, after*
- **Additional language:** *on the way, lessons start, out to play, same, different, routine, bedtime*
- **Revision:** times, daily actions

Materials

- **Flashcards:** daily routine (44–51)

Warmer

- Show the daily routine flashcards in turn and elicit the words. Show them in a different order. Pupils chorus the words.
- Stick the flashcards on the board and number them 1 to 8. Say a sentence about your daily routine using one of the activities. Pupils say the correct number. Repeat with different actions.

Song

PB29. ACTIVITY 1

Listen and match.

- Show Activity 1 on the whiteboard. Focus pupils on the pictures and elicit some of the verbs by asking, e.g. *Tell me something that this boy does every day.*
- Say *Open your Pupil's Books at page 29, please.* Direct pupils to the activity instruction and the example answer. Play the first verse on the Audio. Check understanding. Play the rest of the Audio. Pupils listen and match the pictures with the appropriate lines in the Song. They write the sequence in their notebooks. They check in pairs. Play the Audio again. Check with the class. Check understanding of vocabulary.

Key: 2 f, 3 e, 4 c, 5 a, 6 d

29

As in Pupil's Book

PB29. ACTIVITY 2

Listen and sing. Do karaoke.

- Play the Audio in short sections for pupils to repeat. Pupils sing the Song, verse by verse and then right through. Divide the class into four groups. Pupils take turns to sing their verse and to mime the actions. Swap roles.

29

As in Pupil's Book

- Say *Do karaoke.* Pupils listen to the karaoke version and stand up and sing the Song as a class.

30

Karaoke version of the song

PB29. ACTIVITY 3

Answer the questions.

- Focus pupils on the questions and the example answer. Pupils ask and answer the questions in open pairs around the class. Involve the whole class.
- Pupils ask and answer the questions in closed pairs. Monitor and check they are answering using complete sentences.

Key: **2** He does his homework at eight o'clock. **3** He starts school at nine o'clock. **4** He goes out to play at eleven o'clock. **5** He goes to bed at nine o'clock.

PB29. ACTIVITY 4

Ask and answer.

- Focus pupils on Activity 4 and ask two pupils to read the speech bubbles aloud. Elicit a few more questions from pupils using the table. Other pupils answer them. Check for correct use of *do* in the question. Pupils work in pairs. They take turns to ask and answer. Check by eliciting some questions and answers.

Extra challenge In pairs, pupils create more questions with *before/after* and other activities. They ask and answer their questions with another pair.

AB29. Answer key, see page T98

Ending the lesson

- Pupils sing the Pupil's Book Song again as a class. They mime as they sing.

Digital Classroom

Presentation Plus: Unit 3
Audio 29–30
Digital Flashcards
Practice Extra

Extra Resources

- **Teacher Resources:** Unit 3, Downloadable Activity Book Teaching Notes
- **Teacher Resources:** Unit 3, *Song worksheet*
- **T107 – Consolidation activity 1:** *What's the time, Mr Wolf?*
- **T107 – Consolidation activity 2:** *Set the time*

1 Listen and match. 29

1 – b

a

b

c

d

e

f

I wake up in the morning,
I get up for breakfast,
I have a shower and I get dressed ... 1
Oooh yes, every day.

I catch the bus
to take me to school ...
I do my homework on the way ... 2
Oooh yes, every day.

Lessons start and
I see my teacher ... 3
Eleven o'clock and we're out to play ... 4
Oooh yes, every day.

I wash my hands ... 5
Before I have my dinner ...
I get undressed and I go to bed ... 6
Oooh yes, oooh yes,
Oooh yes, every day, every day,
every day.

2 Listen and sing. Do karaoke. 30

3 Answer the questions.

He gets dressed at seven o'clock.

1 What time does he get dressed?
2 What time does he do his homework?
3 What time does he start school?
4 What time does he go out to play?
5 What time does he go to bed?

4 Ask and answer.

What do you do before breakfast?

I have a shower.

What do you do	before after	breakfast? lunch? dinner? school? bedtime?

Language: present simple

1 31 Say the chant. Ask and answer.

What do you do on Mondays?

I go swimming.

Monday	Tuesday	Wednesday	Thursday	Friday	Saturday/ Sunday

2 32 Listen and say the day.

a

b

c

3 33 Listen again. Choose the right words.

1 Simon **always** / **never** plays in the park on Mondays.
2 Simon **always** / **sometimes** does his homework on Mondays.
3 Simon **sometimes** / **never** goes swimming on Wednesdays.
4 Simon **always** / **never** plays in the park on Sundays.

1 Simon never plays in the park on Mondays.

STUDY

always ✓✓✓
sometimes ✓
never ✗

She **sometimes** plays football in the park.

He **always** wakes up at seven o'clock.

They **never** go to school on Sundays.

Objectives

To name the days of the week and to talk about frequency of routine actions.

Target language

- **Key language:** *Monday, Tuesday, Wednesday, Thursday, Friday, Saturday, Sunday, weekend, always, sometimes, never, every day, How often …?*
- **Revision:** prepositions, sport and activities, present simple for routines, *before, after*

Materials

- **Presentation:** School timetable

Warmer

- Review time and routines by asking questions around the class, e.g. *What time do you get up? Do you have a shower every day? Do you have breakfast after your shower every day?* Include several questions with *every day*, e.g. *Do you do homework every day?*, following *No* responses with *How many times … (in a week)?*

Presentation

- Use the school timetable to introduce/review the days of the week. If you always write the day and the date on the board at the start of the lesson, focus pupils on this. Say *each day*. Pupils repeat. Ask questions, e.g. *When do you have English?* (Monday and Wednesday). *Is that every day?* (no). *How often do you have maths?* Raise awareness of *How often …?*

PB30. ACTIVITY 1

Say the chant. Ask and answer.

- Show Activity 1 on the whiteboard. Say *Open your Pupil's Books at page 30, please*. Pupils stand up. Play the **Audio**. They join in the chant, clapping or snapping their fingers to the rhythm.
- Ask two pupils to read out the question and answer in the example speech bubble. Highlight the 's' on *Mondays* in the question. In pairs, pupils ask and answer about different days of the week.

Extra challenge Tell pupils they must use a different verb for each of their answers.

31

Monday, Tuesday, Wednesday, Thursday, Friday, Saturday, Sunday [x2]

PB30. ACTIVITY 2

Listen and say the day.

- Show Activity 2 on the whiteboard. Elicit who and what they can see. Point out that Simon isn't in the park in picture a. Play the **Audio**. Pupils listen for the day. They whisper it to their partner. Play the **Audio** again. Check with the class. Elicit what Simon does on the different days.
- Focus pupils on the *Study* Box. Elicit some things that pupils always, sometimes and never do. Write some of their examples on the board, underline the frequency words and check understanding of the concept with reference to a week. Pupils copy the examples from the board into their notebooks.
- Watch the **Video**.

Key: a Monday, **b** Wednesday, **c** Sunday

32

Lenny: How often do you play in the park, Simon? Do you play every day?
Simon: Well, no. I never play in the park on Mondays.
Lenny: Yes, we always have lots of homework on Mondays.
Simon: I sometimes play in the park after school on Wednesdays, but I sometimes go swimming with Dad.
Lenny: And what about at the weekend?
Simon: I always play in the park on Sundays. It's my favourite day.
Lenny: Simon … What day is it today?
Simon: It's Sunday! Let's go to the park!

PB30. ACTIVITY 3

Listen again. Choose the right words.

- Focus pupils on Activity 3 and give them time to read the sentences before they listen. Play the **Audio** again. Check with the class, eliciting complete sentences. Pupils write the correct sentences in their notebooks.

Key: **2** always, **3** sometimes, **4** always

33

As in audio script 32 above

AB30. Answer key, see page T98

Ending the lesson

- Do a version of the days of the week chant to end the lesson. First time they hum *Monday* and say the other days, second time they hum *Monday, Tuesday* and say the other days, etc. until they are humming the whole chant.

Digital Classroom

Presentation Plus: Unit 3
Digital Flashcards
Audio 31–33
Practice Extra

Extra Resources

- **Teacher Resources:** Unit 3, Downloadable Activity Book Teaching Notes
- **Teacher Resources:** Unit 3, *Reinforcement worksheet 2*
- **AB86 and PB86 – Grammar reference 3**
- **T107 – Extension activity:** *About me*
- **T107 – Consolidation activity:** *How often?*

Objectives

To have more practice reading and to talk about routines and frequency.

Target language

- **Key language:** *always, sometimes, never*
- **Additional language:** *score a goal*
- **Revision:** present simple, daily activities, days of the week, *holidays, mountains, family, car*

Materials

- Photocopiable 3, copied onto card (one for each pair of pupils)

Warmer

- Say some true and false sentences about yourself using adverbs of frequency, e.g. *I always wear a helmet in class. I always speak English.* Pupils say *Yes* for the true sentences and correct the false sentences (using *you*), e.g. *No, you never wear a helmet in class!*

PB31. ACTIVITY 1

Look, read and complete.

- Show Activity 1 on the whiteboard. Say *Open your Pupil's Books at page 31, please.* Elicit what they can see in the pictures and what the ticks and crosses mean. If they can't remember, refer them to the *Study* Box on the previous page. Direct pupils to the activity instruction and check they know what to do. They read the text in pairs and fill in the gaps. Check with the class by asking pupils to read the sentences aloud.

Key: **2** never, **3** always, **4** sometimes, **5** sometimes, **6** never, **7** sometimes

PB31. ACTIVITY 2

Listen and say 'yes' or 'no'.

- Play the **Audio**. Tell pupils to do thumbs up (yes) and thumbs down (no) to their partner the first time they listen, and not to speak. Play the statements. Pupils do thumbs up / thumbs down. Play the statements again. Pause after each one for pupils to respond. Elicit corrections for the 'no' sentences.

Key: **1** Yes. **2** No, he never plays the piano in his holidays. **3** No, he always plays tennis on Wednesdays. **4** Yes. **5** Yes. **6** No, he sometimes takes his family to the mountains on Sundays. **7** No, they sometimes sing songs in the car.

34

1. James Flunk is a music teacher.
2. He always plays the piano in his holidays.
3. He never plays tennis on Wednesdays.
4. He sometimes plays football with his daughter Jane.
5. He takes his son to the swimming pool every Saturday morning.
6. He always takes his family to the mountains on Sundays.
7. They never sing songs in the car.

- Use Photocopiable 3 from the Teacher Resources.

PB31 ACTIVITY 3

Look and make sentences. Use the words in the boxes.

- Focus pupils on Activity 3 and on the pictures. Elicit some of the activities and focus pupils on the words in the boxes.
- Demonstrate the activity using the example and then in open pairs. Pupils work individually and write sentences in their notebooks. Encourage them to try to make true sentences if they can. Monitor and help/check. Make groups of four. Pupils take turns to say some of their sentences to their group.

Extra challenge Pupils use their sentences to try to find something they all have in common.

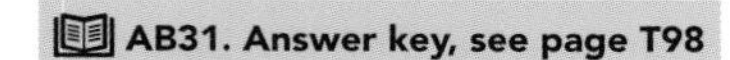

AB31. Answer key, see page T98

Ending the lesson

- Invite seven pupils to the front of the class. Whisper a day of the week to each one. They stand in alphabetical order.

Digital Classroom

Presentation Plus: Unit 3

Digital Flashcards

Audio 34

Practice Extra

Extra Resources

- **Teacher Resources:** Unit 3, Downloadable Activity Book Teaching Notes
- **Teacher Resources:** Unit 3, *Extension worksheet 1*
- **T107 – Extension activity:** *Team quiz*

1 Look, read and complete.

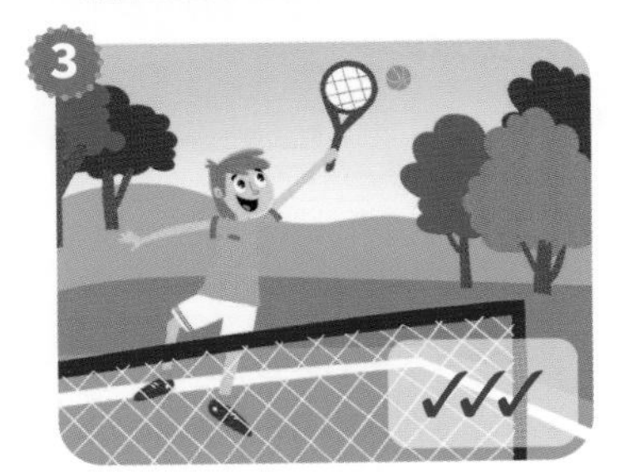

James Flunk is a music teacher. At school he [1] always plays the piano but he [2] ________ plays the piano in his holidays.

James loves playing tennis, so he [3] ________ plays on Wednesdays. He [4] ________ plays football with his daughter Jane, too. She [5] ________ scores a goal.

Every Saturday morning James takes his son for his swimming lesson, but James [6] ________ goes swimming.

He sometimes takes his family to the mountains on Sundays. They [7] ________ sing songs in the car.

2 34 Listen and say 'yes' or 'no'.

3 Look and make sentences. Use the words in the boxes.

always sometimes never

on Saturdays on Wednesdays after school in the morning

I never ride my bike on Wednesdays.

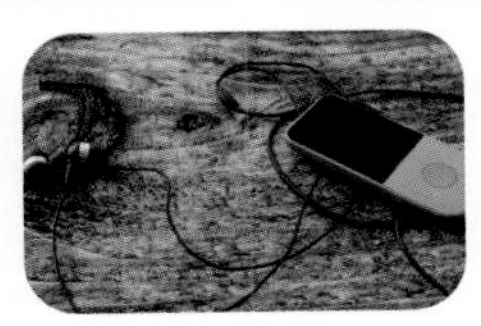
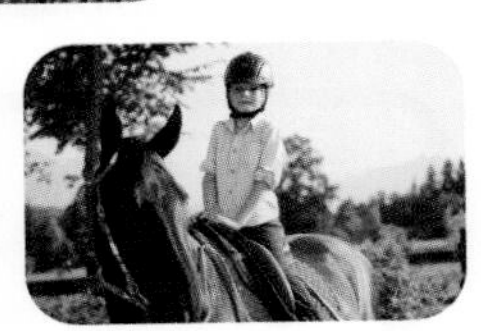

Lock's sounds and spelling

1 35 **Watch the video. Watch again and practise.**

2 **Find and underline or circle the /iz/, /z/, and /s/ sounds.**

Owl dances at night and plays by the moon,
He catches his food and eats before noon.

3 **Work in pairs. Write and say.**

fly dance get up go to bed have a shower wake up wash hands eat brush teeth and hair sing do homework

The bee flies to the flowers after breakfast.

before breakfast has a shower	after lunch	before bed
in the morning	at night	after breakfast
after dinner	before bed	before dinner

Show what you know

The bat __________ and ______ fruit at night.

Objectives

To recognise and practise third person agreement /s/, /z/ and /ɪz/ with a focus on *sh/ch* spelling patterns.

Target language

- **Key language:** the sounds /s/ (*eats*), /z/ (*plays*) and /ɪz/ (*dances*)
- **Additional language:** *bat, moon, noon*
- **Revision:** daily routines, *always, never, sometimes*

Materials

- **Flashcards:** daily routine (44–51)

Warmer

- Show pupils the daily routine flashcards. Say and mime the actions together and stick the flashcards on the board. Pupils stand in two lines facing the board. Whisper *I always have a shower after breakfast* to the last two pupils in each line. Pupils whisper the sentence on down the line. The first two pupils in each line run and touch the correct flashcard (*have a shower*) and say the full sentence. Those two pupils now join the back of each line. Continue in the same way with different sentences.

Presentation

PB32. ACTIVITY 1

Watch the video. Watch again and practise.

- Show Activity 1 on the whiteboard. Watch the ▶ Video. Ask pupils what animal it is and what actions they remember from the ▶ Video. Write the actions on the board.

▶ 35

Voice: /ɪz/ /ɪz/ /z/ /z/ /s/ /s/
Key: /ɪz/ /ɪz/ /z/ /z/ /s/ /s/
Lock: What can you see, Key?
Voice: dances /ɪz/ plays /z/
Lock & Key: Owl dances at night and plays by the moon.
Voice: catches /ɪz/ eats /s/
Lock & Key: He catches his food and eats before noon.
Lock & Voice: Owl dances at night and plays by the moon, He catches his food and eats before noon.
Lock: Come on, everyone. One, two, three … let's say it with Key!
Lock, Key & Voice: Owl dances at night and plays by the moon, He catches his food and eats before noon.
Lock: I say – well done, Key!

- Watch the ▶ Video again, saying and miming the actions. Write more actions from the ▶ Video on the board (*looks, listens, dances, plays, catches, eats*). Say the words together. When saying the /s/ sound ending, make an *s* shape with your arm, like a snake. For the /ɪz/ sound ending, make an *i* shape and then a *z* with your hand. For the /z/ sound ending, make just a *z* with your hand. Circle the /s/ words in green, the /z/ words in red and the /ɪz/ words in blue.

PB32. ACTIVITY 2

Find and underline or circle the *iz*, *z* and *s* sounds.

- Look at the pictures and sentences together. Divide the class into three groups. Tell one group they are the /s/ sound, the second group they are the /z/ sound and the other group they are the /ɪz/ sound. Read out *Owl …* (group /ɪz/ says *dances*) *at night and …* (group /z/ says *plays*) … Continue in this way.
- Ask pupils to underline the *iz*, *z* and *s* sounds in their books.
- Point out the spelling pattern: *sh/c/ch* + *es* = /ɪz/.

Extra support Pupils write the words in their notebooks, using blue for /ɪz/ endings, red for /z/ endings and green for /s/ endings.

PB32. ACTIVITY 3

Work in pairs. Write and say.

- Look at the three animal pictures together and ask pupils what they know about the daily habits of these animals. Look at the word box and ask pupils to mime the words. Pupils choose three activities for each animal, write them in the table and tell their partner, e.g. *The tiger has a shower before breakfast. He brushes his teeth and hair in the morning. He dances after dinner.* Point out the spelling pattern for *brush*: *sh* + *es* = /ɪz/.

Show what you know

- Pupils complete the sentence with the missing words and practise saying it.

Key: dances, eats

AB32. Answer key, see page T98

Ending the lesson

- Stand pupils in two lines at the back of the class. Tell pupils they will zig-zag across the room towards the door. When they zig-zag to the left together, say a word with the /s/ ending sound, and when they zig-zag across to the right, say a word with the /ɪz/ or /z/ ending sound.

Digital Classroom

Audio 35
Practice Extra

Extra Resources

- **Teacher Resources:** Unit 3, Downloadable Activity Book Teaching Notes
- **T107 – Extension activity 1:** *Sound action sentences*
- **T107 – Extension activity 2:** *Animal routines*

Objectives

To watch and read a story and to review language from the unit.

Target language

- **Key language:** language from the unit, *show, Everybody knows …, reporter*
- **Additional language:** *follow, tell, pyjamas*
- **Revision:** language from the story, adjectives (*quiet, clever*), *episode*

Warmer

- Review the story. Teach pupils to respond *Oh, yes, they are! / Oh, no, they're not!* as the audience do in pantomimes. Say some statements to review the story. The class respond in chorus accordingly, e.g. *Lock and Key are doctors.* (*Oh, no, they're not!*)

Extra challenge Invite volunteers to say true or false sentences about Lock and Key.

Story

PB33.

Watch the video.

- Say *Open your Pupil's Books at page 33, please.* Say *This is the next episode of the story.* Use the pictures to teach the words *reporter, follow, pyjamas.* Set the pre-watching questions: *What's the reporter's name? What time do Lock and Key get up? Do Lock and Key always follow people?* Play the ▶ Video. Pupils answer the questions in pairs. Check with the class (Johnny Talkalot; never before ten o'clock; no, sometimes).
- Play the Audio. Pupils listen and repeat. Encourage them to say the words with intonation and feeling.
- Check comprehension by holding up your book and asking, e.g. *What questions is Johnny going to ask?* (about Lock and Key's work). *What time does he think they get up?* (before you and me / early). *What's Key wearing?* (pyjamas). *Is he working?* (no). *Are the detectives clever? Why? / Why not?*

▶ 36

Johnny: Good morning. I'm Johnny Talkalot. On today's show we've got the detectives, Lock and Key, to tell us about their work. We all know detectives work a lot and get up before you and me.

Johnny: Mr Key, this is Johnny Talkalot. It's nine o'clock! Where are you? You aren't in the detective agency.

Key: Oh no, we never get up before ten o'clock.

Johnny: Everybody knows detectives are very clever.

Lock: Yes, sometimes we follow people. We're very quiet so they never know we're behind them.

Key: Yeeoww! My nose!

Johnny: So, girls and boys, what do you think? Do these detectives work a lot? Are they quiet? And are they very clever?

PB33. ACTIVITY 1

Ask and answer the questions in picture 6.

- In pairs, pupils answer the questions that appear in the final frame of the story. Check answers as a class.

AB33. Answer key, see page T98

Ending the lesson

- Say sentences about Lock and Key, based on today's episode of the story, e.g. *Lock and Key are very clever.* Pupils respond *Oh, yes, they are!* or *Oh, no, they're not!* as in the Warmer activity.

Digital Classroom

Presentation Plus: Unit 3

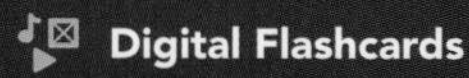

Digital Flashcards

Audio 36

Practice Extra

Extra Resources

- **Teacher Resources:** Unit 3, Downloadable Activity Book Teaching Notes
- **Teacher Resources:** Unit 3, Downloadable Activity Book Audio Script
- **Teacher Resources:** Unit 3, *Extension worksheet 2*
- **Teacher Resources:** Unit 3, *Video, Suzy's room*
- **T108 – Extension activity 1:** *Role play*
- **T108 – Extension activity 2:** *Interview*

Lock & Key!

3

36

1 **Ask and answer the questions in picture 6.**

What do astronauts do in space?

1 37 **Listen and say. Who is Sally? Where does she live?**

2 37 **Listen again and tick the true sentences.**

1 There are other astronauts on the Space Station. ☐
2 Sally works on the Space Station. ☐
3 Sally wears a spacesuit. ☐
4 A robot cleaner does the tidying up. ☐
5 Sally watches films in her free time. ☐

3 **Think about the astronaut's day. How is your day similar or different? Think and say.**

I have breakfast, too.

My food doesn't float.

DIDYOUKNOW...?
There are no showers on the Space Station, but there are toilets!

Unit 3 A day in the life
Pupil's Book p.34

Objectives

To compare and contrast daily routines.

Target language

- **Key language:** language from the unit
- **Additional language:** *cleaner, toilet, astronaut, robot, space, space station, spacesuit*
- **Revision:** *have a shower, watch films, tidy up*

Warmer

- Write *Astronaut* on the board. Brainstorm words associated with astronauts, e.g *the moon, space, spacesuit, spaceship,* and write them on the board. Ask *How many astronauts do you think are in space right now?* Elicit pupils' guesses. Then help them look up the information on a search engine.
- Ask *What do you think astronauts do in space?* Invite pupils to share ideas.

PB34.

What do astronauts do in space?

- Tell pupils that they're going to learn more about what astronauts do in this lesson.
- Watch the ▶ **Video** and answer the questions in the ▶ **Video**.

PB34. ACTIVITY 1

Listen and say. Who is Sally? Where does she live?

- Say *Open your Pupil's Books at page 34, please.* Show Activity 1 on the whiteboard. Focus pupils' attention on the photo. Ask *What do you think this text is about?* Play the **Audio** and have pupils raise their hands when they hear a question. Explain that this is an interview with an astronaut.
- Ask a pupil to read the questions in the rubric. Play the **Audio** again. Check answers as a class. Encourage pupils to explain their answers.

Extra support Play the **Audio**, pausing after each question. Elicit the question and write it on the board. Elicit the answers and continue the **Audio** to check.

37

Interviewer: Today, I'm talking to an astronaut on the Space Station. Hello, Sally! Do you like living in space?
Sally: Yes, I do.
Interviewer: What do you do there?
Sally: I work with five other astronauts.
Interviewer: How is space different?
Sally: Everything floats in space.
Interviewer: Even you?
Sally: Yes!
Interviewer: Wow, that is different! Does the Space Station move?
Sally: Yes, it goes very fast. It goes around the whole Earth in only 90 minutes! It's light for 45 minutes, and then it's dark for 45 minutes.
Interviewer: What do you do every day?
Sally: I wake up at six o'clock, and then I have a …
Interviewer: Wash?
Sally: Yes, but not with water. I wash with a wet towel.
Interviewer: Ah, OK. And do you wear a spacesuit?
Sally: No, I don't wear a spacesuit. I wear a T-shirt and trousers. So I get dressed, I have breakfast and then I work.
Interviewer: Do you ever do chores, like tidying up? Or is there a robot cleaner?
Sally: Actually yes, we all tidy up. But we haven't got a robot cleaner, unfortunately.
Interviewer: What do you like doing in your free time?
Sally: I exercise, I read and watch films. And I love looking at the Earth!
Interviewer: Wow, that sounds amazing! Thank you for talking to me, Sally.

PB34. ACTIVITY 2

Listen again and tick the true sentences.

- Give pupils time to read the sentences. Play the **Audio** for pupils to listen and mark the true sentences. Check answers as a class.

Key: 1, 2, 5

37

PB34. ACTIVITY 3

Think about the astronaut's day. How is your day similar or different? Think and say.

- Read the question and two pupils read the example. In pairs, pupils answer the question.

Did you know …?

- Invite a volunteer to read the information in the box out loud. Ask pupils if this fact surprises them.

AB34. Answer key, see page T98

Ending the lesson

- Play an astronaut memory game. Say *I'm going to the moon and I'm going to take … (my video games).* Throw a soft ball to a volunteer. This pupil repeats your statement, and adds a new thing, e.g. *I'm going to the moon and I'm going to take my video games and my pet cat.* Continue in this way.

Digital Classroom

Presentation Plus: Unit 3
Digital Flashcards
Audio 37
Practice Extra

Extra Resources

- **Teacher Resources:** Unit 3, Downloadable Activity Book Teaching Notes
- **T108 – Consolidation activity:** *Sally's day*
- **T108 – Extension activity:** *Astronaut role play*

Unit 3 A day in the life
Pupil's Book p.35

Objectives
To prepare an interview with an astronaut.

Target language
- **Key language:** language from the unit
- **Additional language:** *amazing, another, doors, excited, half past, o'clock, outside, eggs, bread, spacesuit, spacewalk, view, yum*
- **Revision:** *breakfast, get up, first, put on, open, wash*

Materials
- **Warmer:** Large sheets of black paper, chalk or paint

Warmer
- Ask *What does Sally, the astronaut from the interview, like to do? What is her favourite activity?* (looking at the Earth).
- Divide the class into groups and give each group a large sheet of black paper and coloured chalk (or paint). Ask pupils to draw a view of the Earth from the Space Station.

PB35. ACTIVITY 4

Read Sally's blog. What is special about today?
- Ask pupils to look at the blog. Explain that a blog is like a diary or a journal, except that it's online and usually other people can read it.
- Give pupils time to read the text. Help with vocabulary if needed, but encourage pupils to use context to understand any unfamiliar words.
- Pupils answer the question in the instructions in pairs. Check answers with the class.

Project
- Remember to download your project notes from *Cambridge One*.

Extra support Write activities from the blog on the board in random order, e.g. *I have breakfast. / I go outside. / I get up. / I put on my spacesuit. / I have a wash.* Elicit the first thing Sally does (get up). Write *1* next to it on the board. Continue eliciting the next activity and writing the next number. Confirm the order with the class.

Key: It's Sally's first spacewalk today.

PB35. ACTIVITY 5

Underline the times in Activity 4.
- Read out the times in the box. For each, write the time in numbers on the board. If pupils are familiar with reading analogue clocks, draw the times on clock faces as well.
- Pupils underline the times in the blog. Monitor the activity and check answers as a class.

Extra challenge Say different times, e.g. *three o'clock, half past ten.* Pupils draw the times on the clocks.

Key: six o'clock, half past six, nine o'clock

PB35. ACTIVITY 6

Prepare for an interview with an astronaut. What questions do you want to ask?
- Explain to pupils that they are going to imagine another interview with an astronaut. Suggest that the astronaut could be preparing to go to the Space Station, the moon or Mars.
- Put pupils into pairs and tell them to write between three and five questions to ask their astronaut.
- Invite volunteers to share their questions with the class. Encourage them to guess how the astronaut answers.

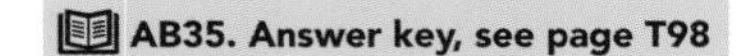

AB35. Answer key, see page T98

Ending the lesson
- Ask pupils which chant/song they'd like to do again from the unit. Do it together to end the lesson.

Digital Classroom

Presentation Plus: Unit 3

Digital Flashcards

Practice Extra

Extra Resources
- **Teacher Resources:** Unit 3, Downloadable Activity Book Teaching Notes
- **Teacher Resources:** Unit 3, *Project notes*
- **PB88–95 – A1 Movers Exam folder**
- **T108 – Consolidation activity:** *Find the lie*

3

4 Read Sally's blog. What is special about today?

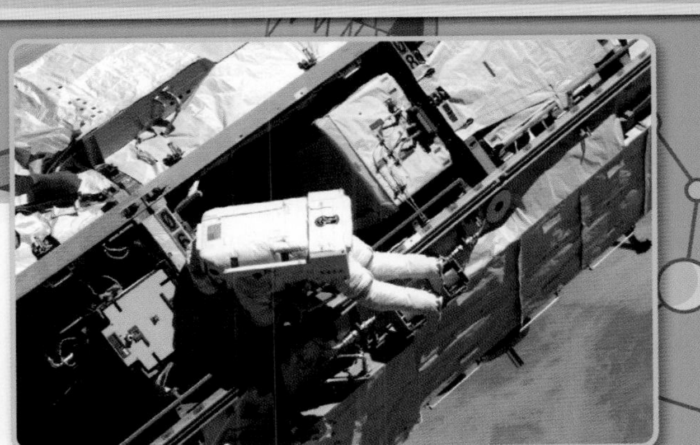

www.myspaceblog.com

24 June

Today is my first spacewalk. I'm so excited!

I get up at six o'clock and I have a wash.

At half past six, I have breakfast. Eggs and bread! Yum!

Then, I put on my spacesuit. Another astronaut helps me and it takes a long time.

Now it's nine o'clock. The doors open and I go outside. Wow! I've got an amazing view of Earth!

5 Underline the times in Activity 4.

Ready to write:

Go to Activity Book page 34.

Learning to write:

Times

six o'clock half past six seven o'clock

6 Prepare for an interview with an astronaut. What questions do you want to ask?

1 Do you sleep in a bed?

2

Project

Role-play an interview with an astronaut.

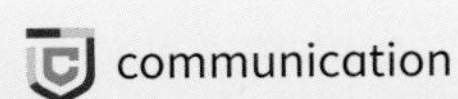

Science: astronauts in space | communication

4 In the city

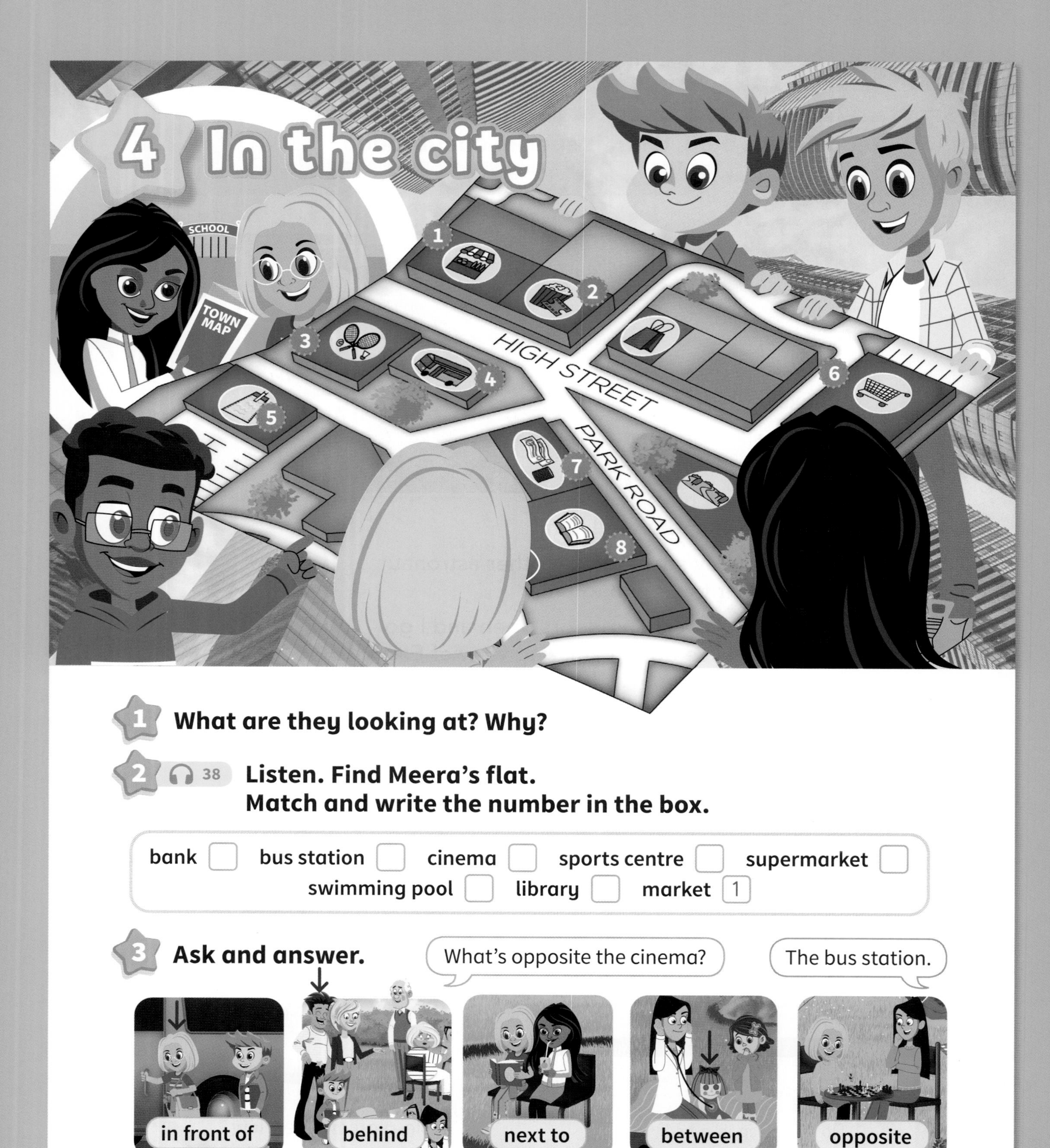

1 **What are they looking at? Why?**

2 38 **Listen. Find Meera's flat. Match and write the number in the box.**

bank ☐ bus station ☐ cinema ☐ sports centre ☐ supermarket ☐ swimming pool ☐ library ☐ market 1

3 **Ask and answer.**

What's opposite the cinema?

The bus station.

in front of

behind

next to

between

opposite

Objectives

To talk about places in a city and say where they are.

Target language

- **Key language:** *bank, bus station, cinema, library, market, sports centre, supermarket, swimming pool, library, next to, opposite, in front of, behind, between*
- **Additional language:** *cool, over here, see you, borrow (books), High Street*
- **Revision:** home, prepositions, *café, hospital, park, town, map, food, look at, Let's … shoe shop, toy shop*

Materials

- **Flashcards:** city (53–62)

Warmer

- Review prepositions *next to, between, in front of, behind.* Invite four pupils to come to the front. Give them instructions, e.g. *Sara, stand between Max and Yasmin. Jordan, stand behind Max.* Give instructions to another group of four.
- Introduce *opposite* and demonstrate using pupils/objects.

Presentation

- Teach/Elicit the new vocabulary using the flashcards. Review *café, park, shop* and *hospital* by drawing pictures.
- Ask *Where can we do our shopping / play sports / watch a film / catch a bus?* Elicit the names of places locally. Develop a mind map around the topic *In the city.*

PB36. ACTIVITY 1

What are they looking at? Why?

- Elicit information about Meera from Unit 2 (she's moving house from a village in the country to a flat in the city). Show Activity 1 on the whiteboard. Focus on the picture. Elicit what they can see. Review/Present *map* and the new vocabulary. Ask questions with *Where* to elicit prepositions, e.g. *Where's the swimming pool?* (behind the sports centre).
- Introduce the words *car park* by asking pupils *What's behind the swimming pool? What do you do in a car park?*
- Say *Open your Pupil's Books at page 36, please.* Ask a pupil to read the questions. Pupils look at the picture, think and answer the questions in pairs. Check with the class.

Key: They're looking at a map. Meera is showing her friends where her new flat is.

PB36. ACTIVITY 2

Listen. Find Meera's flat. Match and write the number in the box.

- Play the **Audio**. Pupils place an eraser on Meera's flat (behind the park, next to the library). They check in pairs.
- Play the **Audio** again. Ask, e.g. *Where's the sports centre?* (next to the bus station). *Where does Meera's family buy their fruit?* (at the market). *What's the name of the street with lots of shops?* (High Street).
- Pupils match the words in the box with the places in the picture. They write the numbers in the boxes.

Key: 7, 4, 2, 3, 6, 5, 8, (1)

38

Meera: Look at this map. My new flat's on it.
Alex: Cool! Is there a sports centre near you?
Meera: Yes, look. It's over here, next to the bus station.
Simon: Wow! And there's a really big swimming pool behind it!
Stella: Look. Here's Park Road. There's a big library … Mmm. Lots of books there.
Meera: Yes, that's next to the bank, where my dad works.
Simon: What's this, next to the cinema?
Meera: That's the market. We get our fruit there.
Alex: Oh, we go to the supermarket to get our food.
Simon: Food … Come on! Let's go for lunch.
Alex & Lenny: Yeah, good idea, Simon. See you, Meera! See you, Stella!
Meera: See you!
Stella: So where is your flat, Meera?
Meera: It's here, behind the park, next to the library.

PB36. ACTIVITY 3

Ask and answer.

- Two pupils read the question and answer aloud. Practise other questions and answers in open pairs.
- Pupils work in pairs. They study the map for one minute. Then they take turns to ask and answer.
- Ask questions around the class about local places. Pupils ask and answer in open pairs.

AB36. Answer key, see pages T98–9

Ending the lesson

- Review vocabulary by asking, e.g. *Where can I borrow books? Where can I buy food? Where can I go when I'm not well?*

Digital Classroom

- **Presentation Plus:** Unit 4
- **Audio 38**
- **Digital Flashcards**
- **Practice Extra**

Extra Resources

- **Teacher Resources:** Unit 4, Downloadable Activity Book Teaching Notes
- **Teacher Resources:** Unit 4, *Reinforcement worksheet 1*
- **T108 – Consolidation activity 1:** *Listen and draw*
- **T108 – Consolidation activity 2:** *Patterns*

Objectives

To practise talking and writing about places in a city and their location.

Target language

- **Key language:** infinitive of purpose: *You go there to buy food. Where do you go to see a film? fruit, vegetables, money, bank, hospital, hotel, swimsuit*
- **Additional language:** *volleyball*
- **Revision:** city, prepositions, *doctor, swim, play badminton, fly a kite, buy, tennis*

Materials

- **Flashcards:** city (53–62)

Warmer

- Review city vocabulary using a mind map. Write *In the city* in the centre of the board and elicit the words from the previous lesson, e.g. *cinema, library*. Check for correct pronunciation. Pupils copy the mind map into their notebooks. Practise the words again using the flashcards.
- Ask one or two questions to prepare for Pupil's Book Activity 1, e.g. *Where do you go to see a film?* (cinema).

PB37. ACTIVITY 1

Look at the picture. Listen and answer.

- Show Activity 1 on the whiteboard. Focus pupils on the picture and elicit some of the places they can see.
- Say *Open your Pupil's Books at page 37, please.* Direct them to the Activity 1 instructions and check understanding. Play the first sentence and point out the example answer. Give pupils time to study the picture and find the places. Play the rest of the **Audio**. Pupils whisper the answer to their partner. Play the **Audio** again. Check after each one to elicit the answer from the class, or from groups of pupils.

Key: It's next to the cinema. It's between the supermarket and the hotel. It's next to the hospital. It's between the bank and the hospital. It's next to the swimming pool. It's next to the bus station. It's next to the supermarket. It's behind the park.

39

Where's the park?
Where's the bus station?
Where's the hospital?
Where's the hotel?
Where's the supermarket?
Where's the sports centre?
Where's the cinema?
Where's the bank?
Where's the swimming pool?

PB37. ACTIVITY 2

Ask and answer.

- Ask two pupils to read the speech bubbles aloud. Pupils play the memory game in pairs. Pupil A closes his/her book and Pupil B looks at the picture and asks questions. Pupil A answers. Then they swap roles.

PB37. ACTIVITY 3

Read and complete with words from the picture in Activity 1.

- Focus pupils' attention on the text in Activity 3. Look at the example answer. Pupils look at the picture from Activity 1, read the text and write the correct town word in each of the spaces.

Key: **2** supermarket, **3** hospital, **4** bank, **5** bus station, **6** cinema, **7** hotel

PB37. ACTIVITY 4

Listen and answer.

- Focus pupils on Activity 4 and on the example question and answer in the speech bubbles. Elicit understanding of impersonal *you* and that it doesn't refer to individual pupils. Play the **Audio**. Pupils listen and point to the correct place on the map. Play the **Audio** again. Pause after each question for pupils to answer in pairs. Check with the class.

Extra challenge More confident pupils can ask other questions with *Where do you go to …?* in pairs.

Key: **2** the sports centre, **3** the market/supermarket, **4** the car park, **5** the bus station, **6** the hospital, **7** the park, **8** the swimming pool

40

Where do you go to see a film?
Where do you go to play badminton?
Where do you go to buy food?
Where do you go to get some money?
Where do you go to catch a bus?
Where do you sleep when you're on holiday?
Where do you go to see a doctor?
Where do you go to fly a kite?
Where do you wear a swimsuit?
Where do you put your rubbish?

AB37. Answer key, see page T99

Ending the lesson

- Elicit from different pupils what their favourite place in their own town/city is and why.

Digital Classroom

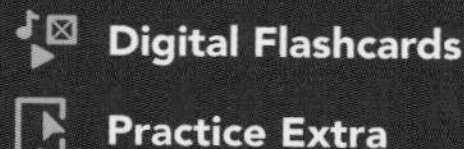

Presentation Plus: Unit 4
Audio 39–40
Digital Flashcards
Practice Extra

Extra Resources

- **Teacher Resources:** Unit 4, Downloadable Activity Book Teaching Notes
- **Teacher Resources:** Unit 4, *Extension worksheet 1*
- **T108 – Consolidation activity 1:** *True or false*
- **T108 – Consolidation activity 2:** *Hot seats*

Look at the picture. Listen and answer.

Where's the park?

It's in front of the swimming pool.

Ask and answer.

Where's the bin?

It's in front of the hotel.

Read and complete with words from the picture in Activity 1.

This is a picture of my town. Look at the [1] swimming pool opposite the park. I sometimes go there to swim with Stella. We always take our swimsuits and towels with us. We go to the [2] ______________ to buy our food. It's between the bank and the [3] ______________. Where do my parents go to get money? They go to the [4] ______________. Can you see the [5] ______________? I go there to catch the bus to school. Where do I love going on Saturdays? I love going to the [6] ______________ to see a film. The cinema's my favourite place in the town. When my grandparents come to town, they stay in the [7] ______________.

Listen and answer.

Where do you go to see a film?

I go to the cinema to see a film.

Language: prepositions of place and infinitive of purpose

1 Look, think and answer. Listen and check.

1 Where are the children?
2 Which children are happy?
3 What book has Lenny got?
4 What time is it?

2 Listen and say 'yes' or 'no'.

3 Ask and answer.

When do you go to the library?

I go to the library on Saturdays.

1 When do you go to the library?
2 What do you enjoy reading?
3 When do you read?
4 Do your family read?
5 Why do you read?

STUDY

Simon **must** be quiet in the library.
They **must** catch the bus.
She **must** do her homework.

Objectives

To talk about obligations using *must*.

Target language

- **Key language:** *must* for obligation, impersonal *you*, *tidy*
- **Additional language:** *book about football, now*
- **Revision:** *quiet, come back*

Warmer

- Show the class a book and say *I'm reading this book. It isn't my book. It's from a …* Elicit *library*. Ask pupils *What do I do when I finish the book?* Check they are familiar with the idea of borrowing a book from a library and then taking it back. Make sure they don't confuse *library* and *bookshop*. Ask different pupils *Do you sometimes go to the library? How often do you go?* Discuss in L1 what other things we can do at the library (e.g. borrow CDs, use the internet, listen to a story).

PB38. ACTIVITY 1

Look, think and answer. Listen and check.

- Show Activity 1 on the whiteboard. Focus pupils on the pictures and elicit who and where the characters are.
- Say *Open your Pupil's Books at page 38, please.* Ask a pupil to read the activity instruction aloud and others to take turns to read the four questions. Pupils compare their answers/ predictions in pairs, looking for clues in the pictures.
- Play the **Audio**. Pupils listen for the answers. They check in pairs. Play the **Audio** again. Check with the class. Elicit complete sentences for the answers. Focus on the sentence *We must go and catch the bus now.* Point out to pupils that *must* is the same for all persons (*I must, She must, You must,* etc.). Focus pupils on the *Study* Box. Ask *Why does Stella say 'Shh' to Lenny?* (they're in the library and they must be quiet).

Key: **1** They are in the library. **2** Lenny, Alex and Simon are happy. **3** He's got a book about football. **4** It's five o'clock.

41

Narrator: The children are in the library, looking at books.
Lenny: Look at this book, Stella! It's about football.
Stella: Shh, Lenny! We're in a library. We must be quiet.
Lenny: Oops, sorry. Meera, look what I've got.
Meera: That's nice, Lenny.
Lenny: It's about football! It's got lots of pictures of my favourite players!
Meera: Shhhh, Lenny. You must be quiet in the library!
Lenny: Sorry!
Alex: Hey, Lenny. What have you got?
Lenny: It's a book about football.
Simon: Cool! That's GREAT! Can I see? Look, it says football is …
Stella & Meera: SHHHH, SIMON! YOU MUST BE QUIET IN THE LIBRARY!
Grandpa Star: Come on, everybody. It's five o'clock. We must go and catch the bus now.
Lenny: OK, OK. Can we come back next week?
Grandpa Star: Yes, I think so … but you must be quiet!

PB38. ACTIVITY 2

Listen and say 'yes' or 'no'.

- Focus pupils on the activity instruction and tell them to whisper to their partner the first time. Play the **Audio**. Pupils listen and whisper. Play the **Audio** again. Pause after each one. Elicit *yes* or *no* and a correct sentence for 'no' responses.

Key: **1** No, they're at the library. **2** Yes. **3** No, he's got a book about football. **4** Yes. **5** No, they must catch a bus. **6** Yes.

42

1 The children are at the bank.
2 You must be quiet in the library.
3 Lenny's got a book about art.
4 The book's got lots of pictures of Lenny's favourite football players.
5 Grandpa Star and the children must catch a plane.
6 The children want to come back next week.

PB38. ACTIVITY 3

Ask and answer.

- Focus pupils on the activity instruction. Ask two pupils to read the example question and answer in the speech bubbles.
- Pupils ask and answer the questions in pairs. Check with the class, inviting pupils to ask and answer in open pairs.

Extra support Invite pupils to ask you the questions first. Answer truthfully for yourself using simple model language.

AB38. Answer key, see page T99

Ending the lesson

- Tell pupils what to do, using *must*, to close the lesson, e.g. *You must put your pencils in your pencil case. You must put your books in your bag. You must put your hands on your desk. You must stand up.*

Digital Classroom

Presentation Plus: Unit 4
Audio 41–42
Digital Flashcards
Practice Extra

Extra Resources

- **Teacher Resources:** Unit 4, Downloadable Activity Book Teaching Notes
- **Teacher Resources:** Unit 4, *Reinforcement worksheet 2*
- **AB87 and PB87 – Grammar reference 4**
- **T108 – Extension activity 1:** *Role play*
- **T108 – Extension activity 2:** *Word search*

Objectives

To have more practice using *must* for obligations and to sing a song.

Target language

- **Key language:** *must* for obligation, *can* for permission
- **Revision:** *city, school, clothes, lunch*

Materials

- Photocopiable 4 (one for each pupil)

Warmer

- Review *must* by asking *What must you do at home to help your mum and dad?* Pupils respond *I must …* Write the ideas on the board.

Song

PB39. ACTIVITY 1

Read and match. Listen and check.

- Show Activity 1 on the whiteboard. Focus on the pictures and elicit what pupils can see.
- Say *Open your Pupil's Books at page 39, please.* Direct pupils to the activity instructions and the example answer. Give pupils time to read all the sentences. Check understanding. Pupils match the rest of the sentences with the pictures. They write the numbers and letters in their notebooks. They check in pairs. Check with the class. Elicit/Teach the difference between *must* (obligation / it's very important / it's a rule) and *can* (permission). Provide other examples which are in daily use in the classroom, e.g. *You must do your homework. You can work with a partner.*
- **Note:** Pupils are only familiar with *can* for ability.

Key: **2** f, **3** b, **4** a, **5** e, **6** c

43

As in Pupil's Book

PB39. ACTIVITY 2

Listen and sing. Do karaoke.

- Focus pupils on Activity 2. Teach the **Song** to pupils line by line with actions. Encourage them to use appropriate intonation for the dad and the girl. Repeat the **Song** with the class until they are confident. Make two groups: dads and girls. They sing in role and then swap roles and repeat.

43

As in Pupil's Book

- Say *Do karaoke.* Pupils listen to the karaoke version and stand up and sing the **Song** as a class.

44

Karaoke version of the song

PB39. ACTIVITY 3

Ask and answer.

- Focus pupils on Activity 3. Check understanding of the phrases in the box. Ask two pupils to read the example question and answer. In pairs, pupils ask their partner the same question. Their partner says which of the tasks in the box they must do at home.

Extra challenge Encourage pupils to use their own ideas as well as the suggestions in the box.

- Check with the class by asking a pupil *What must you do at home?* When the pupil answers, everyone else in the class who must also do that task at home puts up their hand.
- Use Photocopiable 4 from the Teacher Resources.

AB39. Answer key, see page T99

Ending the lesson

- Start a chain around the class, selecting pupils at random to continue. Start, e.g. *At home I must clean my room.* Pupil 1: *At home I must clean my room and help my mum.* Pupil 2: *At home I must clean my room, help my mum and feed my hamster*, etc. Stop the chain when it gets to about six activities and start another one about rules in a different place, e.g. *At school … / At the swimming pool …*

Digital Classroom

Presentation Plus: Unit 4

Audio 43–44

Digital Flashcards

Practice Extra

Extra Resources

- **Teacher Resources:** Unit 4, Downloadable Activity Book Teaching Notes
- **Teacher Resources:** Unit 4, Downloadable Activity Book Audio Script
- **Teacher Resources:** Unit 4, *Song worksheet*
- **T108 – Extension activity:** *Crazy school*

Read and match. Listen and check.

1 – d

1	Must I make my bed, Dad?	Yes, you must.
2	Must I wear a skirt, Dad?	Yes, you must.
3	Must I go to school, Dad?	Yes, you must.
4	Must I do my homework, Dad?	Yes, you must.
5	Must I clean my shoes, Dad?	Yes, you must.
6	Can I play in the park, Dad?	Yes, you can!

Listen and sing. Do karaoke.

Ask and answer.

make the bed | clean your room
clean your shoes | help in the kitchen
wash the car | help Mum and Dad

What must you do at home?

I must clean my room.

Language: *must* for obligation

Lock's sounds and spelling

1 45 **Watch the video. Watch again and practise.**

2 **Find and circle the sounds. Say.**

Where's the bear with purple hair?
He's over there, on the chair!

3 **Draw lines. Then ask, answer and draw.**

Where's the small bear?

The small bear is in the bank.

Show what you know

There's a small ______ with yellow ______.

Objectives

To recognise and practise /eə/ in familiar vocabulary and practise spelling patterns *-ear*, *-air* and *-ere* in context.

Target language

- **Key language:** the sound /eə/ (*bear, pear, hair, chair, where, there*)
- **Revision:** *Where's the …*, places in town, prepositions of place

Materials

- **Flashcards:** *bank* (53), *bus station* (54), *cinema* (55), *sports centre* (60), *supermarket* (61), *market* (58), *swimming pool* (62), *library* (57)

Warmer

- Show pupils the places in the city flashcards and say them together. Stick the flashcards on the walls around the room. Start at the first place together and ask pupils what you can do there, e.g. *the bank – you can get money / you can keep money*. Divide the class into groups, with one group starting at each flashcard / place in the city. In these groups, pupils say what you can do at each of the places in the city. Move groups on to the next card, clockwise.
- Continue around until every group has been to each flashcard / place in the city.

Presentation

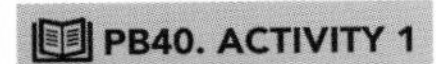

PB40. ACTIVITY 1

Watch the video. Watch again and practise.

- Watch the ▶ Video and ask pupils which animal they were looking for (a bear), and where it was (on the chair). Ask pupils what other detail they remember from the ▶ Video, (*purple hair, chair*).

🔊 ▶ 45

Voice & Key: /eə/ /eə/ /eə/
Lock: What can you see, Key?
Voice: Where /eə/ bear /eə/ hair /eə/
Lock & Key: Where's the bear with purple hair?
Voice: there /eə/ chair /eə/
Lock & Key: He's over there, on the chair!
Lock & Voice: Where's the bear with purple hair? He's over there, on the chair!
Lock: Come on, everyone. One, two, three … let's say it with Key!
Voice, Lock & Key: Where's the bear with purple hair? He's over there, on the chair!
Lock: I say – well done, Key!

PB40. ACTIVITY 2

Find and circle the sounds. Say.

- Watch the ▶ Video again and ask pupils to tell you the details of finding the bear in the library (with his purple hair and sitting on a chair). Ask pupils to look at the sentences on the page and circle the words with the /eə/ sound.
- Write *-ere*, *-ear* and *-air* as headings on the board. Point to each spelling pattern and say /eə/ for pupils to repeat. Ask volunteers to come to the board and write a word from the sentences under each spelling pattern heading.

Key: Pupils circle: Where's, bear, hair, there, chair

PB40. ACTIVITY 3

Draw lines. Then ask, answer and draw.

- Focus pupils' attention on the two pictures of the city and the pictures below. Elicit what pupils can see and say the words together. Tell pupils to look at the picture of the city on the left-hand side and to decide where they want to put each of the items below in the city picture. Pupils work alone and draw lines to the places they want the item to be in the city.

Extra support Before pupils start the speaking part, drill pronunciation of each of the items in the row of pictures.

- Put pupils into pairs A and B. B asks A *Where is the (bear)?* A answers, telling B where they put their bear. B draws a line for A's answer on the city picture on the right-hand side of the page. The pairs continue, asking, answering and drawing lines on the city picture on the right.
- Once both pairs have finished, tell pupils to look and check.

Show what you know

- Focus on the *Show what you know* Box. Pupils complete the sentence with the missing words and practise saying it.

Key: bear, hair

AB40. Answer key, see page T99

Ending the lesson

- Put pupils in three groups. Tell group 1 they are spelling pattern *-ere*, group 2 that they are *-ear* and group 3, *-air*. Call out a mix of words from the unit (without the target sound) and words from the ▶ Video with the target sound. When a group hears their spelling pattern, they raise their hands and say the sound and the word.

Digital Classroom

Presentation Plus: Unit 4

Digital Flashcards

Audio 45

Practice Extra

Extra Resources

- **Teacher Resources:** Unit 4, Downloadable Activity Book Teaching Notes
- **T108 – Consolidation activity 1:** *Word tracing game*
- **T108 – Consolidation activity 2:** *Sound mini-book*

Objectives

To read a story and review language from the unit.

Target language

- **Key language:** language from the unit, *robber, look for, Give me …*
- **Additional language:** *I need …*
- **Revision:** *episode, cash, money, Lock and Key, No problem, must, shopping, lovely day, Let's go, Don't touch*

Warmer

- Review the Lock and Key story so far. Select six to eight speech bubbles from previous episodes and write them on the board. Elicit who said them and what's happening in that episode.

Story

PB41.

Watch the video.

- Say *Open your Pupil's Books at page 41, please.* Elicit which episode this is (five). Focus pupils on the Wanted notice on the computer screen. Use the picture to teach *bank robber.*

Extra support Before watching the ▶ **Video**, elicit who and what pupils can see in each picture and where they are.

- Set the pre-watching questions: *What's the bank robber's name? Does Mrs Potts' friend like shopping? Do Lock and Key catch the bank robber?* Watch the ▶ **Video** with the class. Pupils answer the questions and check in pairs. Check with the class (Lottie Cash; yes, she loves it; no, they catch Mrs Potts' friend!)
- Play the **Audio**. Pupils listen and repeat. Encourage them to say the words with intonation and feeling.
- Check comprehension by pointing to the pictures on the whiteboard and asking, e.g. *Why must Mrs Potts' friend go to the bank?* (she needs some money). *Where are they going shopping?* (in the city). *Who does Key think he sees?* (Lottie Cash). *What does Lock say?* (*We must stop her*). Elicit what Key's favourite phrase is (*No problem, Lock*). Ask if it's true (no).

▶ 46

Narrator: Lock and Key are looking for work on the computer.
Lock: Hmm, Lottie Cash, the bank robber. We can find her.
Key: No problem, Lock!
Woman: I need some money. I must go to the bank.
Mrs Potts: Today is a lovely day for shopping in the city.
Woman: Come on then, let's go. I love shopping.
Key: It's her! It's Lottie Cash, the bank robber! She's going to the bank now.
Lock: We must stop her! We need to get there before her.
Key: Give me that money, Lottie Cash!
Woman: Lottie who?
Mrs Potts: Don't touch her money!
Mrs Potts: What? Not you again, Mr Key!
Lock: Stand up, Key. You and I need to talk!
Key: No problem, Lock!

PB41. ACTIVITY 1

Where must Mrs Potts go? Why? Where must Lock and Key go? Why?

- Ask a pupil to read the questions aloud. Give pupils time to talk about them in pairs. They can reread the story if necessary. Check answers as a class.

Key: Mrs Potts must go to the bank to get some money. Lock and Key must go to the bank to find Lottie Cash, the bank robber.

AB41. Answer key, see page T99

Ending the lesson

- Say lines from today's episode of Lock and Key. Try to say the lines with intonation and feeling. Pupils listen and say who said it.

Digital Classroom

Presentation Plus: Unit 4
Audio 46

Digital Flashcards
Practice Extra

Extra Resources

- **Teacher Resources:** Unit 4, Downloadable Activity Book Teaching Notes
- **Teacher Resources:** Unit 4, *Extension worksheet 2*
- **Teacher Resources:** Unit 4, *Video, Suzy's room*
- **T108 – Extension activity:** *Role play*
- **T108 – Consolidation activity:** *Mime game*

1 **Where must Mrs Potts go? Why? Where must Lock and Key go? Why?**

Where do we go shopping?

1 47 **Listen and read. Which shop is interesting to you? Why?**

Candylawa

Riyadh, Saudi Arabia

Do you like sweets? Candylawa has got it all: sweets, cakes and popcorn. After buying some treats, you can buy nice gifts, such as T-shirts and animal toys. There's also a café for visitors.

Brooklyn Superhero Supply Company

New York City, USA

Are you a superhero? Do you want to be one? This shop has got superhero costumes, such as masks and capes. You can also buy fun toys and science kits to make things! You can build a robot or write a secret message with invisible ink.

2 Read and match. Then write.

		What do both shops sell?
Brooklyn Superhero Supply Company	a in Saudi Arabia	
	b in the USA	
	c costumes	
Candylawa	d a café	
	e sweet treats	

3 What shops do you like? What do you buy there? Think and say.

I like craft shops.

I buy paint and crayons.

DIDYOUKNOW...?

Clothes and shoes are the most popular items for online shopping.

Objectives

To be able to describe shops, saying what pupils like and why.

Target language

- **Key language:** language from the unit
- **Additional language:** *buy, cape, costume, gift, mask, online, popcorn, robot, shopping, superhero, sweets*
- **Revision:** *café, shoes, T-shirt, toy*

Warmer

- Draw a large bank note on the board. Ask pupils to imagine that they've got a lot of money. Put pupils in pairs or small groups and ask *What do you want to buy with all that money?* Encourage volunteers to share ideas with the class.

PB42.

Where do we go shopping?

- Tell pupils that they're going to learn more about shops in this lesson.
- Watch the ▶ Video and answer the questions in the ▶ Video.

PB42. ACTIVITY 1

Listen and read. Which shop is interesting to you? Why?

- Say *Open your Pupil's Books at page 42, please.* Focus pupils on Activity 1. Ask them to look at the two shop descriptions. Ask *What do you think the shops sell?* Play the Audio for pupils to follow along in their books.
- Ask the questions in the rubric. Pupils discuss their answers in pairs and then share their opinions with the class. Encourage pupils to explain their answers.

Extra support Play the Audio again. Pupils raise their hands when they hear what the shops sell. They underline the words, e.g. *cakes, popcorn, gifts, T-shirts, toys, sweets, superhero costumes, masks, capes, fun toys, science kits, a robot, invisible ink.*

47

Boy: Candylawa, Riyadh, Saudi Arabia
Do you like sweets? Candylawa has got it all: sweets, cakes and popcorn. After buying some treats, you can buy nice gifts, such as T-shirts and animal toys. There's also a café for visitors.

Girl: Brooklyn Superhero Supply Company
New York City, USA
Are you a superhero? Do you want to be one? This shop has got superhero costumes such as masks and capes. You can also buy fun toys and science kits to make things! You can build a robot or write a secret message with invisible ink.

PB42. ACTIVITY 2

Read and match. Then write.

- Focus pupils on Activity 2. In pairs, they match the shops with the phrases. Then they write the answer to the question on the line. Monitor pupils' progress. Check answers as a class.
- Put pupils into pairs to take turns making sentences about the shops in Activity 1.

Key: Brooklyn Superhero Supply Company: b, c;
Candylawa: a, d, e; toys

PB42. ACTIVITY 3

What shops do you like? What do you buy there? Think and say.

- Focus on Activity 3 and ask a pupil to read the instructions aloud.
- Put pupils into small groups to discuss shops they like and the things they buy there.

Did you know ...?

- Ask *Do you ever buy things online?* Encourage pupils to give examples of things they or their parents buy online. Invite a volunteer to read the information in the box out loud. Ask pupils if this fact surprises them.

AB42. Answer key, see page T99

Ending the lesson

- Ask pupils to imagine an interaction in one of the shops, Brooklyn Superhero Supply Company or Candylawa. Brainstorm things sales assistants and customers say, e.g. *Can I help you? That's £15. Excuse me. I'm looking for ...* Put pupils into pairs or small groups to role-play shop interactions.

Digital Classroom

Audio 47
Practice Extra

Extra Resources

- **Teacher Resources:** Unit 4, Downloadable Activity Book Teaching Notes
- **T109 – Extension activity:** *Shop symbols*

Objectives

To describe their own imaginary shop.

Target language

- **Key language:** language from the unit
- **Additional language:** *coconut water, delicious, yummy, ice cream van, sell, thirsty, van*
- **Revision:** *book, dog, beach, drive, music*

Materials

- **Warmer:** Photos of shop signs

Warmer

- Display photos of shop signs around the room. Invite pupils to stand up and identify the shops, saying or guessing what they sell.
- Ask *What do you notice about shop signs?* Encourage pupils to comment.

PB43. ACTIVITY 4

Why are these shops different? Read and match.

- Show Activity 4 on the whiteboard. Focus pupils' attention on the photos and ask them what they can see in each.
- Read out the question in the rubric and give pupils time to read the text. Help with vocabulary if needed, but encourage pupils to use context to understand any unfamiliar words.
- Pupils answer the question in the instructions. Ask which of the shops they like the most, and if they have ever seen shops like these.

Project

- Remember to download your project notes from *Cambridge One*.

Key: 2, 3, 1

PB43. ACTIVITY 5

Underline the nouns in Activity 4.

- Read out the sentence in the box. Ask pupils what words for people, places and things they can find in Activity 4, e.g. *books*. Ask *Is it a person, place or thing?* (yes, it's a thing). Tell pupils to underline the other nouns in Activity 4, and check answers with a partner.
- Monitor the activity and review as a class.

Extra support For extra practice of identifying nouns, ask pupils to underline the nouns in the Candylawa shop advert in Activity 1. Invite volunteers to write the nouns on the board. Check by having pupils confirm that each word is a person, place or thing.

Key: Pupils underline: books, van, field, car park, space, storybooks, notebooks; coconut water, beach; ice cream, music, ice cream van, street, school

PB43. ACTIVITY 6

Imagine you want to open a shop. What do you sell? Think and say.

- Explain to pupils that they are going to imagine a new shop. Give them time to think and draw or make notes about their shop. Encourage pupils to think about features, such as a café or a children's area, to attract customers.
- Put pupils into pairs or small groups to discuss their shops and the features they've got.
- Invite volunteers to share their ideas with the class.

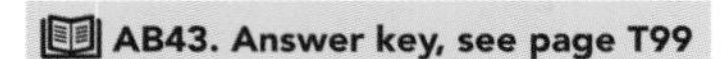
AB43. Answer key, see page T99

Ending the lesson

- Ask pupils which chant or song they'd like to do again from the unit. Do it together to end the lesson.

Digital Classroom

Presentation Plus: Unit 4
Digital Flashcards

Practice Extra

Extra Resources

- **Teacher Resources:** Unit 4, Downloadable Activity Book Teaching Notes
- **Teacher Resources:** Unit 4, *Project notes*
- **PB88–95 – A1 Movers Exam folder**
- **T109 – Consolidation activity:** *Odd word out*

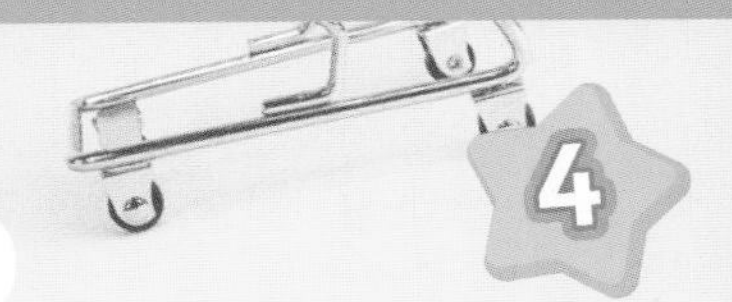

4 Why are these shops different? Read and match.

1

MOVING BOOKS

Imagine a van that drives around and sells books! You can buy books in a field or in the car park. Books about space, storybooks, notebooks… you can find them all here!

2

COCONUT DELIGHT

Thirsty? Come and drink some delicious coconut water. You can find us by the beach.

3

C+M ice cream

Can you hear the music? The ice cream van is coming!! It drives to your street or your school and you can buy yummy ice cream.

5 Underline the nouns in Activity 4.

Learning to write:

Nouns

A noun is a word for a person, place or thing.

6 Imagine you want to open a shop. What do you sell? Think and say.

Ready to write:

Go to Activity Book page 42.

Project

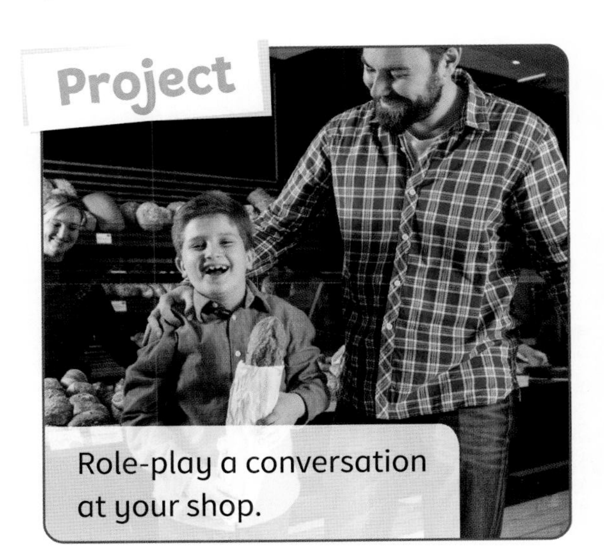

Role-play a conversation at your shop.

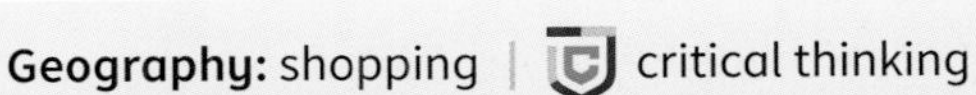

Geography: shopping | critical thinking

Review Units 3 and 4

1 Play the game.

START

go to the bus station

go to the hospital

go to the library

go to the market

go to the funfair

go to the supermarket

go to the sports centre

go to the cinema

FINISH

Objectives

To review language from Units 3 and 4 and play a game.

Target language

- **Key language:** vocabulary and language from Units 3 and 4
- **Revision:** procedural language, language for games, instructions, *go to …*

Materials

- Dice and four different coloured counters for each group of four pupils
- **Flashcards:** city (53–62)

Warmer

- Review places in a city using the flashcards. Show the flashcards. Elicit the words chorally. Place the flashcards on the board. Choose volunteers to say them in order. Turn the cards over. See if pupils can remember the order. Turn them back to check.
- Give definitions for each place, e.g. *I can go here on Saturdays. I must be quiet here. I can read here.* (library). Say several sentences for each place, starting with more general clues to encourage pupils to think before they guess.

PB44. ACTIVITY 1

Play the game.

- Say *Open your Pupil's Books at page 44, please.* Elicit what they can see (a game). Say *Can you remember some of the language we use in games?* Elicit/Prompt, e.g. *It's my turn, Pass the dice, I'm red, I've won, That's cheating.*

Extra support Write useful language on the board for pupils to refer to during the game.

- Remind pupils to use English. Say *You speak* (their mother tongue), *you miss a turn!* Check understanding of *miss a turn.* Check pupils know how to play and demonstrate the game. They throw the dice and go around the board. When they come to a 'go to …' square, they move to that place and say the name aloud. They start their next turn there.
- Pupils make groups of four. They clear their desks and place one book in the centre. Hand out a dice and four different coloured counters to each group. They throw the dice to see who starts. Play moves from Start to Finish. The first pupil in each group to reach the finish is the winner.

AB44. Answer key, see pages T99–100

Ending the lesson

- Write the following parts of phrases/words in two columns on the board:

1	*wake*	*suit*
2	*super*	*off*
3	*lib*	*hero*
4	*space*	*up*
5	*have a*	*market*
6	*super*	*on*
7	*take*	*station*
8	*bus*	*bed*
9	*put*	*rary*
10	*go to*	*shower*

- Pupils take turns to come to the board and match the halves to make words and phrases from Units 3 and 4. Check comprehension of all the words and practise pronunciation with the whole class.

Key: 1 wake up, **2** supermarket / superhero, **3** library, **4** spacesuit, **5** have a shower, **6** superhero / supermarket, **7** take off, **8** bus station, **9** put on, **10** go to bed

Digital Classroom

Presentation Plus: Unit 4

Practice Extra

Digital Flashcards

Extra Resources

- **Teacher Resources:** Unit 4, Downloadable Activity Book Teaching Notes
- **T109 – Consolidation activity:** *Sing a song*

Objectives

To review language from Units 3 and 4 and practise listening.

Target language

- **Key language:** vocabulary and language from Units 3 and 4
- **Revision:** *crossword*

Warmer

- Ask questions around the class to prepare pupils for the listening activity, e.g. *What do you do on Sunday afternoons? / Friday evenings? What time do you get home from school? / get up in the mornings? What do you do before/after dinner?*

PB45. ACTIVITY 2

Listen and choose the correct picture.

- Say *Open your Pupil's Books at page 45, please.* Play the **Audio**. Pupils listen and circle the correct picture in pencil. They check in pairs. Play the **Audio** again. Check with the class.

Extra support The first time they listen, encourage pupils to cross out any answer they think is incorrect even if they are not sure which is correct. Then they can check again the second time.

Key: **2** b, **3** a, **4** a, **5** c

48

1 Do you play in the park on Saturday, Jack?
No. I always go out with my mum on Saturdays.
Oh, that's nice! Where do you go?
We go to the cinema.

2 Do you finish school at three o'clock, Daisy?
Yes, but I don't come home then.
Really? Why not? Where do you go?
I go to the swimming pool after school.
So, what time do you come home?
I come home at five o'clock.

3 When do you do your homework, Paul?
I do it before dinner.
What do you do after dinner?
I always watch TV.

4 Do you walk to school, Vicky?
No. I never walk to school. I catch the bus every day.
Oh, do you go to the bus station every morning?
No. I catch the bus in front of my house.

5 Are you going into town, John?
Yes. I need a new book.
Are you going to the library?
No. I'm going to that big new bookshop next to the hospital.
Oh, can I come with you?

PB45.

Quiz

- Say *Now let's read and remember.* Remind pupils of the meaning of *quiz*. Focus pupils on the questions. Pupils look back through Units 3 and 4 and find the answers to the questions. They discuss them in groups of four. Check with the class.

Key: **1** She catches the bus to school at eight o'clock. **2** He takes his son for a swimming lesson. **3** No, they don't. **4** She works on the Space Station. **5** The sports centre. **6** You go to the cinema. **7** He's over there, on a chair. **8** Because the friend needs some money.

AB45. Answer key, see page T100

Ending the lesson

- Pupils work in groups of four. They need one 'Do you remember?' (Activity Book page 43 activity 1). Two pupils (A) cover the words from Unit 3. The other two pupils (B) take turns to say what each picture is and spell the word. 'A's look and check. They reverse roles for Unit 4.

Digital Classroom

Audio 48

Extra Resources

- **Teacher Resources:** Unit 4, Downloadable Activity Book Teaching Notes
- **T109 – Consolidation activity 1:** *Play the game*

2 🎧 48 Listen and choose the correct picture.

1 What does Jack do on Saturday afternoons?

a 

b 

✓

c 

2 What time does Daisy come home from school?

a 

b 

c 

3 What does Paul do after dinner?

a 

b 

c 

4 Where does Vicky catch the bus?

a 

b 

c 

5 Where's John going?

a 

b 

c 

1 What time does Stella catch the bus to school? (p28)

2 What does James Flunk do every Saturday morning? (p31)

3 Do Lock and Key get up before ten o'clock? (p33)

4 Where does Sally work? (p34)

5 On Meera's map, what's opposite the market? (p36)

6 Where do you go to see a film? (p37)

7 Where's the bear with the purple hair? (p40)

8 Why must Mrs Potts and her friend go to the bank? (p41)

5 Fit and well

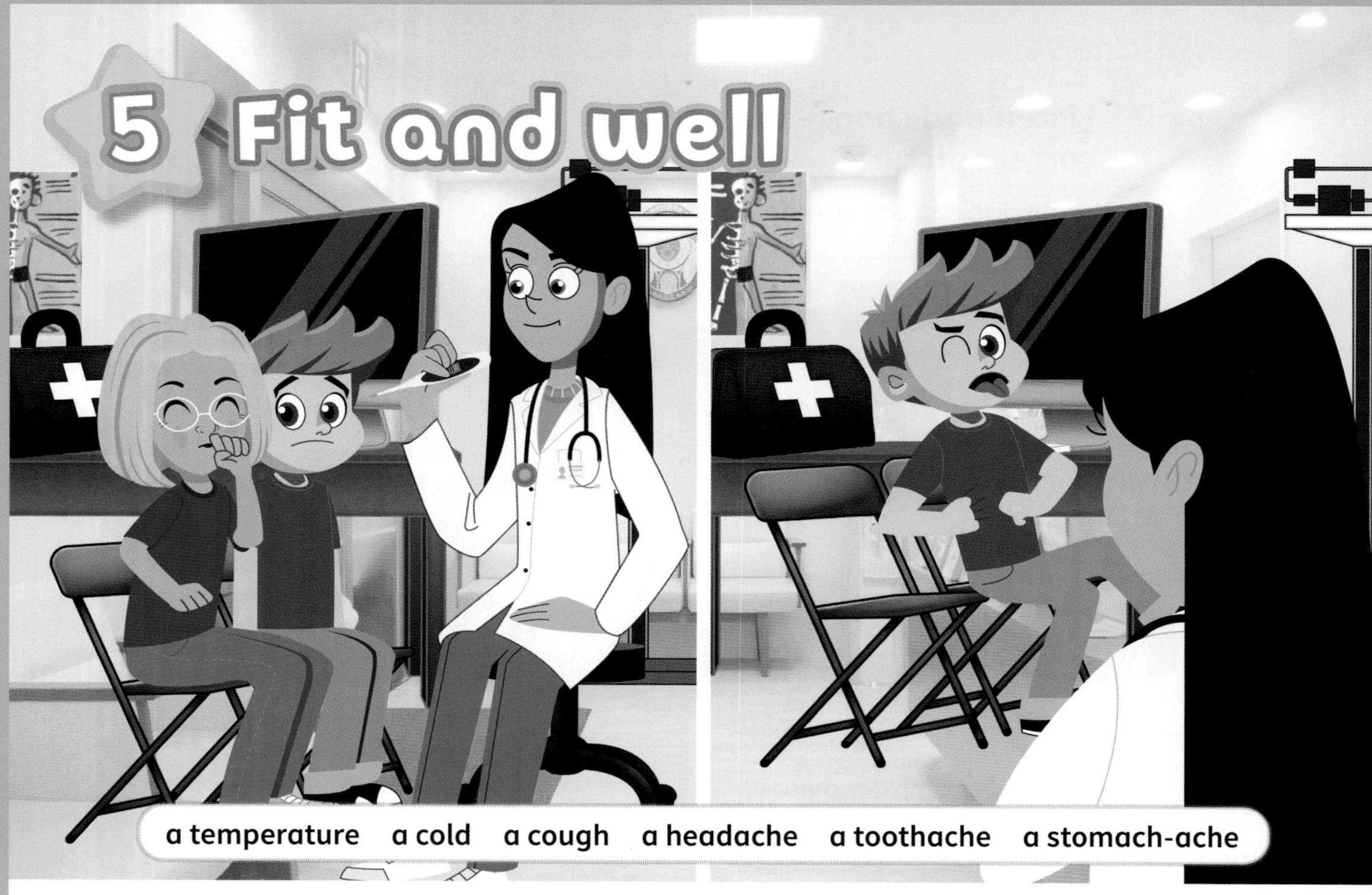

1 49 Look, think and answer. Listen and check.

1 Where are Stella and Simon?
2 Who's the doctor?
3 Is Stella hot?
4 Is Simon ill?

2 What's the matter? Act it out.

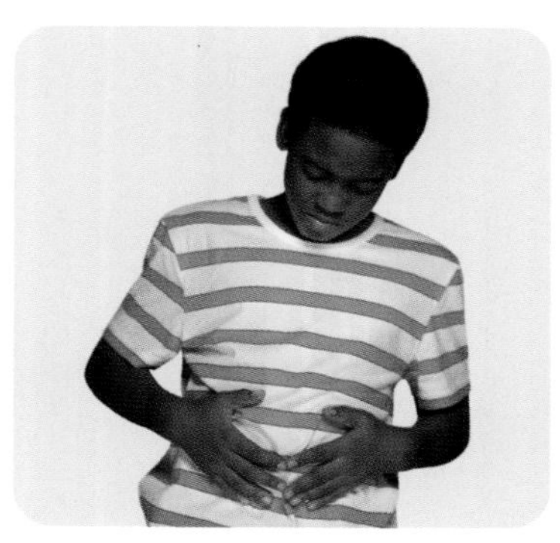

What's the matter?

He's got a cough/stomach-ache.

STUDY

What's the matter?
He**'s got** a cough.
She**'s got** a temperature.
I**'ve got** a stomach-ache.

3 50 Listen and do the actions.

Unit 5 Fit and well
Pupil's Book p.46

Objectives

To understand and talk about common illnesses.

Target language

- **Key language:** *What's the matter? I've got …, I'm not very well, ill, a cold, a cough, a stomach-ache, a headache, a temperature, a toothache*
- **Additional language:** *My head hurts, degrees*
- **Revision:** food, body parts, *have got, must, Let's …, a lot, want, Don't (eat), Who …? hot, happy*

Materials

- **Flashcards:** illness (63–70)

Warmer

- Review body vocabulary. Pupils stand up. Say *Touch your ears.* Pupils touch their ears. Give other instructions quickly, including *head, eye, nose, mouth, foot/feet, tooth/teeth, face, hair, hand, leg, arm.* Present *stomach, back, shoulder* by pointing. Continue the game, including the new words.

Presentation

- Elicit/Teach the illnesses, showing the flashcards and saying the words. Pupils repeat. Teach *ill,* using mime. Say *How are you? I'm very well, thank you. How are you? I'm not very well. I'm ill.*

PB46. ACTIVITY 1

Look, think and answer. Listen and check.

- Show Activity 1 on the whiteboard. Focus pupils on the picture and elicit who/what they can see (Stella and Simon with Aunt May at the doctor's).
- Say *Open your Pupil's Books at page 46, please.* Ask a pupil to read the activity instruction aloud and others to read the four questions. Pupils compare predictions in pairs.
- Play the Audio. Pupils listen for the answers. They check in pairs. Play the Audio again.
- Check with the class. Elicit complete sentences for the answers. Play the Audio again. Pupils listen. Check understanding of *sweets, cold, cough, temperature.* Focus pupils on the *Study* Box at the bottom of the page. Check comprehension. Explain that *My stomach hurts* and *I've got a stomach-ache* mean the same thing.

Key: **1** They're at the doctor's. **2** The doctor is Aunt May. **3** Yes, she is. **4** No, he isn't.

49

Aunt May: Good morning. How are you today, Stella?
Stella: Oh, I'm not very well. I've got a cold.
Aunt May: And you've got a cough. Have you got a headache?
Stella: Oh, yes. My head hurts a lot, and I'm very hot.
Aunt May: OK. Put this under your arm. Oh, yes. 39 degrees. You've got a temperature. So you must drink lots of water and orange juice. Now, what's the matter with you, Simon?
Simon: My stomach hurts a lot and I don't want to eat.
Aunt May: Have you got a toothache?
Simon: No.
Aunt May: I see, so … you've got a stomach-ache. Well, go to bed and don't eat any cake, sweets or chocolate today.
Simon: I think I'm OK now. Can I go and play?
Aunt May: Hmm …

PB46. ACTIVITY 2

What's the matter? Act it out.

- Show Activity 2 on the whiteboard and point to the photo. Ask *What's the matter?* (he's got a cough or stomach-ache).
- Demonstrate the activity first. Mime an illness, e.g. *headache.* Say *My head hurts.* Elicit the response from pupils, e.g. *You've got a headache.* Pupils work in small groups, taking turns to act out an illness and to respond, as in the speech bubbles.

Extra support Before completing the activity in small groups, invite volunteers to mime some of the other illnesses for the whole class to guess.

PB46. ACTIVITY 3

Listen and do the actions.

- Pupils stand up. Play the Audio. Pupils mime actions for the illnesses.
- Divide the class into six groups. Play the Audio again. Point to a group each time for them to mime.
- Do further practice in open pairs. One pupil says the problem, e.g. *You've got a headache.* Another pupil mimes.

50

You've got a headache. You've got a temperature. You've got a toothache. You've got a stomach-ache. You've got a cough. You've got a cold.

AB46. Answer key, see page T100

Ending the lesson

- Pupils close their books. Dictate the new words for pupils to write in their notebooks. They swap notebooks and check each other's work. Check with the class and elicit the spellings.

Digital Classroom

Presentation Plus: Unit 5

Digital Flashcards

Audio 49–50

Practice Extra

Extra Resources

- **Teacher Resources:** Unit 5, Downloadable Activity Book Teaching Notes
- **Teacher Resources:** Unit 5, *Reinforcement worksheet 1*
- **T109 – Extension activity:** *Role play*
- **T109 – Consolidation activity:** *Label it*

Objectives

To talk and write about common illnesses.

Target language

- **Key language:** *What's the matter* (*with him/her/them/you*)? *backache, earache, hurt*
- **Revision:** illnesses, body, *have got, can't* (lack of ability), *go to school, eat sweets*

Materials

- **Flashcards:** illness (63–70)

Warmer

- Review illnesses. Show the flashcards. Elicit the words. Stick the flashcards on the board and number them 1 to 8. Say a word and pupils say the correct number. Say a number. Pupils chorus the correct word. Review the new parts of the body: *stomach, shoulder, back*. Point and elicit.
- Write gapped words on the board for pupils to complete, e.g. *_t_ _ _ _ _-a_h_* (*stomach-ache*). Include *temperature, cough, cold, toothache, headache*.

PB47. ACTIVITY 1

Listen and say the letter.

- Show Activity 1 on the whiteboard. Focus pupils on the pictures of the illnesses and on the activity instruction.
- Say *Open your Pupil's Books at page 47, please.* Play the **Audio**. Pupils listen and whisper the illness to their partner. Play the **Audio** again. Check with the class, e.g. *h, headache.*

Key: h, g, c, b, e, f, a, d

51

Girl: What's the matter?
Boy: Oh, I've got a headache.
Boy: What's the matter with you?
Boy & Girl: We've got colds.
Man: What's the matter with him?
Girl: He's got a cough.
Man: What's the matter with them?
Girl: They've got a temperature.
Woman: What's the matter with your grandfather?
Boy: He's got a backache.
Woman: What's the matter with your dad?
Boy: He's got a toothache.
Man: What's the matter with your grandmother?
Girl: She's got a stomach-ache.
Woman: What's the matter with your mum?
Boy: She's got an earache.

Practice

- Invite ten pupils to the front. Explain that they are going to mime being the people in the pictures in Activity 1. Secretly whisper a letter (a–h) to each pupil / pair of pupils (corresponding to the pictures). Pupils mime appropriately (e.g. the pupil with letter f mimes having toothache, the pupils with letter b mime having a temperature). Ask a pupil *What's the matter with you?* He/She responds *I've got …* Ask the class *What's the matter with him/her?* The class responds *He's/She's got …* Repeat with the other pupils and pairs, involving the class in the questioning. Use *What's the matter with them? They've got …* as well as singular *you*.

PB47. ACTIVITY 2

Make sentences. Say the letter.

- Focus pupils on Activity 2. Invite two pupils to read the speech bubbles aloud. One makes a sentence, the other says the letter for the picture in Activity 1. Do a few more examples around the class. Pupils work in pairs, taking turns.
- Check as a class.

Extra support Allow pupils to work in pairs to prepare sentences. Then they join with another pair to complete the task.

Key: a She's got a stomach-ache. **b** They've got a temperature. **c** He's got a cough. (**d** She's got an earache.) **e** He's got a backache. **f** He's got a toothache. **g** They've got a cold. **h** He's got a headache.

PB47. ACTIVITY 3

Read and say 'yes' or 'no'.

- Focus pupils on Activity 3. Check understanding of the instructions. Pupils read the text. Then they read the sentences and, in pairs, say *yes* if the sentence is true or *no* if it's false.
- Check with the class.

Key: 1 No, **2** Yes, **3** Yes, **4** Yes, **5** No, **6** No

---

PB47. ACTIVITY 4

Work in pairs. Say and guess.

- Ask two pupils to read the speech bubbles aloud. Say *My head hurts* and encourage pupils to guess what's the matter. (You've got a headache.) In pairs, pupils continue the activity with *ear, back* and *tooth*.

AB47. Answer key, see page T100

Ending the lesson

- Call out illnesses for pupils to mime.

Digital Classroom

Presentation Plus: Unit 5
Digital Flashcards
Audio 51
Practice Extra

Extra Resources

- **Teacher Resources:** Unit 5, Downloadable Activity Book Teaching Notes
- **T109 – Extension activity 1:** *Chant*
- **T109 – Extension activity 2:** *Draw and write*

1 Listen and say the letter.

a

b

c

d

e

f

g

h

2 Make sentences. Say the letter.

He's She's They've	got	a toothache. a backache. a stomach-ache. a headache.	an earache. a temperature. a cold. a cough.

She's got an earache.

d

3 Read and say 'yes' or 'no'.

Poor Stella! Her head hurts and she's very hot. She's got a temperature. She isn't very well because she's got a cough and a bad cold. She must stay in bed and drink lots of water and orange juice. She's sad because she wants to go to school but she can't.

Simon mustn't eat sweets or chocolate today because he says he's got a stomach-ache. Do you think he's got a stomach-ache or do you think he's OK?

1 Stella's back hurts.
2 She's got a temperature.
3 She must stay in bed.
4 She must drink lots of orange juice.
5 Simon says he's got a toothache.
6 He must eat sweets and chocolate today.

4 Work in pairs. Say and guess.

My stomach hurts.

You've got a stomach-ache.

Language: *have got* and *has got*

Look, think and answer. Listen and check.

1 Where's Stella?
2 Who's Mrs Star talking to?
3 What's the matter with Stella?
4 Can she go to school?

Make more sentences.

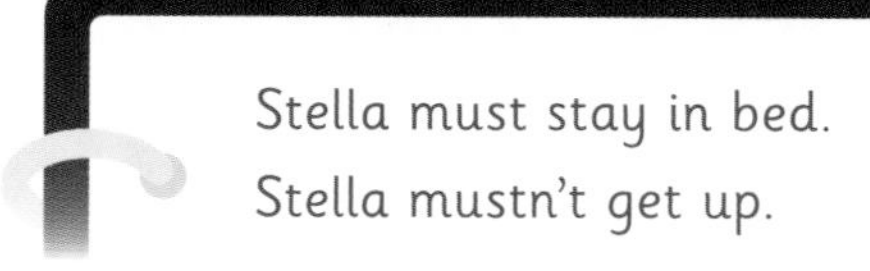

Listen and say '*must*' or '*mustn't*'.

When you've got a cough you … go out.

mustn't

When you've got a headache you … go to bed.

must

STUDY

You **must** stay in bed.
She **mustn't** go out.

Language: *must* and *mustn't* for obligation

Objectives

To talk about obligations using *must* and *mustn't*.

Target language

- **Key language:** positive and negative obligations, *must, mustn't*, permission, *can't*, clauses with *when, get up*
- **Additional language:** *How often …? medicine, blanket, meal*
- **Revision:** illnesses, daily routines, activities, food

Materials

- Photocopiable 5, on thin card, one copy for each pupil

Warmer

- Review some of the classroom rules with *must* from Unit 4, e.g. *You must speak English in class. You must do your homework.* Elicit others that pupils remember.

Presentation

- Write on the board: *eat in class, talk in the library, run in the classroom, shout the answers.* Say, e.g. *You must eat in class.* Pupils respond *No, that's not right. You mustn't eat in class!* Repeat with the other sentences. Focus pupils on the *Study* Box.

PB48. ACTIVITY 1

Look, think and answer. Listen and check.

- Show Activity 1 on the whiteboard. Elicit who they can see.
- Say *Open your Pupil's Books at page 48, please.* Ask a pupil to read the activity instruction aloud and others to take turns to read the four questions. Pupils compare their predictions in pairs.
- Play the Audio. Pupils listen for the answers. They check in pairs. Play the Audio again. Check *medicine, blanket, meal.*
- Watch the ▶ Video.

Key: **1** She's in bed. **2** She's talking to Grandpa Star. **3** She's got a temperature. **4** No, she can't.

▶ 52

Grandpa Star: Oh, dear. What's the matter with Stella?
Mrs Star: Hmm. She's got a temperature. Look, 39 degrees!
Stella: Can I go to school, Mum?
Mrs Star: No, you can't go to school today.
Grandpa Star: Go to school! She mustn't go out!
Stella: Can I get up?
Mrs Star: No, sorry, Stella. You mustn't get up.
Grandpa Star: You must stay in bed and put this blanket on you.
Stella: Can I read?
Mrs Star: Yes, you can read. And you must take this.
Grandpa Star: Oh, how often must she take it?
Mrs Star: She must take it after every meal for a week.
Stella: A week? … Oh, no!

PB48. ACTIVITY 2

Make more sentences.

- Focus pupils on the *Study* Box. Point out the negative form *mustn't*. Practise pronunciation, without saying the first 't'.
- Focus pupils on Activity 2. Ask a pupil to read the examples.

Extra support In pairs, pupils talk about other things that Stella must and mustn't do.

- Pupils write sentences with *must* and *mustn't* in their notebooks. Monitor and help with language as necessary.

PB48. ACTIVITY 3

Listen and say 'must' or 'mustn't'.

- Focus pupils on Activity 3. Read out the example sentences, saying *beep* instead of the missing word. Ask *Must or mustn't?*
- Play the Audio. In pairs, pupils listen and whisper *must* or *mustn't* to their partner. Play the Audio again, pausing after each sentence to elicit the answer from the class.

Key: **3** mustn't, **4** mustn't, **5** mustn't, **6** mustn't, **7** must, **8** must

53

1 When you've got a cough you … go out.
2 When you've got a headache you … go to bed.
3 When you've got a backache you … do sport.
4 When you've got a temperature you … go to school.
5 When you've got an earache you … listen to music.
6 When you've got a stomach-ache you … eat sweets.
7 When you've got a toothache you … go to the dentist.
8 When you've got a cold you … drink a lot of orange juice.

- Use Photocopiable 5 from the Teacher Resources.

AB48. Answer key, see page T100

Ending the lesson

- Say, e.g. *Stella's got a cough. Stella must take her medicine after breakfast.* Pupils correct you (e.g. *Stella's got a temperature. Stella must take her medicine after every meal.*).

Digital Classroom

Presentation Plus: Unit 5
Audio 52–53

Digital Flashcards
Practice Extra

Extra Resources

- **Teacher Resources:** Unit 5, Downloadable Activity Book Teaching Notes
- **Teacher Resources:** Unit 5, Downloadable Activity Book Audio Script
- **Teacher Resources:** Unit 5, *Reinforcement worksheet 2*
- **Teacher Resources:** Unit 5, *Extension worksheet 1*
- **AB87 and PB87 – Grammar reference 5**
- **T109 – Extension activity:** *Class rules*

Objectives

To have more practice reading about obligations using *must* and *mustn't* and to sing a song.

Target language

- **Additional language:** *says*
- **Revision:** obligations, *must/mustn't, Don't …,* illnesses, daily routines, activities and actions, *swim, skip, jump, hop, climb, run, dance*

Materials

- **Flashcards:** illness (63–70) and word cards

Warmer

- Review the illnesses using the flashcards. Show the flashcards and elicit the words. Stick the flashcards on the board in a column, with the word cards at the bottom of the board in random order. Pupils come to the front in turn and match a word card with a flashcard.
- Remove the flashcards from the board. Mime having a headache to elicit the sentence *You've got a headache* from the class. When they guess correctly, show them the flashcard to confirm. Call a pupil to the front. Give him/her a different illness flashcard. The pupil mimes for the class to guess. The pupil who guesses correctly has the next turn at the front. Repeat until all the flashcards have been used.

PB49. ACTIVITY 1

Read the story. Look at the pictures. Write the correct word next to numbers 1–6.

- Elicit from pupils who they go to with a stomach-ache, and who they go to with a toothache.
- Say *Open your Pupil's Books at page 49, please.* Focus pupils on the pictures and elicit what they can see. Focus pupils on the activity instruction and check understanding, using number 1 as an example. Pupils complete the sentences with the correct words.

Key: **2** cough, **3** doctor, **4** sleep, **5** swimming, **6** bed

Song

PB49. ACTIVITY 2

Listen and move.

- Focus pupils on Activity 2. Elicit the activities in the photos. Say and mime each activity for pupils to repeat and copy the action. Say one of the activities. Pupils mime. Repeat for all the activities.
- Focus pupils on the activity instruction and say *What are you going to do?* Pupils say *Listen and move.* Tell them to listen and follow the first time. Play the **Audio**. Pupils read silently as they listen the first time. Pupils stand up. Play the **Audio** again, for pupils to listen and mime each action.

54
As in Pupil's Book

PB49. ACTIVITY 3

Listen and sing. Do karaoke.

- Play the **Audio** again, pausing to teach the **Song** line by line. Pupils repeat the **Song** as a whole class and then in groups. Make two groups. Each group sings and moves for their verse. Change groups and repeat.

54
As in Pupil's Book

- Say *Do karaoke.* Pupils listen to the karaoke version. They sing the **Song** as a class and mime the actions.

Extra support Put the class in two groups. One group sings the first verse of the **Song** without doing the actions and does the actions for the second verse without singing. The other group does the actions for the first verse and sings the second verse.

55
Karaoke version of the song

AB49. Answer key, see page T100

Ending the lesson

- Mime an illness, e.g. *a cough.* Elicit some responses from different pupils using *mustn't/don't/must,* e.g. *You mustn't go swimming. You mustn't talk a lot. You must drink orange juice. Don't go out.* Say *Thank you.* Repeat with pupils coming to the front in turn to mime another illness.

Digital Classroom

Presentation Plus: Unit 5
Digital Flashcards

Practice Extra

Extra Resources

- **Teacher Resources:** Unit 5, Downloadable Activity Book Teaching Notes
- **T109 – Consolidation activity:** *Do what I say …*
- **T109 – Extension activity:** *Consequences*

Read the story. Look at the pictures. Write the correct word next to numbers 1–6.

swimming

cough

bed

~~school~~

sleep

doctor

It's Tuesday and Paul's at home. He can't go to 1 school because he's ill. He's got a temperature. He mustn't get up. He must stay in bed. He's got a 2 ________ and a cold. His 3 ________ says he mustn't run or play. He must 4 ________ and drink a lot. Paul always has a 5 ________ lesson on Tuesdays but he can't go today. He isn't sad because he can listen to music in 6 ________!

Listen and move.

Move, move, move.
To be fit and well.
Come on move your body ...

Let's have a good time.
Run, swim and climb.
Move, move, move.
Move your body.

Dance, dance, dance.
Don't stop until you drop.
Come on, you know it's fun.

Dance, dance, dance.
Hop, skip and jump.
Come on, you know it's fun.

Let's have a good time ...

Listen and sing. Do karaoke.

Lock's sounds and spelling

 **Watch the video. Watch again and practise.**

 **Listen and write.**

He's got a cold and he's feeling ill – poor farmer Bill!
The sheep ate all the cake – now they've got a stomach-ache!

 **Work in pairs. Describe and say.**

She's got a toothache. She mustn't eat sweets.

Show what you know

_____'__ got a cough and ____'_ got a cold.

Objectives

To recognise and practise /v/ and /z/ in contracted verbs with *he, she, they, we* forms in context and to notice spelling patterns *'s* and *'ve*.

Target language

- **Key language:** the sounds /z/ (*he's, she's*) and /v/ (*they've, we've*)
- **Revision:** *have/has got (a temperature, a cold, a cough, a headache, a toothache, a stomach-ache)*

Warmer

- Elicit activities pupils enjoy and write them on the board (e.g. *play football, go swimming, ride a bike, watch TV*). Draw a tick or a cross next to each activity. Tell pupils the cross means *I can't* and the tick means *I can*. Point to an activity with a cross and say, e.g. *I can't go swimming*. Pupils give a reason, e.g. *You've got a temperature*. In groups of four, pupils take turns to say an *I can / I can't* sentence. For *I can't*, the rest of the group say a reason.

Presentation

PB50. ACTIVITY 1

Watch the video. Watch again and practise.

- Write *farmer* and *sheep* on the board and tell pupils that the farmer and the sheep can't work. Elicit guesses as to why. Tell pupils you're going to watch a ▶ **Video** to find out.
- Watch the ▶ **Video** and ask *What's the matter with the farmer and the sheep?* Ask what else they remember from the ▶ **Video** and write key words on the board.

▶ 56

Voice & Key: /z/ /z/ /v/ /v/
Lock: What can you see, Key?
Voice: he's /z/
Lock & Key: He's got a cold and he's feeling ill – poor farmer Bill!
Voice: they've /v/
Lock & Key: The sheep ate all the cake, now they've got a stomach-ache!
Lock & Voice: He's got a cold and he's feeling ill – poor farmer Bill! The sheep ate all the cake – now they've got a stomach-ache!
Lock: Come on, everyone. One, two, three … let's say it with Key!
Voice, Lock & Key: He's got a cold and he's feeling ill – poor farmer Bill! The sheep ate all the cake, now they've got a stomach-ache!
Lock: I say – well done, Key!

- Watch the ▶ **Video** again. Ask pupils *Who's got a cold?* and elicit *He's got a cold*. Repeat with *stomach-ache* to elicit *They've*. Write *he's* and *they've* on the board. Underline the *'s* and the *'ve* and check understanding that they are the contractions *has/have*. Say the sounds /z/ and /v/ for pupils to repeat. Repeat with the pronouns (*he's, they've*).

PB50. ACTIVITY 2

Listen and write.

- Wipe out the *'s* and *'ve* from *he's* and *they've* on the board and ask pupils to say the sound and write the letters in the air with their finger. Ask pupils what's the matter with farmer Bill, to elicit *he's got a cold* for pupils to write. Ask pupils *How is he feeling?* to elicit *He's feeling ill*. Ask what the sheep ate (cake) and what's the matter with them to elicit *They've got a stomach-ache*. Pupils write each of the words and phrases you elicit. In pairs, they compare the words they've written and try to reconstruct the rhyme from the key words they have. Then they check in their Pupil's Books.
- Divide the class into two groups, A and B. Say the first line from the ▶ **Video**, *He's got a cold and he's feeling ill – poor farmer Bill!* Group A say the line with *he's got* and group B say the line with *they've got*. Groups swap roles.

Extra challenge Tell pupils in group A that they are now the sheep and elicit the sentences with the pronouns *you've* and *we've*. Invite a pupil to take the role of the farmer and elicit sentences with *I've* and *she's/he's*.

PB50. ACTIVITY 3

Work in pairs. Describe and say.

- Focus pupils on the first picture and ask what they can see to elicit *They've got* + illness. Ask pupils to suggest what they can or can't do and what they must do. In pairs, pupils say what illnesses the others have got and what they must do.

Show what you know

- Focus on the *Show what you know* Box. Pupils complete the sentence with the missing words and practise saying it.

Key: They've, she's

AB50. Answer key, see pages T100

Ending the lesson

- Say a sentence with *'s* or *'ve*, but say *beep* in place of the contracted verb, e.g. *I beep got a cold*. Pupils say the missing contraction sound /z/ or /v/. Repeat with other sentences.

Digital Classroom

Presentation Plus: Unit 5
Digital Flashcards
Audio 56
Practice Extra

Extra Resources

- **Teacher Resources:** Unit 5, Downloadable Activity Book Teaching Notes
- **T109 – Consolidation activity:** *Whisper and write*
- **T109 – Extension activity:** *Picture gallery*

Objectives

To read a story and to review language from the unit.

Target language

- **Key language:** language from the unit, *look after, rich*
- **Additional language:** *party, waiter*
- **Revision:** language from the story, *have got, episode, beautiful painting, cake, Which cake would you like? I'd like …, not good for you, stomach-ache, What's the matter?*

Materials

- **Flashcards:** illness (63–70)

Warmer

- Review the Lock and Key story so far. Write *Lock and Key* in the centre of the board and build a mind map by eliciting what pupils remember, e.g. *detectives, no problem, not clever, robber, pet thief, never get up before ten o'clock.*

Story

PB51.

Watch the video.

- Say *Open your Pupil's Books at page 51, please.* Elicit which episode this is (six). Focus pupils on the first frame and elicit the woman's name (Miss Rich). Check understanding of *rich*.

Extra support Use the pictures to guide pupils to predict the story.

- Set the pre-watching questions: *What's the name of the painting? What has Key got? Who's got the painting?*
- Watch the ▶ **Video**. Pupils answer the questions and check in pairs. Check with the class ('The Toothache'; cakes and a stomach-ache; a thief).
- Play the 🔊 **Audio**. Pupils listen and repeat. Encourage them to say the words with intonation and feeling.
- Check comprehension by pointing to the pictures on the whiteboard and asking, e.g. *What does Miss Rich want the detectives to do?* (look after the painting). *What does Key see?* (a lot of cakes). *What does this man* (point to the waiter) *say?* (Would you like a cake, Sir?). *Who is he?* (a waiter). *How many cakes has Key got?* (four). *Which is your favourite?*

🔊▶ 57

Miss Rich: I'm having a big party and I need some detectives to look after my beautiful painting, 'The Toothache'.
Key: No problem, Miss Rich.
Miss Rich: This is my beautiful painting.
Key: Ooh, there are a lot of cakes!
Key: There's a lemon cake, a chocolate cake, an apple cake and a carrot cake.
Butler: Would you like a cake, Sir?
Lock: I'd like a lemon cake, please. Which cake would you like, Key?
Key: Er …, I can't choose. Oooh … Which cake?
Key: Look. I've got an apple cake, I've got a carrot cake, I've got a lemon cake and I've got a chocolate cake.
Lock: Oh Key. That's not good for you.
Lock: Hmm, what's the matter, Key?
Key: I've got some chocolate cake and now I've got a stomach-ache, too.
Miss Rich: … and I haven't got my beautiful painting!

PB51. ACTIVITY 1

How many cakes does Key have? Which cakes are they?

- Ask a pupil to read the questions aloud. Give pupils time to talk about them in pairs. They can reread the story if necessary. Check answers as a class.

Key: Lock has got four cakes. He's got an apple cake, a carrot cake, a lemon cake and a chocolate cake.

AB51. Answer key, see page T100

Ending the lesson

- Say true and false sentences about today's episode of Lock and Key, e.g. *Miss Rich is having a party. The painting is called 'The Headache'. The waiter gives Lock and Key some drinks. Key has a stomach-ache.* Pupils listen and call out *yes* or *no*.

Digital Classroom

Presentation Plus: Unit 5
Audio 57

Digital Flashcards
Practice Extra

Extra Resources

- **Teacher Resources:** Unit 5, Downloadable Activity Book Teaching Notes
- **Teacher Resources:** Unit 5, *Extension worksheet 2*
- **Teacher Resources:** Unit 5, *Video, Suzy's room*
- **T110 – Extension activity:** *Role play*
- **T110 – Consolidation activity:** *Play the game*

1 **How many cakes does Key have? Which cakes are they?**

What remedies do we use?

1 58 **Listen and read. Do you use any of these remedies? Do you think they work?**

What do you do when you're ill? Here are some common home remedies!

Soup – have you got a cold or the flu? Chicken soup is a famous food remedy. In some countries, lizard soup is popular!

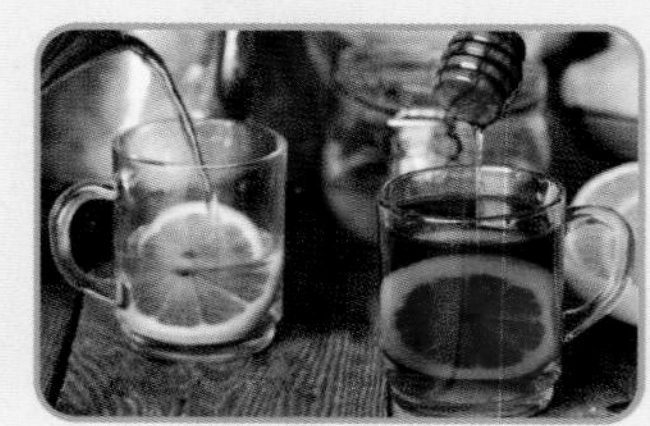

Herbal tea – hot tea is a popular remedy. Herbal teas come from different parts of plants. Have you got a sore throat or stomach-ache? These teas can help you.

Essential oils – essential oils come from plants, too. You can use essential oils on your skin for headaches and muscle aches. But be careful! One or two drops is enough.

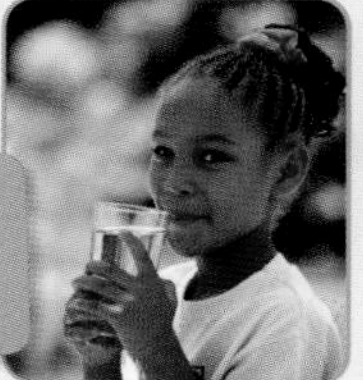

REMEMBER! Water's always good for you!

2 **Look and suggest a remedy from the text. Write your answer on the lines.**

1 

essential oils

2 

3 

4

3 **What other home remedies or health advice can you think of? Think and say.**

Take vitamin C.

Stay in bed.

Put ice on it.

DIDYOUKNOW...?
Most remedies come from plants – about 70%!

Objectives

To discuss illnesses and home remedies.

Target language

- **Key language:** language from the unit
- **Additional language:** *drops, essential oil, flu, good for you, herbal, home remedy, ill, illness, lizard, medicine, muscle ache, skin, sore throat*
- **Revision:** *chicken, help, popular, soup, tea, water*

Warmer

- Write *Achoo!* on the board and mime sneezing. Brainstorm illnesses and symptoms, e.g. *temperature, headache, stomach-ache, sore throat,* and write them on the board. Ask *What do you do to feel better when you're ill?* Invite pupils to give suggestions.
- You are now ready to watch the ▶ Video.

PB52.

What remedies do we use?

- Tell pupils that they're going to learn more about home remedies in this lesson.
- Watch the ▶ Video and answer the questions in the ▶ Video.

PB52. ACTIVITY 1

Listen and read. Do you use any of these remedies? Do you think they work?

- Show Activity 1 on the whiteboard and focus pupils on the remedies in the pictures. Ask *What do you think this text is about?* Play the Audio for pupils to follow along in their books.
- Ask the questions in the rubric. Pupils discuss the questions in pairs. Encourage them to explain their answers. Check with the class. Ask *What are some other things that are good for you?*

Extra support Tell pupils to underline the words for illnesses in red (*a cold, the flu, sore throat, stomach-ache, headaches, muscle aches*) and remedies in blue (*chicken soup, lizard soup, hot tea, herbal teas, essential oils*).

Extra challenge Make sentences about the home remedies from the text, e.g. *One or two drops is enough.* Pupils say what the remedy is.

58

As in Pupil's Book

PB52. ACTIVITY 2

Look and suggest a remedy from the text. Write your answer on the lines.

- Point to the photos of illnesses. Ask what the first illness is (a headache). Elicit a remedy from the text: *essential oils.* Put pupils into pairs to write remedies for the other illnesses. Monitor pupils' progress. Check answers as a class.

Key: **2** herbal tea, **3** soup, **4** herbal tea

PB52. ACTIVITY 3

What other home remedies or health advice can you think of? Think and say.

- Read the question in the rubric aloud and ask volunteers to read the examples. Put pupils into small groups to discuss other home remedies and health advice they know of.

Did you know ...?

- Invite a volunteer to read the information in the box aloud. Ask pupils if this fact surprises them. Point to the photo and say *This is eucalyptus. It has a strong smell. People use it for cold and flu symptoms.*

AB52. Answer key, see page T100

Ending the lesson

- Play a game. Write *Illness or remedy?* on the board. Divide the class into teams. Say an illness or a remedy, e.g. *stomach-ache.* If it's an illness, pupils raise their left hand. If it's a remedy, they raise their right hand.

Digital Classroom

Presentation Plus: Unit 5
Digital Flashcards
Audio 58
Practice Extra

Extra Resources

- **Teacher Resources:** Unit 5, Downloadable Activity Book Teaching Notes
- **T110 – Consolidation activity:** *Class survey*

Objectives

To write a leaflet about an illness.

Target language

- **Additional language:** *hiccups, hold your breath, honey, movements, muscle, noise, spoon*
- **Revision:** *cold, count, sugar, worry*

Materials

- **Warmer:** Realia related to illnesses and remedies, e.g. tissues, masks, hand sanitiser, herbal tea, a thermometer

Warmer

- Display illnesses and remedies realia, e.g. tissues, masks, hand sanitiser, herbal tea, a thermometer. Pupils look at the items and say what they are for.

PB53. ACTIVITY 4

Read the leaflet. What is the problem? How can you treat it?

- Show Activity 4 on the whiteboard. Focus pupils on the leaflet and ask *What are the hiccups?* Mime having the hiccups. Ask *Have you ever had the hiccups?*
- Say *Open your Pupil's Books at page 53, please.* Give pupils time to read the text. Help with vocabulary if needed, but encourage pupils to use context to understand any unfamiliar words.
- Pupils answer the questions in the rubric.

Key: The problem is hiccups. You can treat it by holding your breath and counting to ten or by eating a spoon of honey or sugar.

Project

- Remember to download your project notes from *Cambridge One*.

PB53. ACTIVITY 5

Underline the imperative verbs in Activity 4.

- Read the sentences in the box aloud. Point out the underlined words. Explain that we use sentences like these to give advice and commands. Tell pupils to underline the imperative verbs in Activity 4, and check answers with a partner.
- Monitor the activity and review as a class.

Extra challenge Elicit examples of affirmative and negative imperatives from everyday life, e.g. rules like *Walk. Don't run.* Invite volunteers to write the advice/rules on the board.

Key: Help, Hold, count, Eat, Don't worry

PB53. ACTIVITY 6

In pairs, give examples of other illnesses. Complete the table in your notebook.

- Explain to pupils that they are going to think about other illnesses, remedies and advice. Pupils work together in pairs to complete the table in their notebooks.
- Elicit pupils' ideas and write them on the board.

AB53. Answer key, see page T100

Ending the lesson

- Write five illnesses on the board with the letters scrambled, e.g. *acothhtoe* (toothache). In small groups, pupils unscramble the words.

Digital Classroom

Digital Flashcards

Extra Resources

- **Teacher Resources:** Unit 5, Downloadable Activity Book Teaching Notes
- **Teacher Resources:** Unit 5, *Project notes*
- **PB88–95 – A1 Movers Exam folder**
- **T110 – Extension activity:** *Silly remedies*
- **T110 – Consolidation activity:** *Simon says*

4 Read the leaflet. What is the problem? How can you treat it?

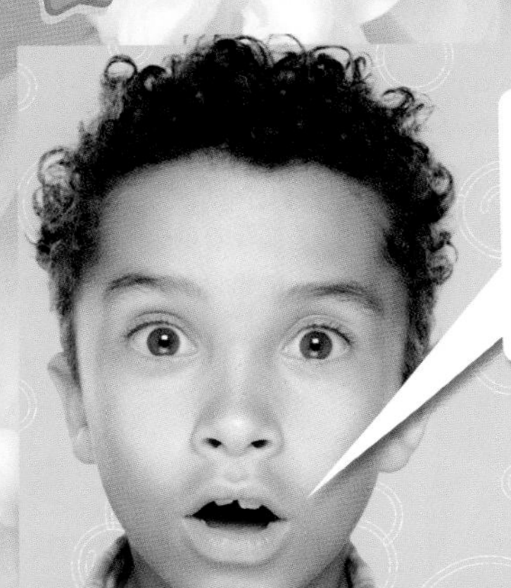

Hiccup facts

Hiccups can happen when you're cold or when you eat too fast.

Hiccups come from muscle movements. They cause you to make a "hiccup" noise. You can't control the hiccups.

How to treat the hiccups

✓ Hold your breath and count to ten.

✓ Eat a spoon of honey or sugar.

✗ Don't worry. Hiccups usually stop after a few minutes.

5 Underline the imperative verbs in Activity 4.

Learning to write:

Imperatives

Count to ten. Don't worry.

Ready to write:

Go to Activity Book page 52.

6 In pairs, give examples of other illnesses. Complete the table in your notebook.

Illness	Do	Don't
toothache		

Project

Make a class book of remedies.

6 In the countryside

1 59 Look, think and answer. Listen and check.

1 Where do they want to go?
2 Does Mr Star want to play tennis?
3 What does Simon want to do?
4 What does Stella want to do?

2 60 Listen and say the letter.

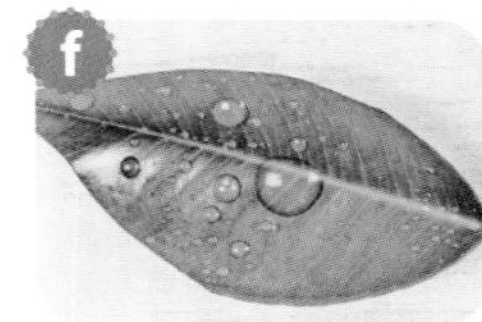

3 Ask and answer.

What do you want to do in the countryside?

I want to have a picnic and swim in the river.

Objectives

To name and talk about places in the countryside.

Target language

- **Key language:** *field, forest, grass, lake, leaf/leaves, picnic, plant, river, countryside*
- **Additional language:** *part, on the ground, stay, other, blanket, towel*
- **Revision:** adjectives, prepositions, activities and actions, characters, *want to, like, love, enjoy, would like to, map, a good idea, lunch, Sunday, must, sometimes, animals*

Materials

- **Flashcards:** countryside (71–78)

Warmer

- Draw pupils' attention to the window in your classroom. Elicit what they can see outside.
- Say *So, where do we live? In the city?* If your school is in the countryside, supply the sentence *We live in the countryside.* If not, say *We don't live in the countryside.*

Presentation

- Elicit different places where people can live: *city, town, village* and *countryside*. Write *Countryside* in a circle in the centre of the board. Elicit what pupils can find in the countryside. Use the flashcards to teach *field, forest, grass, lake, leaf/leaves, plant, river.*

PB54. ACTIVITY 1

Look, think and answer. Listen and check.

- Show Activity 1 on the whiteboard. Focus pupils on the picture. Ask *Who can you see?* (the Star family). *What are they looking at?* (a map).
- Say *Open your Pupil's Books at page 54, please.* Pupils find a field, a forest, grass, a lake, a leaf, a plant and a river in the picture. Ask a pupil to read the activity instruction aloud and others to take turns to read the four questions. Pupils compare their answers/predictions in pairs, looking for clues in the picture.
- Play the **Audio**. Pupils check in pairs. Play the **Audio** again. Check with the class. Check comprehension and understanding of *blanket, picnic* and *towel* with the picture and ask questions, e.g. *Are they going to eat outside? What's this called? Do you have picnics with your family?*

Key: **1** They want to go to the countryside for a picnic on Sunday. **2** No. He wants to go for a picnic. **3** He wants to go swimming. **4** She wants to look at some plants and draw their leaves.

59

Mr Star: Look at this map of the countryside. Let's go there for a picnic on Sunday. We can take a blanket and have our lunch on the grass, next to that big rock.
Grandpa: That's a good idea. I like picnics. Ooh, there's a river here with a waterfall. I'd like to go fishing.
Simon: And I'd like to go swimming. There's a lake next to the river.
Mr Star: OK, so you need to take a towel.
Stella: Look! Here's a big forest. I want to look at some plants and draw their leaves.
Suzy: Is there any grass to play on, Dad?
Mr Star: Yes, Suzy. Look at the map. These green parts are fields. There's a lot of grass.
Grandpa: Hmm, lots of grass and a blanket … That's great … for a nice sleep after lunch. Hmm.

PB54. ACTIVITY 2

Listen and say the letter.

- Focus pupils on the Activity 2 pictures. Pupils point to each one and name it. Direct pupils to the activity instruction. Play the **Audio**. Pupils point or whisper to their partner. Play the **Audio** again. Check with the class by asking, e.g. *What's 'e'?* or *Which one's 'grass'?*
- In pairs, pupils ask and answer about the pictures.

Key: d, a, h, j, g, f, c, b, i

60

a forest, a lake, a picnic, a field, a waterfall, grass, a leaf, a river, a plant, a rock

PB54. ACTIVITY 3

Ask and answer.

- Focus pupils on Activity 3. Ask two pupils to read the example.
- In pairs, pupils ask and answer and then swap roles.

Extra challenge Pupils can stand up and walk around the classroom asking the question to as many of their classmates as possible.

AB54. Answer key, see page T101

Ending the lesson

- Write the key words from the lesson on the board. Elicit connections between them, e.g. *Leaves and grass are both green. You need a blanket for a picnic.* Help pupils by pointing to two or three, e.g. *lake, river, towel* and asking *What's the connection between these three?*

Digital Classroom

Audio 59–60

Extra Resources

- **Teacher Resources:** Unit 6, Downloadable Activity Book Teaching Notes
- **Teacher Resources:** Unit 6, *Reinforcement worksheet 1*
- **T110 – Consolidation activity:** *Spell it*
- **T110 – Extension activity:** *Things I enjoy*

Objectives

To read a story about the countryside and complete a questionnaire.

Target language

- **Key language:** present continuous for narrating a story with pictures, *duck, free time*
- **Additional language:** *at the moment, because, so, looks* (*sad*)
- **Revision:** countryside, family, prepositions, adjectives, food, *can't*

Materials

- **Flashcards:** countryside (71–78)

Warmer

- Review the countryside words using the flashcards.
- Write the first letter and one other letter of *blanket, field, forest, grass, lake, leaf, picnic, plant, river, towel* on the board, followed by dashes for the other letters, e.g. *f_ _ _ s _*.
- Pupils guess and give the spellings. Display the flashcards on the board for pupils to check their spelling, or ask the class to correct.

PB55. ACTIVITY 1

Read and complete.

- Show Activity 1 on the whiteboard. Focus them on the picture and the text. Say *Find the names of the boy and the girl.*
- Say *Open your Pupil's Books at page 55, please.* Pupils scan the text. Check with the class (Charlie, Lily). Pupils take turns to read the text aloud around the class. Check understanding by asking, e.g. *Where are they?* (in the forest). *Who are they with?* (their grandmother). *What have they got on the blanket?* (a picnic). Focus pupils on the incomplete sentences under the text and the example. In pairs, pupils complete the sentences orally. They can use one, two, three or four words for each sentence. Check by eliciting sentences from different pairs around the class.

Extra support Before completing the task orally, pupils can find and underline the answers in the text.

Key: **2** Charlie, **3** it's very old, **4** on the blanket, **5** the ducks, **6** the family's new bread

PB55. ACTIVITY 2

Complete the story. Use words from the box.

- Focus pupils on Activity 2. They work in pairs and complete the summary of the story. Monitor the class as pupils are working. Remind them to use the text in Activity 1 to help them.

Key: **2** countryside, **3** his, **4** grandmother, **5** blanket, **6** very, **7** old, **8** eat, **9** lake, **10** ducks, **11** picnic

AB55. Answer key, see page T101

Ending the lesson

- Do a quick hands-up survey about free-time activities, e.g. *Who likes climbing trees? Hands up!* Write *Climbing trees* and the number of pupils on the board. Repeat for other free-time activities. Review the numbers on the board and say which is/are the favourite(s).

Digital Classroom

- **Presentation Plus:** Unit 6
- **Practice Extra**
- **Digital Flashcards**

Extra Resources

- **Teacher Resources:** Unit 6, Downloadable Activity Book Teaching Notes
- **Teacher Resources:** Unit 6, *Extension worksheet 1*
- **T110 – Consolidation activity:** *True or false*
- **T110 – Extension activity:** *Picture dictation*

1 Read and complete.

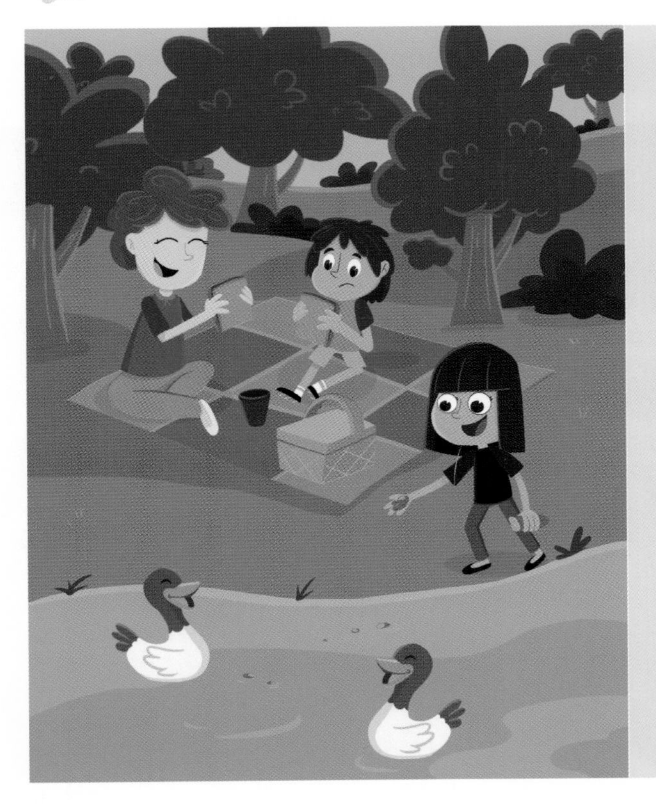

A picnic without bread

Charlie and his sister Lily enjoy having picnics in the countryside. Today they're having a picnic in the forest with their grandmother.

Charlie and his grandmother are sitting on a blanket. They're putting the picnic on it. After lunch, Charlie wants to do his homework. He must look at the plants and draw their leaves.

Charlie looks sad because the bread's very old and they can't eat it for lunch …

Lily's standing next to the lake! She looks happy because she's throwing bread to the ducks. It isn't the bread for the ducks, it's the new bread for their picnic.

The ducks are eating the family's lunch!

1 Today Charlie and Lily are eating lunch in …
2 … wants to draw the plants and their leaves.
3 Charlie doesn't like his bread because …
4 Lily isn't sitting … with her brother and grandmother.
5 She's giving the new bread to …
6 The ducks are having … for lunch!

Today Charlie and Lily are eating lunch in the forest.

2 Complete the story. Use words from the box.

countryside ~~picnics~~ old blanket grandmother his very lake eat picnic ducks

Charlie and Lily like going for [1] picnics in the countryside. Today they are in the [2] ________ with their grandmother. Charlie and [3] ________ [4] ________ are putting the food on the [5] ________ . Charlie's looking at the bread because it's [6] ________ , so they can't [7] ________ it. Next to the [8] ________ , Lily's throwing bread to the [9] ________ . It's the nice new bread for the family's [10] ________ !

Language: present continuous

1 Look, think and say the name. Listen and check.

1 … puts the table under a tree.
2 … helps Simon.
3 … wants some food.
4 … isn't happy with her drawing.

2 Close your books. Listen and answer.

3 Mime and guess.

Are you thirsty?

Yes, I am.

LOOK

Shall I help you with the blanket?

Yes, please.

Objectives

To describe a scene using adjectives and make suggestions.

Target language

- **Key language:** suggestions and offers: *Shall I …?*, adjectives: *bad, cold, fat, good, hot, hungry, loud, quiet, strong, thirsty, tired, thin, weak*
- **Additional language:** *baby cow (calf)*
- **Revision:** countryside, food, adjectives, *have got, eat, sleep, drink, listen, radio, help, Let's …*

Warmer

- Start a chain to review unit vocabulary: *In the countryside you can see … grass.* Volunteers continue the chain, e.g. *In the countryside you can see grass and lakes.*

PB56. ACTIVITY 1

Look, think and say the name. Listen and check.

- Show Activity 1 on the whiteboard. Focus pupils on the picture. Elicit who/what they can see. Ask a pupil to read the activity instruction aloud and others to read the four sentences. Pupils compare their predictions in pairs.
- Say *Open your Pupil's Books at page 56, please.* Play the **Audio**. Pupils listen for the answers. They check in pairs. Play the **Audio** again. Check with the class. Discuss the picture, using information from the **Audio**, and elicit/teach the new adjectives: *cold, fat, hot, hungry*, e.g. *Look at Simon. He's thinking about food. He's hungry!*
- Say, e.g. *Shall we listen to the audio again?* Prompt the response *Yes, let's.* Play the first part up to *Yes, please!* Elicit what Stella says (she wants to help). Ask *What does she say?* (*Shall I help you put the blanket on the grass, Simon?*) Focus pupils on the *Look* Box. Invite a pupil to read it aloud and check comprehension. Elicit other examples in a classroom context, e.g. *Shall I open the door? Shall I clean the board?*

Key: **1** Mr Star, **2** Stella, **3** Simon, **4** Stella

61

1 **Mr Star:** OK. Now, where shall I put the picnic table?
Mrs Star: Put it over there under that tree, please.
Simon: Oof, I can't do this!
Stella: Shall I help you put the blanket on the grass, Simon?
Simon: Yes, please!

2 **Narrator:** Later …
Simon's cold and hungry. He wants to eat.
Suzy's hot and thirsty. She wants a drink.
Grandpa Star is catching a big fish. He's very strong.
Grandma Star's near the cows in the field. She's very quiet.
She's painting a baby cow. It's got thin legs and it's very weak.
The big cow is fat.
Stella isn't happy because her drawing's bad.
Mr Star's listening to the radio. His music is very loud.
Oh, yes! And finally, Mrs Star. She's sleeping because she's very tired.

PB56. ACTIVITY 2

Close your books. Listen and answer.

- Play the **Audio**. Pupils listen and quietly say the answers. Play the **Audio** again. Check with the class. Elicit the answers from different pairs each time. Make sure they use the correct pronouns with the adjectives.

Key: **1** It's bad. **2** He's cold. **3** It's loud. **4** She's thirsty. **5** He's strong. **6** She's tired. **7** It's fat. **8** She's quiet.

62

1 Is Stella's drawing good or bad?
2 Is Simon hot or cold?
3 Is the music quiet or loud?
4 Is Suzy hungry or thirsty?
5 Is Grandpa strong or weak?
6 Is Mrs Star tired or hungry?
7 Is the big cow fat or thin?
8 Is Grandma tired or quiet?

PB56. ACTIVITY 3

Mime and guess.

- Mime being thirsty. A pupil reads the speech bubble. Reply *Yes, I am.*
- In groups, a pupil mimes an adjective. The others ask, e.g. *Are you (hungry)?*

Extra support Do more examples together.

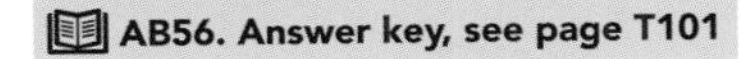
AB56. Answer key, see page T101

Ending the lesson

- Do a clapping chant of the word pairs, e.g. Teacher: (Clap, clap) *Bad.* Pupils: (Clap, clap) *Good.*

Digital Classroom

Presentation Plus: Unit 6

Digital Flashcards
Audio 61–62
Practice Extra

Extra Resources

- **Teacher Resources:** Unit 6, Downloadable Activity Book Teaching Notes
- **Teacher Resources:** Unit 6, *Reinforcement worksheet 2*
- **AB87 and PB87 – Grammar reference 6**
- **T110 – Consolidation activity:** *Fill the gaps*
- **T110 – Extension activity:** *What's the situation?*

Objectives

To have practice using adjectives and to sing a song.

Target language

- **Key language:** rhyming words, *skin, angry*
- **Additional language:** *everywhere, that*
- **Revision:** adjectives, food, clothes, illnesses, town, body, people, *here, there*

Materials

- Photocopiable 6, one copy for each pupil copied onto thin card.

Warmer

- Review adjectives using mime. Say, e.g. *Tall*. Pupils reach up to show they're tall. Continue with other adjectives: *short, big, small, hungry, thirsty, weak, strong, fat, thin, happy, sad, young, old*.

Song

PB57. ACTIVITY 1

Read and complete. Listen and check.

- Show Activity 1 on the whiteboard. Focus pupils on the pictures and encourage them to describe the people.
- Say *Open your Pupil's Books at page 57, please*. In pairs, pupils quickly look through the Song lyrics and try to guess what the missing words are. Remind them to use the ones in the box. They write the words in pencil.
- Play the Audio. Pupils listen and check/complete. Check with the class. Elicit the patterns (rhyme and opposites). Check general comprehension and understanding of new words, e.g. *skin*.

Key: **2** long, **3** hair, **4** bad, **5** tall, **6** quiet

63

As in Pupil's Book

PB57. ACTIVITY 2

Listen and sing. Do karaoke.

- Play the Audio again in sections. Pupils join in with the Song.

Extra challenge Encourage pupils to suggest actions for each of the adjectives in the Song.

- Play the Audio right through for pupils to sing. Practise the Song with the class. Encourage them to mime, too: it will help them remember.

63

As in Pupil's Book

- Say *Do karaoke*. Pupils listen to the karaoke version. They sing the Song as a class and mime the actions.

64

Karaoke version of the song

PB57. ACTIVITY 3

Listen and write. Match the words and the pictures.

- Focus pupils on Activity 3 and on the activity instructions. Check understanding. Play the example. Check understanding of *angry*. Pupils write the word as it's being spelt and then match it with a picture. Play the rest of the Audio. Pupils check in pairs. Play the Audio again. Check with the class.

Key: **2** thirsty – d, **3** clever – h, **4** cold – b, **5** loud – f, **6** hungry – c, **7** strong – a, **8** tired – g

65

1 a-n-g-r-y
2 t-h-i-r-s-t-y
3 c-l-e-v-e-r
4 c-o-l-d
5 l-o-u-d
6 h-u-n-g-r-y
7 s-t-r-o-n-g
8 t-i-r-e-d

- Use Photocopiable 6 from the Teacher Resources.

AB57. Answer key, see page T101

Ending the lesson

- Sing the Song again as a whole class or in groups.

Digital Classroom

Presentation Plus: Unit 6
Audio 63–65
Digital Flashcards
Practice Extra

Extra Resources

- **Teacher Resources:** Unit 6, Downloadable Activity Book Teaching Notes
- **Teacher Resources:** Unit 6, *Song worksheet*
- **T110 – Consolidation activity:** *Mime game*

1 Read and complete. Listen and check.

bad hair long quiet tall ~~thin~~

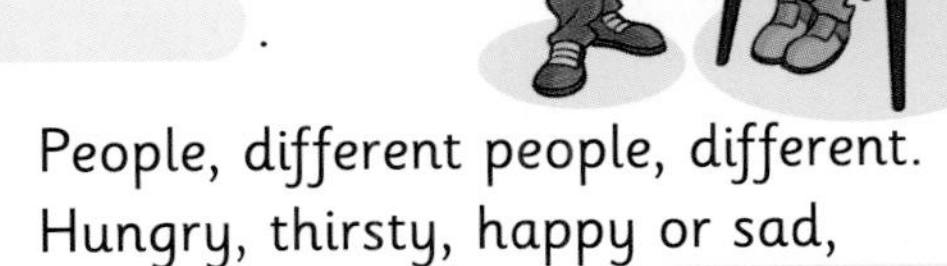

People, people here or there.
People, people everywhere.
Different colours, different skin.
Bodies that are fat, bodies that are [1] thin.

Some are weak, some are strong,
With hair that's short or hair that's [2] ______.
Straight, curly, dark or fair.
Different people, different [3] ______.

People, different people, different.
Hungry, thirsty, happy or sad,
Young or old, good or [4] ______.
People are big, people are small.
People are short, people are [5] ______.

People, different people, different.
Funny, naughty, angry or tired,
Clever, beautiful, loud or [6] ______.
People, people here or there.
People, people everywhere.

2 Listen and sing. Do karaoke.

3 Listen and write. Match the words and the pictures.

1 A-N-G-R-Y

Angry – d

Lock's sounds and spelling

1 66 **Watch the video. Watch again and practise.**

In the forest, parrots sit on the grass by the river. They watch their bread and grapes so crocodiles can't steal their dinner!

2 **Listen and write.**

3 **Look, ask and answer.** What's the big crocodile doing? It's sitting by the river.

Show what you know

The ______________ is swimming in the ________.

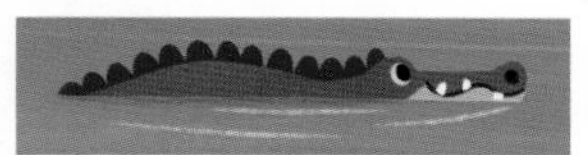

Unit 6 In the countryside
Pupil's Book p.58

Objectives
To recognise and practise /r/ in various positions in familiar vocabulary.

Target language
- **Key language:** the sound /r/ (*river, grass, forest*)
- **Additional language:** *parrot, crocodile, steal*
- **Revision:** *hungry, thirsty, bread, grapes, sit, watch, dinner*

Materials
- **Flashcards:** river (78), field (71), forest (72), lake (74)

Warmer
- Show pupils the field, river, forest, lake flashcards and stick them on the board. Focus on the field flashcard and ask pupils what you can do in a field, what they mustn't do in a field and what they want to do in a field. Share ideas together and repeat with the other three flashcards.

Presentation

PB58. ACTIVITY 1

Watch the video. Watch again and practise.
- Write the word *forest* on the board. Ask pupils what animals live in the forest and what those animals do there.
- Watch the ▶ **Video** together and ask pupils what animals are in the ▶ **Video**. Elicit *parrots* and *crocodiles* and write them on the board. Ask pupils where they are (on the grass by the river) and ask pupils what they are doing there (having dinner).

▶ 66

Voice: /r/ /r/
Key: Who's there, Lock?
Lock: Go and see, turn the key!
Lock: Aha! A good detective looks and listens. What can you hear, Key?
Voice: /r/ /r/
Key: /r/ /r/
Lock: What can you see, Key?
Voice: forest /r/ parrots /r/ grass /r/ river /r/
Lock & Key: In the forest, parrots sit on the grass by the river.
Voice: bread /r/ grapes /r/ crocodiles /r/
Lock & Key: They watch their bread and grapes so crocodiles can't steal their dinner.
Lock & Voice: In the forest, parrots sit on the grass by the river. They watch their bread and grapes so crocodiles can't steal their dinner.
Lock: Come on, everybody. One, two, three … let's say it with Key!
Voice, Lock & Key: In the forest, parrots sit on the grass by the river. They watch their bread and grapes so crocodiles can't steal their dinner.
Lock: I say, well done, Key!

- Watch the ▶ **Video** again. Ask pupils if they remember the food they have and write the answers on the board (*bread* and *grapes*). Ask them what sound they can see and hear that is the same in each word, to elicit /r/. Say the sound for pupils to repeat. Say the phrases from the ▶ **Video** together and pupils mime the actions. Pairs practise saying the rhyme.

Extra challenge In pairs, pupils say the rhyme together, with one pupil saying only the /r/ words and the other pupil saying the rest of the rhyme.

PB58. ACTIVITY 2

Listen and write.
- Show Activity 2 on the whiteboard. Pupils close their books. Say *forest* for pupils to write the word in their notebooks.
- Ask pupils what animals are in the forest to elicit *crocodiles* and *parrots* for pupils to write. Ask pupils where the animals are, to elicit *grass* and *river*. Ask what the parrots are eating to elicit *bread* and *grapes*. Pupils write each of the words and phrases you elicit. In pairs, they compare the words they've written and try to reconstruct the rhyme from the key words they have. Then they check in their Pupil's Books.

PB58. ACTIVITY 3

Look, ask and answer.
- Focus pupils on Activity 3. Ask them to look at the picture and elicit what they can see. In pairs, pupils ask and answer questions about the picture, e.g. *What is the crocodile doing? Who's hungry?*

Extra challenge In pairs, pupils write two more sentence starters, using the picture, for another pair to finish.

Show what you know
- Focus on the *Show what you know* Box. Pupils complete the sentence with the missing words and practise saying it.

Key: crocodile, river

AB58. Answer key, see page T101

Ending the lesson
- Tell pupils you're going to talk about what you did in today's lesson, and they must listen and put their hand up each time they hear the /r/ sound. Say the following sentences slowly: *Today we watched a video and we read a rhyme. The rhyme was about some parrots. The parrots were by a river in a forest. The parrots had grapes and bread.*

Digital Classroom

Presentation Plus: Unit 6
Audio 66
Digital Flashcards
Practice Extra

Extra Resources
- **Teacher Resources:** Unit 6, Downloadable Activity Book Teaching Notes
- **T111 – Consolidation activity:** *Rhyme orchestra*
- **T111 – Extension activity:** *Writing rhymes*

Objectives

To read a story and review language from the unit.

Target language

- **Key language:** language from the unit
- **Additional language:** *Please go and ask her, too. Don't be silly.*
- **Revision:** language from the story, countryside, *Let's go …, Shall we/I …? stand, a long walk, up the mountain*

Warmer

- Review the story and the characters with pupils. Elicit what happened in the last episode by asking, e.g. *Remember. Lock and Key are at a party. What happens? What's the name of the picture? What do they eat?*
- Say *Today Lock and Key are going for a picnic in the countryside. Mrs Potts is going, too. What do you think happens?* Elicit some ideas. Write them on the board. Help pupils formulate the ideas if necessary and provide the language, e.g. *They fall into the river. They haven't got the picnic. Mrs Potts catches a fish.*

Story

PB59.

Watch the video.

- Say *Open your Pupil's Books at page 59, please.* Elicit which episode this is (seven). Set the pre-watching questions, using pupils' predictions from the Warmer, e.g. *Do they fall into the river?* Watch the ▶ Video. Pupils answer the questions and check in pairs. Check with the class.
- Play the Audio. Pupils listen and repeat. Encourage them to say the words with intonation and feeling.
- Check comprehension by pointing to the pictures on the whiteboard and asking, e.g. *Who suggests asking Mrs Potts?* (Key). *What's happening to the picnic?* (it's falling out). *What does Key suggest to Mrs Potts first?* (*Shall I take a photo of you?*). *What does she say?* (*No, thank you.*). *What does he suggest to Lock?* (*Shall I go and catch some fish?*). *Why does Key go for a long walk?* (he's annoyed with them).

▶ 67

Lock: Let's go to the countryside for a picnic, Key.
Key: Great idea, Lock!
Key: Shall we ask Mrs Potts, too?
Lock: Yes, Key. Please go and ask her.
Key: Shall I take a photo of you, Mrs Potts? Go and stand in front of our car.
Mrs Potts: No, thank you, Mr Key. I can take one of the lake.
Key: Are you hungry, Lock? Shall I go to the river and catch some fish to eat?
Lock: Don't be silly, Key. We've got a big picnic.
Key: Are you cold, Mrs Potts. Shall I put this blanket on you?
Mrs Potts: No, thank you. It's hot. I don't need a blanket.
Key: Well, I can't get you food or a blanket and I can't help you … No problem, I can go for a long walk up the mountain.
Lock: Yes, Key!
Mrs Potts: Good idea!

PB59. ACTIVITY 1

Describe the pictures. What are they doing?

- Ask a pupil to read the instruction and question aloud. In pairs, they use the question to talk about what is happening in each frame of the story. Check with the class by pointing to each frame on the whiteboard and eliciting pupils' descriptions.

Extra support Elicit a description of the first picture as a class before pupils complete the activity in pairs.

AB59. Answer key, see page T101

Ending the lesson

- Ask pupils which chant/song they'd like to do again from the unit. Do it together to end the lesson.

Digital Classroom

Presentation Plus: Unit 6
Digital Flashcards
Audio 67
Practice Extra

Extra Resources

- **Teacher Resources:** Unit 6, Downloadable Activity Book Teaching Notes
- **Teacher Resources:** Unit 2, *Extension worksheet 2*
- **Teacher Resources:** Unit 2, *Video, Suzy's room*
- **T109 – Extension activity:** *Role play*

1 **Describe the pictures. What are they doing?**

Why do we live in different places?

1 68 **Listen and read. Which place do you prefer? Why?**

City: Singapore

Hi! I'm Tara. I'm a teenager and I live in Singapore. I love my city because it's really big and there's lots to do. I live on the 36th floor and from my window I can see shops and the skate park. The city is great, but I think there's a lot of traffic and pollution, and that isn't good for us.

Countryside: Argentina

Hello, I'm Emilio. I live in the countryside in Argentina because my dad's a farm worker. My mum's English and she's a writer. I like my life in the countryside because it's quiet and we've got a big garden with apple trees. I love nature, but sometimes it's a bit boring because I don't meet many people and it's difficult to make friends. All my friends live far away!

2 **Read and put a tick in the correct column.**

	City	Countryside
1 People have got more space to live.		✓
2 The air isn't clean.		
3 There's less noise.		
4 There's more public transport.		
5 People can enjoy nature more.		

3 **What are the advantages and disadvantages of living in the city? Think and say.**

It's very noisy.

Disadvantage!

DIDYOUKNOW...?

Most people in the world live in towns and cities – about 60%!

Objectives

To compare and contrast living in the city versus living in the countryside.

Target language

- **Key language:** language from the unit
- **Additional language:** *boring, countryside, make friends, nature, pollution, public transport, skate park, teenager, traffic, worker, writer*
- **Revision:** *city, quiet*

Materials

- **Warmer:** Photo of the Earth at night

Warmer

- Show pupils a photo of the Earth at night and encourage them to find where they live. Point out areas with lots of lights and ask what they show (cities, areas with lots of people).
- You are now ready to watch the ▶ Video.

PB60.

Why do we live in different places?

- Tell pupils that they're going to learn more about places where people live in this lesson.
- Watch the ▶ Video and answer the questions in the ▶ Video.

PB60. ACTIVITY 1

Listen and read. Which place do you prefer? Why?

- Show Activity 1 on the whiteboard. Focus pupils on the photos. Ask *What do you think this text is about?* Ask a pupil to read the questions in the rubric aloud.
- Say *Open your Pupil's Books at page 60, please.* Play the Audio while pupils follow along in their books.

Extra support Before discussing the questions in the rubric, ask *Where does Tara live? Where does Emilio live? How are the places different?*

- Pupils discuss the questions in pairs. Invite volunteers to share their opinions with the class. Encourage them to explain their answers.

68
As in Pupil's Book

PB60. ACTIVITY 2

Read and put a tick in the correct column.

- Focus pupils on Activity 2. Write *City* and *Countryside* on the board. Discuss the general characteristics of both places with the class.
- Pupils read the sentences and identify whether it describes the city or the countryside. Do the first one together as an example.

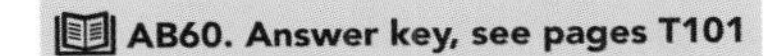

Key: 2 City, **3** Countryside, **4** City, **5** Countryside

Did you know ...?

- Invite a volunteer to read the information in the box aloud. Ask pupils if this fact surprises them.

PB60. ACTIVITY 3

What are the advantages and disadvantages of living in the city? Think and say.

- Focus pupils on Activity 3. Read the instructions aloud and ask two pupils to read the example. In small groups, pupils discuss the advantages and disadvantages of living in the city. One pupil says a sentence and the others identify whether it's an advantage or disadvantage. Invite groups to share their ideas with the class.

AB60. Answer key, see pages T101

Ending the lesson

- Ask pupils whether they live in the city or in the countryside. Encourage them to give examples to support their answers.

Digital Classroom

Presentation Plus: Unit 6
Audio 68
Digital Flashcards
Practice Extra

Extra Resources

- **Teacher Resources:** Unit 6, Downloadable Activity Book Teaching Notes
- **T111 – Consolidation activity:** *Word sort*
- **T111 – Extension activity:** *Murals*

Objectives

To write an email about where they live.

Target language

- **Key language:** language from the unit
- **Additional language:** *builder, skateboarding*
- **Revision:** city, countryside, *horse, park, pollution*

Materials

- **Warmer:** Photos of different places in cities and in the countryside

Warmer

- Show the class photos of different places in cities and in the countryside. Pupils call out *city* or *countryside.*

PB61. ACTIVITY 4

Read the emails. Underline the advantages of each place in green and the disadvantages in blue.

- Show Activity 4 on the whiteboard. Ask *What are their names? Where do they live?* Pupils scan the emails for the names of the people and places (Metin, Ruby; Kemble Creek in Australia, Istanbul). Give pupils time to read the text. Help with vocabulary if needed but encourage them to use context to understand any unfamiliar words.
- Say *Open your Pupil's Books at page 61, please.* Pupils underline the advantages and disadvantages in the corresponding colours. Do the first one together.
- Monitor the activity and review as a class.

Extra challenge Say a sentence from one of the emails, e.g. *I live in the Outback.* Pupils call out the name of the person.

> **Key:** Pupils underline in green: I like riding horses, lots to do; Pupils underline in blue: I don't see my friends a lot because they live far away, there's a lot of pollution

---

PB61. ACTIVITY 5

Circle the capital letters in names and places in Activity 4.

- Focus pupils on the sentences in the box. Ask *Which letters are capital letters?* Circle them on the board. Ask *Why do we capitalise these letters?* Explain that we use capital letters for the names of people and places. We also capitalise the first word in a sentence and the pronoun *I.*
- Pupils circle the capital letters in names and places in the emails. They do not need to circle all the capital letters.

> **Key:** Pupils circle the initial capital letter in the following words: Metin, Ruby, Australia, Outback, Kemble Creek, Zara, Istanbul, Defne

Project

- Remember to download your project notes from *Cambridge One.*

PB61. ACTIVITY 6

In pairs, say advantages and disadvantages of the place where you live. Complete the table in your notebook.

- In pairs, pupils discuss the advantages and disadvantages of the place where they live. They complete the table in their notebooks.
- Elicit pupils' ideas and write them on the board.

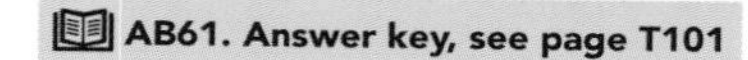

AB61. Answer key, see page T101

Ending the lesson

- Encourage pupils to imagine a city with no disadvantages. Give them time to discuss ideas in small groups. Then elicit ideas as a class.

Digital Classroom

Presentation Plus: Unit 6
Practice Extra
Digital Flashcards

Extra Resources

- **Teacher Resources:** Unit 6, Downloadable Activity Book Teaching Notes
- **Teacher Resources:** Unit 6, Downloadable Activity Book Audio Script
- **Teacher Resources:** Unit 6, *Project notes*
- **T111 – Consolidation activity:** *Name game*

4 **Read the emails. Underline the advantages of each place in green and the disadvantages in blue.**

Dear Metin,

I'm Ruby, and I'm from Australia. I live in the Outback in a small town called Kemble Creek.

I love living in the countryside because I like riding horses. My horse is called Zara and she loves it when we ride out to visit my aunt. I don't see my friends a lot because they live far away.

Please write soon!

Ruby

Hi Ruby,

I'm Metin. I'm a teenager and I live in Istanbul. It's a huge city with lots to do. I go skateboarding in the park with my friends every day.

I live with my sister, Defne, and my mum. My mum is a builder!

I love the city, but there's a lot of pollution. I don't like that!

Take care,

Metin

5 **Circle the capital letters in names and places in Activity 4.**

Ready to write:

Go to Activity Book page 65.

Learning to write:

Capitalisation

I'm Leo. I live in New York.

6 **In pairs, say advantages and disadvantages of the place where you live. Complete the table in your notebook.**

I live in ______	
Advantages of living here	Disadvantages of living here

Project

Do an interview on life in the city or the countryside.

Review Units 5 and 6

1 Play the game.

Objectives

To review language from Units 5 and 6 and play a game.

Target language

- **Key language:** vocabulary and language from Units 5 and 6, *adventure, bridge, mountain*
- **Additional language:** *choose, so, remember to …*
- **Revision:** language for games, *beach*

Materials

- **Flashcards:** countryside (71–78)
- Dice and four different coloured counters for each group of four pupils
- **Warmer:** paper with key words written on, or word cards

Warmer

- Hand out pieces of paper with key words from Units 5 and 6, or word cards (one for each pupil). Make groups of six. Pupils take turns to say what their word is and to give a sentence including their word. The other pupils in the group decide if it's correct or not. Monitor and help as necessary. Elicit an example sentence for each word.

PB62. ACTIVITY 1

Play the game.

- Use the countryside flashcards to review vocabulary from Unit 6. Draw a bridge and a mountain on the board and elicit the words.
- Say *Open your Pupil's Books at page 62, please.* Elicit what they can see (a game). Say *Can you remember some of the language we use in games?* Elicit/Prompt, e.g. *Whose turn is it? Pass the dice. I'm red. What does … mean? You've won. That's not fair.* Remind pupils to use English. Say *You speak* (their mother tongue)*, you miss a turn!* Check understanding of *miss a turn*. Check pupils know how to play and demonstrate the game. They throw the dice and go around the board. When they land on an instruction square, they must read it aloud and follow the instruction. Check understanding of *go forward, go back, throw again, throw a six.*

Extra support Write the useful language for games on the board so that pupils can refer to it during the game.

- Pupils make groups of four. They clear their desks and place one book in the centre. Hand out a dice and four different coloured counters to each group. They throw the dice to see who starts. Play moves from Start to Finish. The first pupil in each group to reach the finish is the winner.

AB62. **Answer key, see page T101**

Ending the lesson

- Mime carrying heavy bags and/or say *These bags are heavy!* to elicit the suggestion *Shall I help you?* Use other mimes/prompts, e.g. *I'm tired, I'm not well, I'm hungry, I'm thirsty, I'm cold, The board is dirty,* to elicit similar suggestions.

Digital Classroom

Presentation Plus: Unit 6

Practice Extra

Extra Resources

- **Teacher Resources:** Unit 6, Downloadable Activity Book Teaching Notes
- **T111 – Consolidation activity:** *Sing a song*

Review Units 5 and 6
Pupil's Book p.63

Objectives

To review language from Units 5 and 6 and talk about differences between pictures.

Target language

- **Key language:** vocabulary and language from Units 5 and 6, *differences*, *place*
- **Additional language:** *odd one out*
- **Revision:** countryside, town, illnesses, adjectives, jobs, actions and activities, *can see …*

Materials

- **Flashcards:** illness (63–70)

Warmer

- Say, e.g. *I can see something in the classroom. It's big and it's blue. It's on the floor near the door.* Pupils take turns to guess, using *Is it … (a book)?* Repeat. Pupils can take turns to name and define objects for the others to guess.

PB63. ACTIVITY 2

Find eight more differences.

- Show Activity 2 on the whiteboard. Focus pupils on the two pictures. Say *They're not the same.* There are some differences. Read the example speech bubble and check comprehension. Provide pupils with the language to use: *I can see … There is/are … The boy is eating …* Write the prompts on the board and check pupils know what they're going to do (take turns to describe parts of the two pictures where there are differences).
- Say *Open your Pupil's Books at page 63, please.* Pupils work in pairs to do the activity. Monitor to help and prompt. Elicit the differences.

Extra support Give pupils time to find and circle the eight differences before they start the speaking activity.

Key: There 1) are two oranges, 2) is one orange.
A man and a woman are sitting on 1) a blanket, 2) chairs.
A boy is eating 1) a sandwich, 2) an apple.
A woman has got 1) no sunglasses and apple juice, 2) sunglasses and orange juice.
A boy has got 1) a black T-shirt and a green towel, 2) a red T-shirt and a blue towel.
A girl is 1) drawing, 2) reading.
The girl is wearing 1) blue trousers, 2) orange trousers.
There 1) are flowers, 2) is a tree.

PB63. ACTIVITY 3

Choose the right words. Say.

- Review illness vocabulary with the flashcards.
- Focus pupils on Activity 3 and on the activity instruction. Do the first one as an example. Invite one pupil to read the definition and another to supply the word (*a field*). Pupils work individually and complete the activity. They check in pairs. Ask pupils which item is not used (a picnic).

Key: **2** a river, **3** chocolate, **4** a headache, **5** a temperature, **6** a blanket

---

PB63.

Quiz

- Say *Now let's read and remember*. Remind pupils of the meaning of *quiz*. Focus pupils on the questions. Pupils look back through Units 5 and 6 and find the answers to the questions. They discuss them in groups of four. Check with the class.
- Pupils write two more questions of their own to help them remember the language and/or vocabulary from the units. They write the questions in their notebooks. Pupils close their Pupil's Books. Volunteers ask the class one of their questions.

Key: **1** She's got a temperature. **2** He's got a cough and a cold. **3** The Toothache. **4** They're having a picnic. **5** She's thirsty. **6** The countryside. **7** There's lots to do. **8** Australia / In the Outback / Kemble Creek.

AB63. Answer key, see page T101

Ending the lesson

- Ask pupils which lessons, topics and/or activities were their favourites.

Digital Classroom

Presentation Plus: Unit 6
Practice Extra
Digital Flashcards

Extra Resources

- **Teacher Resources:** Unit 6, Downloadable Activity Book Teaching Notes
- **T111 – Consolidation activity:** *Play a game*

Find eight more differences.

In picture 1, there are five bananas. In picture 2, there are four bananas.

Choose the right words. Say.

chocolate

a field

a river

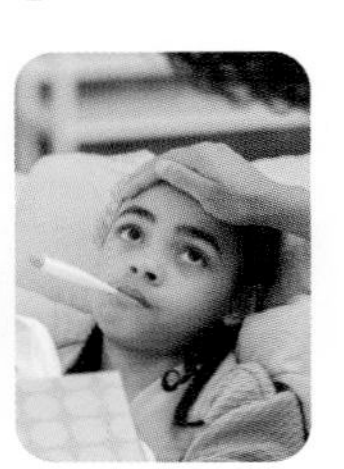
a temperature

a picnic

a headache

a blanket

1 Cows and sheep sometimes live here. A field.
2 Fish can swim here.
3 Charlie's got a toothache. He mustn't eat this.
4 This is when your head hurts.
5 You have this when you aren't well and you're very hot.
6 You put this on your bed when you're cold.

Quiz

1 Why must Stella go to bed? (p46)
2 What's the matter with Paul? (p49)
3 What's Miss Rich's beautiful painting called? (p51)
4 What are Lily and her family doing in the forest? (p55)
5 Is Suzy hungry or thirsty? (p56)
6 Where do Lock and Key want to go for a picnic? (p 59)
7 What's an advantage of living in the city? (p60)
8 Where does Ruby live? (p61)

7 World of animals

 69 **Look, think and answer. Listen and check.**

1 What are Simon and Stella doing?
2 Which animals are strong?
3 Which animal does Stella like?
4 Which animals talk a lot?

 **Ask and answer.**

Which animals do you like?

I like pandas.

Where do they live?

They live in the forests and mountains in China.

  70 **Complete with the words in the box. Listen and check.**

night sleep ~~sea~~ leaves meat

1 Dolphins, jellyfish, whales and sharks live in the ___sea___.
2 Bears eat fish, fruit, plants and ________.
3 Kangaroos eat ________.
4 Lions are strong and they ________ a lot.
5 Bats sleep in the day and get their food at ________.

Objectives

To talk about wild animals and their habitats.

Target language

- **Key language:** *world, dolphin, kangaroo, lion, panda, shark, whale, parrot, bear, bat, jellyfish*
- **Additional language:** *China, insect, quick*
- **Revision:** characters, animals, adjectives, routine actions, e.g. *eat, sleep; sea,* present simple

Materials

- **Flashcards:** wild animals (93–102)

Warmer

- Review known wild animals by giving clues, e.g. *I'm thinking about an animal. It's a bird. It's black and white. It can swim, but it can't fly* (penguin). As pupils guess the animals, write them on the board around a mind map. Write *Wild animals* in the centre. Introduce *huge.*
- Say *Huge is very, very big,* and write it on the board. Ask *Fish, whale, which is huge?* Elicit further examples of things that are huge from pupils (e.g. the sea, a huge country (China, Russia, etc.), a building, the sun, a forest).

Presentation

- Teach/Elicit the new animals using the animal flashcards. Elicit what pupils know about each one (e.g. colours, where they live, what they eat). Add them to the mind map.

PB64. ACTIVITY 1

Look, think and answer. Listen and check.

- Show Activity 1 on the whiteboard. Check comprehension of the unit title (especially *world*). Focus pupils on the picture. Elicit what animals they can see.
- Say *Open your Pupil's Books at page 64, please.* Ask a pupil to read the activity instruction aloud and others to take turns to read the four questions. Pupils compare their predictions in pairs, looking for clues in the picture.
- Play the Audio. Pupils listen and check. Play the Audio again.
- Check with the class. Set more listening questions, e.g. *Which animals live in the sea? Which animal sleeps a lot?* Play the Audio again. Pupils listen for the answers. They check in pairs. Check general understanding, e.g. *What do bears eat?* Check understanding of *quick* and *insect.*

Key: **1** They are looking at animals of the world on the computer. **2** Bears and lions are strong. **3** She likes pandas. **4** Parrots talk a lot.

69

Stella: Ooh. 'Animals of the world' … Dolphins, whales and sharks live in the sea. Dolphins eat fish.
Simon: Yeah, and bears eat fish, too. They eat everything – fish, fruit, plants, meat … Look at this one. It's big and strong.
Stella: Yes, lions are strong, too. They sleep a lot.
Simon: Here's a kangaroo. It eats leaves.
Stella: I like pandas. They're black and white, and they live in China.
Simon: Wow! These small brown bats sleep in the day and get their food at night … They're really quick. They can eat 100 insects in five minutes.
Stella: Yuk. Here are Suzy's favourite animals. These parrots are beautiful. They're red, yellow, green, blue …
Simon: And they talk a lot, too. Just like Suzy!

PB64. ACTIVITY 2

Ask and answer.

- Focus pupils on the picture in Activity 2 and elicit the animal (panda). Ask two pupils to read the speech bubbles. Elicit different habitats (e.g. sea, forest, trees) and continents (e.g. Africa, America, Europe).

Extra support Write the habitats and continents on the board for pupils to refer to during the task.

- In pairs, pupils ask and answer the questions. Then they share their ideas with the class.

PB64. ACTIVITY 3

Complete with the words in the box. Listen and check.

- Focus pupils on Activity 3. Read the instruction aloud and check understanding. Pupils listen to the Audio again and complete the sentences using words from the box. They compare answers in pairs. Then they listen again and check. Check with the class.

Key: **2** meat, **3** leaves, **4** sleep, **5** night

70

1 Dolphins, jellyfish, whales and sharks live in the sea.
2 Bears eat fish, fruit, plants and meat.
3 Kangaroos eat leaves.
4 Lions are strong and they sleep a lot.
5 Bats sleep in the day and get their food at night.

AB64. Answer key, see page T101

Ending the lesson

- Review the new animals from the lesson. Provide clues, e.g. *It lives in the sea. It eats fish. It's very, very big.* (whale).

Digital Classroom

Presentation Plus: Unit 7

Digital Flashcards

Audio 69–70
Practice Extra

Extra Resources

- **Teacher Resources:** Unit 7, Downloadable Activity Book Teaching Notes
- **Teacher Resources:** Unit 7, *Reinforcement worksheet 1*
- **T111 – Extension activity:** *Animal categories*

Objectives

To write descriptions of wild animals, their habits and habitats.

Target language

- **Key language:** adjective order
- **Revision:** wild animals, body parts, adjectives, *have got*, descriptions, *can*

Materials

- **Flashcards:** wild animals (91–99)
- **Warmer: Word word cards from** *Teacher Resources*

Warmer

- Review the wild animals (*panda, kangaroo, lion, dolphin, shark, whale, bat, bear, parrot, jellyfish*) using the animal flashcards. Stick them on the board. Invite pupils to come up in turn and write the name of the animal under each picture. Encourage other pupils to help with the spelling. Use the word cards from the *Teacher Resources* to check spelling if you wish.

PB65. ACTIVITY 1

Read and match.

- Show Activity 1 on the whiteboard. Focus pupils on the pictures and elicit what some of them are, e.g. *What's picture b?* Direct pupils to the activity instruction and check understanding. Remind them to look for the key words as they read to help them match. Point out that the sentences match just six of the ten photos.

Extra support Encourage pupils to underline the key words in each text.

- Say *Open your Pupil's Books at page 65, please.* Pupils read the texts silently and match them with the pictures. They check in pairs. Check by asking pupils to read the texts and then eliciting from the class which picture it describes. Elicit what key words pupils found.
- Check general understanding of the texts and of any new vocabulary.
- Focus pupils on some of the lists of adjectives, e.g. *huge grey / big brown*, and elicit what they notice about the order (size + colour).

Key: **2** a, **3** b, **4** g, **5** h, **6** i

PB65. ACTIVITY 2

Play the game.

- Focus pupils on Activity 2 and the instruction. Ask two pupils to read the example speech bubbles. Pupils work in pairs. They cover the texts in Activity 1. They take turns to say a sentence about one of the animals and guess what it is. Encourage pupils to ask questions if they can't guess the animal from the first sentence. Monitor and help as necessary. Elicit some exchanges from pairs.

PB65. ACTIVITY 3

Read and complete with the words in the box.

- Focus pupils on the text and the picture in Activity 3. Elicit the name of the animal (whale). Remind pupils where to find the words to complete the text (in the box). Pupils work individually and write the words in pencil. Monitor pupils as they are working. Remind them to ask their friends if they need help. Check with the class by asking pupils in turn to read out the sentences. Pupils correct/check their work. Check understanding of the text by asking, e.g. *What colour are whales? Where do they live?*

Key: **2** grey, **3** sea, **4** cold, **5** eats, **6** animals, **7** sometimes

AB65. **Answer key, see page T102**

Ending the lesson

- Elicit which animals pupils wrote about in Activity Book page 65 Activity 2. Write the animals on the board. Find out how many pupils wrote about each one with a 'hands up'. Write the totals on the board, draw a simple bar chart and announce the class's favourite wild animal.

Digital Classroom

Presentation Plus: Unit 7
Practice Extra
Digital Flashcards

Extra Resources

- **Teacher Resources:** Unit 7, Downloadable Activity Book Teaching Notes
- **T111 – Consolidation activity:** *Whisper and draw*
- **T111 – Extension activity:** *Animal profiles*

Read and match.

    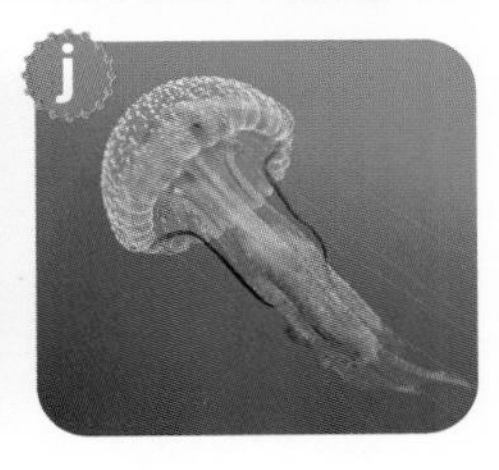

1 This huge grey animal lives in the sea. It's got a very big mouth and a lot of teeth. It can sometimes eat people. [e]

2 This grey animal lives in the sea. It's got a long nose and small teeth. It's very clever and it likes playing. [ ]

3 This big brown animal lives in Australia. It's got two long, strong legs and two short, thin arms. It can jump. [ ]

4 This animal can fly. It eats fruit. It can be red, green and blue and it's very loud. [ ]

5 This big animal is grey, brown or white. It's big and it can stand on two legs. It eats fish, meat, fruit and plants. It sleeps when it's cold. [ ]

6 This black and white bird can swim, but it can't fly. It lives in very cold water and it eats fish. [ ]

Play the game.

This animal has got a long nose and small teeth.

It's a dolphin.

Read and complete with the words in the box.

eats cold sometimes ~~huge~~ grey sea animals

This [1] huge blue or [2] ______ animal lives in the [3] ______
It likes very [4] ______ water. It [5] ______ a lot of small sea
[6] ______ and plants. It's [7] ______ very long.

Look and answer. Listen and check.

1 Who's doing a project on animals?
2 Which two animals are they looking at?
3 Can bats carry trees?
4 Are elephants strong?

What do you think? Read and say 'yes' or 'no'.

1 Whales are bigger than penguins.
2 Dolphins are longer than whales.
3 Lions are quicker than pandas.
4 Bats are dirtier than elephants.
5 Jellyfish are better at climbing than pandas.
6 Sharks are worse at swimming than kangaroos.

STUDY

Regular:

clean + er – clean**er**

big + g + er – big**ger**

dirty - y + ier – dirt**ier**

Irregular:

good – **better**

bad – **worse**

Objectives

To compare animals using comparative adjectives.

Target language

- **Key language:** comparative of common irregular and one- and two-syllable regular adjectives, *bad/worse, good/bad, -y, -ier, -er,* doubling of consonants: *thin/thinner, than*
- **Additional language:** *centimetres,* land animals
- **Revision:** adjectives, wild animals, body parts, *Shall we …? Let's …, the internet*

Warmer

- Elicit known adjectives using mime and pictures. Write the adjectives on the board. Elicit *good, bad, quick, big, long, small, short, dirty, strong, nice, hungry, clean, weak, fat, easy, thin, quiet, hot.* Ask pupils to make pairs from some of the adjectives, e.g. *strong – weak.*

Presentation

- Use classroom objects to introduce the notion of comparison. Take two fairly short pencils (one shorter than the other). Hold up the longer one and say *This pencil's short.* Hold up the other one and say *This pencil's short too.* Hold them both up and say *This pencil's shorter than that pencil.* Repeat with other objects and adjectives, e.g. *book / thin, bag / clean, hair / long, exercise / easy.* Pupils repeat the comparative sentences after you. Listen for correct pronunciation of *than* – the weak form /ðan/.

PB66. ACTIVITY 1

Look and answer. Listen and check.

- Show Activity 1 on the whiteboard. Focus pupils on the picture. Ask a pupil to read the activity instruction aloud and others to take turns to read the four questions.
- Say *Open your Pupil's Books at page 66, please.* Pupils compare their predictions in pairs, looking for clues in the picture.
- Play the **Audio**. Pupils listen for the answers. They check in pairs. Play the **Audio** again if necessary. Check with the class.
- Watch the ▶ **Video.**

Key: 1 Lenny, Simon and Stella. **2** Elephants and bats. **3** No, they can't. **4** Yes, they are.

▶ 71

Lenny: We've got homework on animals today.
Simon: Let's use the internet. It's quicker than using a book.
Lenny: Cool, look at this elephant. It's bigger than all the other land animals in the world.
Stella: Shall we look at another animal?
Stella: Look at this.
Lenny: A bat.
Stella: It's much smaller than the elephant. It says that some bats are only four centimetres long!
Lenny: The elephant is stronger – it says it can carry trees!
Simon: And the elephant is much dirtier than the bat. Elephants like swimming in dirty rivers and lakes when it's hot. Just like Dotty!

PB66. ACTIVITY 2

What do you think? Read and say 'yes' or 'no'.

- Focus pupils on Activity 2 and on the activity instructions. Do the first one as an example. Pupils whisper *yes* or *no* to their partner. Check with the class.

Extra challenge Pupils correct the false sentences.

Key: 1 Yes, **2** No, **3** Yes, **4** No, **5** No, **6** No

Practice

- Focus pupils on the *Study* Box. Explain that these are called *comparatives* if you wish. Elicit what pupils notice about the spellings of the different words. Write them on the board to help. Make four columns. Write *clean* at the top of one, *big* at the top of the next, *dirty* at the top of the next and *good/bad* at the top of the next. Elicit the comparatives for each word and write them in the appropriate column, e.g. *cleaner.* Focus pupils on the different spellings of the comparatives and elicit the spelling rules for the three examples: *clean/cleaner, big/bigger, dirty/dirtier.* Remind pupils that *good* and *bad* are irregular.

AB66. Answer key, see page T102

Ending the lesson

- Hold up pairs of classroom objects for pupils to offer comparative sentences. Supply an adjective for them to use if necessary, e.g. *clean.*

Digital Classroom

Presentation Plus: Unit 7
Audio 71
Digital Flashcards
Practice Extra

Extra Resources

- **Teacher Resources:** Unit 7, Downloadable Activity Book Teaching Notes
- **Teacher Resources:** Unit 7, *Reinforcement worksheet 2*
- **AB87 and PB87 – Grammar reference 7**
- **T111 – Consolidation activity:** *Sentences*
- **T111 – Extension activity:** *Picture dictation*

Objectives

To have further practice using comparative adjectives and to sing a song.

Target language

- **Key language:** *uglier, the (white) one*
- **Revision:** adjectives, present continuous
- Photocopiable 7, one for each pair of pupils

Warmer

- Do a chant to review the comparatives. Say a simple adjective, e.g. *Clean*. Pupils chant *Cleaner*. Use all the adjectives from the previous lesson. Vary the activity by sometimes chanting the comparative for pupils to respond with the simple adjective.

Song

PB67. ACTIVITY 1

Listen and complete. Sing the song.

- Show Activity 1 on the whiteboard. Focus pupils on Activity 1 and elicit what they can see in the pictures around the text, e.g. *a lion, a snake*. Read the first part of the activity instructions aloud and make sure pupils know what to do.
- Say *Open your Pupil's Books at page 67, please*. In pairs, pupils try to guess which words go in the gaps. They write the words in pencil.
- Elicit ideas. Play the **Audio** for pupils to listen and check their answers. Check with the class.
- Play the **Audio** again, line by line and then verse by verse, for pupils to repeat. Continue until pupils are confident with the **Song**.
- Teach the following actions for the words of the **Song**:
  walking = walking on the spot
  What can I see? = hand held horizontally on forehead above eyes
  lion = lion roaring and pouncing
  swimming = moving arms as if swimming a crawl stroke
  shark = hand on head as if a shark's fin
  standing = standing still
  snake = moving arm as if a snake slithering
  hiding = hands in front of face, hiding features
  bat = arms outstretched as if they are wings
  sitting = sitting down
  monkey = arms up as if hanging from a tree branch
- Pupils stand up, sing and mime as a whole class and then in five groups, one group for each verse.

Key: **2** can, **3** than, **4** snake, **5** hiding, **6** smaller, **7** see, **8** me

72
As in Pupil's Book

PB67. ACTIVITY 2

Listen and sing. Do karaoke.

- Focus pupils on Activity 2. Say *Do karaoke*. Pupils listen to the karaoke version. They sing the **Song** as a class and mime the actions.

73
Karaoke version of the song

PB67. ACTIVITY 3

Make sentences. Use the words in the boxes.

- Focus pupils on Activity 3. Draw attention to the first picture, the adjectives and the example sentence. Elicit one or two comparative sentences about another picture. Pupils work in pairs and make sentences about the pictures. Monitor and help if they can't think of sentences.
- Elicit the sentences and write them on the board.

Key: **1** The lion's stronger than the cat. The cat's quieter/(weaker) than the lion. **2** The whale's longer/bigger than the snake. **3** The panda's fatter/slower than the tiger. **4** The elephant is worse at jumping than the frog. The frog is better at jumping than the elephant.

Extra challenge Encourage pupils to think of some more sentences with different adjectives to compare the animals.

AB67. Answer key, see page T102

- Use Photocopiable 7 from the Teacher Resources.

Ending the lesson

- Sing the **Song** from the beginning of the lesson, with the extra verses if pupils did Extension activity 1.

Digital Classroom

Presentation Plus: Unit 7

Digital Flashcards

Audio 72–73

Practice Extra

Extra Resources

- **Teacher Resources:** Unit 7, Downloadable Activity Book Teaching Notes
- **Teacher Resources:** Unit 7, *Extension worksheet 1*
- **Teacher Resources:** Unit 7, *Song worksheet*
- **T111 – Extension activity 1:** *Our song*
- **T111 – Extension activity 2:** *Finding out*

1 72 Listen and complete. Sing the song.

~~bigger~~ see me hiding snake smaller can than

I'm walking,
I'm walking.
What can I see?
I can see a lion and it's [1] bigger
than me.

I'm swimming,
I'm swimming.
What can I see?
I [2] ______ see a shark
and it's uglier [3] ______ me.

I'm standing,
I'm standing.
What can I see?
I can see a [4] ______
and it's thinner than me.

I'm hiding,
I'm [5] ______.
What can I see?
I can see a bat
and it's [6] ______ than me.

I'm sitting,
I'm sitting.
What can I see?
I can [7] ______ a monkey
and it's naughtier than [8] ______.

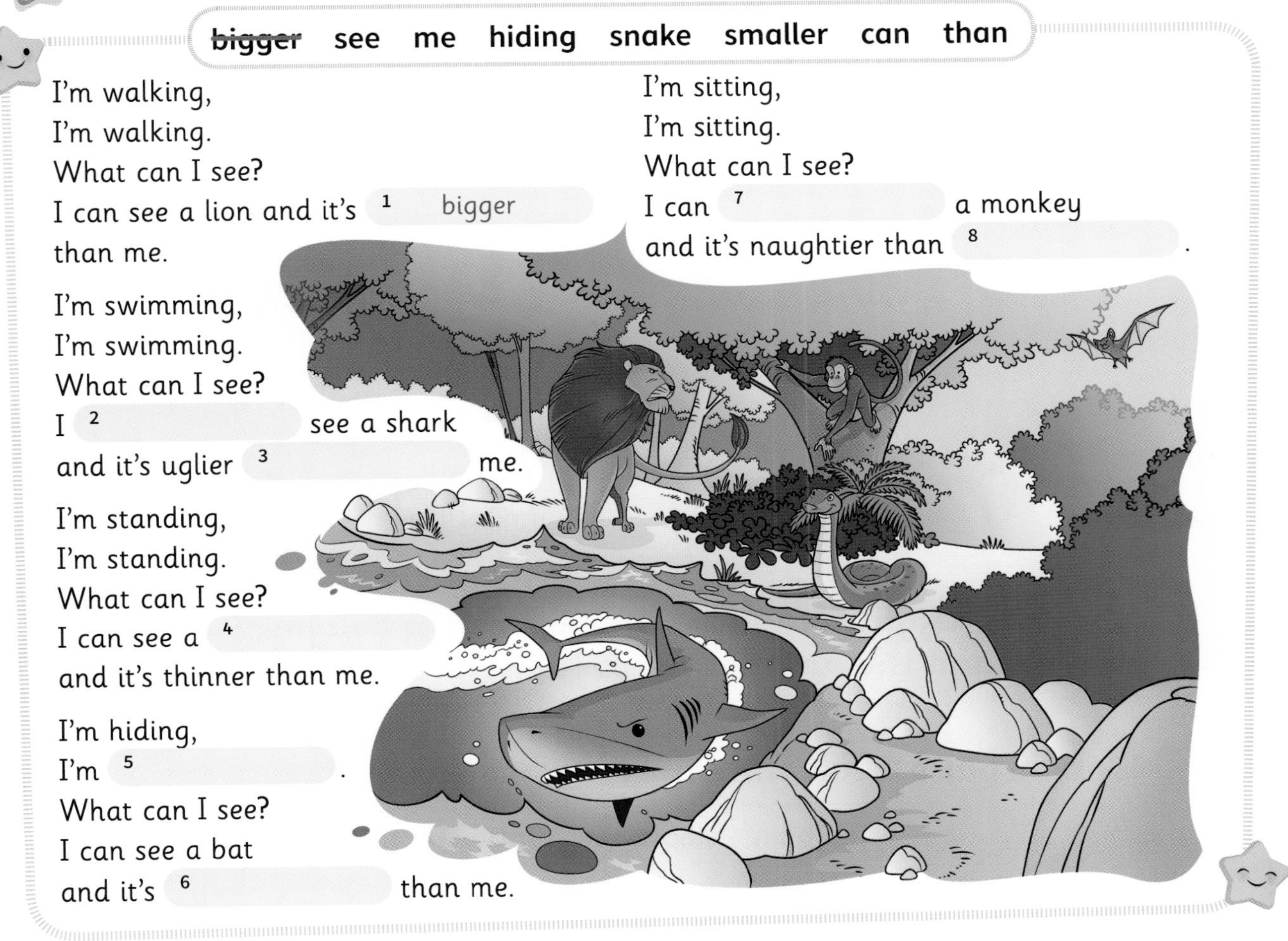

2 73 Listen and sing. Do karaoke.

3 Make sentences. Use the words in the boxes.

The cat's weaker than the lion.

quiet
strong
weak

long
big

fat
slow

bad/good at jumping

Language: comparative adjectives and present continuous

Lock's sounds and spelling

1 74 **Watch the video. Watch again and practise.**

2 **Find and underline the sounds.**

3 **Work in pairs. Look and say.**

dolphin elephant giraffe frog

coughing laughing taking a photo flying

boat forest sea desert tree

1

2
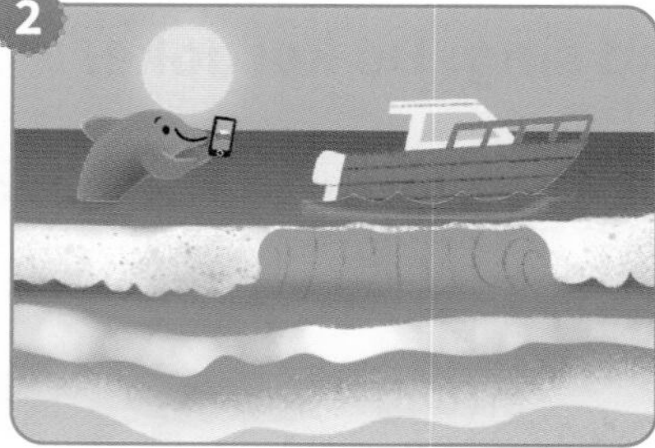

3

In the sea, there's a dolphin with a phone.

Number 2!

Show what you know

The ______ takes a ________ of the __________.

Objectives

To recognise and practise /f/ and practise *f, ff, ph* and *gh* spelling patterns.

Target language

- **Key language:** the sound /f/ (*funny, giraffe, dolphin, laugh*)
- **Additional language:** *flamingo, frog, cough*
- **Revision:** animals, comparatives

Materials

- **Picture download:** Letter cards f / ff / ph / gh
- **Presentation:** flamingo / giraffe
- **Flashcards:** wild animals (91–99)
- **Warmer:** Small pieces of paper (one for each pupil)

Warmer

- Stick the animal flashcards on the board. Give pupils a small piece of paper each. On one side of the paper, they write two adjectives (e.g. *small / big / clever / slow*). On the other side, they write the name of one of the animals on the board.
- Put pupils in pairs with a partner with a different animal. They put their paper on the table with the animal side up. Pupils turn over their paper to reveal the adjectives. They use the adjectives to compare their animals.

Presentation

PB68. ACTIVITY 1

Watch the video. Watch again and practise.

- Show Activity 1 on the whiteboard. Show pupils the flamingo and giraffe pictures and ask them to imagine where they are (jungle, sea, forest, etc.), who they are with and what they are doing. Pupils discuss in pairs and then as a class. Tell pupils they will watch the ▶ **Video** to find out.
- Watch the ▶ **Video**. Ask where the animals are (the countryside) and what animals are in the ▶ **Video** (flamingo, frog, giraffe, dolphin). Ask what each animal is doing (coughing, laughing, taking a photo). Mime the actions.

▶ 74

Voice & Key: /f/ /f/ /f/
Lock: What can you see, Key?
Voice & Key: giraffe /f/ laughs /f/ frog /f/ coughs /f/
Lock & Key: The giraffe laughs when the frog coughs.
Voice: dolphin /f/ funny /f/ photographs /f/
Lock & Key: And the dolphin takes funny photographs.
Lock & Voice: The giraffe laughs when the frog coughs. And the dolphin takes funny photographs.
Lock: Come on, everybody. One, two, three … let's say it with Key!
Voice, Lock & Key: The giraffe laughs when the frog coughs. And the dolphin takes funny photographs.
Lock: I say, well done, Key!

- Watch the ▶ **Video** again and say the sentences together. On the words with a single *f* spelling, raise one arm; for words with a *ff* spelling, raise both arms; for words with a *ph* spelling, clap; and for words with a *gh* spelling, stamp.
- In small groups, pupils practise the movements.

PB68. ACTIVITY 2

Find and underline the sounds.

- Focus pupils on Activity 2. Show pupils the letter cards *f, ff, ph, gh* and stick them on the board. Say the /f/ sound for each and do the movements (one arm, two arms, clap, stamp).
- Pupils look at the sentences in the book and underline the /f/ sound words and the four spelling patterns. Point to each of the letter cards on the board. Pupils tell you the corresponding word(s) from the sentences.

Extra challenge Point to a letter card. Pupils write the words they remember for this spelling in their notebooks.

PB68. ACTIVITY 3

Work in pairs. Look and say.

- Focus pupils on the pictures in Activity 3 and elicit the habitat (*forest, sea, desert*).
- Tell pupils that they will choose a picture and describe what is happening in the picture using words from the boxes. Ask a pupil to read the example sentence.
- In pairs, one pupil will say a sentence about one of the pictures and the other pupil will say which picture it is. Then they stand up and mingle, telling each other about their habitats.

Show what you know

- Focus on the *Show what you know* Box. Pupils complete the sentence with the missing words and practise saying it.

Key: frog, photo, giraffe

AB68. Answer key, see page T102

Ending the lesson

- Divide the class into four groups f, ff, ph and gh. Call out words with these spellings, for the matching group to do their mime.

Digital Classroom

Presentation Plus: Unit 7
Audio 74
Digital Flashcards
Practice Extra

Extra Resources

- **Teacher Resources:** Unit 7, Downloadable Activity Book Teaching Notes
- **T111–2 – Consolidation activity:** *Letter race*

Objectives

To read a story and review language from the unit.

Target language

- **Key language:** language from the unit
- **Additional language:** *in town, everybody, office, the wrong man*
- **Revision:** comparative adjectives, present continuous, *need, Shall we …?, Let's go, Don't look, Be quiet, He can hear you*

Warmer

- Review the story so far. Play short sections of earlier story episodes on the Audio and elicit from pupils what happens in those parts of the story.

  Note: Pupils use the present simple to talk about previous episodes.

Story

PB69.

Watch the video.

- Say *Open your Pupil's Books at page 69, please.* Elicit which episode this is (eight). Set the pre-watching questions: *Where do Lock and Key go? Who do they think they see? What happens at the end of the episode?* Watch the ▶ Video. Pupils answer the questions and check in pairs. Check with the class (to a café in town; Robin Motors, the car thief; he takes their car).
- Watch the ▶ Video. Pupils listen and repeat. Encourage them to say the words with intonation and feeling.

Extra support Half the class can say Lock's lines and the other half can say Key's lines.

- Check comprehension by pointing to the pictures on the whiteboard and asking, e.g. *Where are they?* (in the office). *Are they hot or cold?* (hot). *Why does Lock say 'Don't look'?* (he doesn't want the man to see them). *Who is Key talking about?* (the man at the other table and Robin Motors). *Can the man hear them?* (yes). Check understanding of *office* and *the wrong man*.

▶ 75

Narrator: It's Thursday morning. Lock and Key are in their office. It's hot. They're tired and thirsty.
Lock: Hmm … Robin Motors, the car thief.
Key: I need a cold drink. Shall we stop?
Lock: Yes, let's go to that new café in town.
Lock: Don't look, Key, but Robin Motors is sitting at the table next to us.
Key: No, that man's uglier then Robin Motors. His nose is bigger and his hair's longer.
Lock: Be quiet, Key. He can hear you, and he's looking at us.
Key: That's not him, Lock. He's the wrong man. Robin Motors is thinner and taller than him.
Lock: Sssh, Key! Everybody can hear you!
Key: But he isn't Robin Motors!
Lock: Oh yes he is, and … HE'S TAKING OUR CAR!

PB69. ACTIVITY 1

Why does Key think the man isn't Robin Motors? Say 5 things.

- Show Activity 1 on the whiteboard. Ask a pupil to read the question aloud. Give pupils time to talk about it in pairs. They can reread the story if necessary. Check answers as a class.

Key: The man is uglier than Robin Motors. His nose is bigger than Robin Motors' nose. His hair is longer than Robin Motors'. Robin Motors is thinner than the man. Robin Motors is taller than the man.

AB69. Answer key, see page T102

Ending the lesson

- Ask pupils which chant or song they'd like to do again from the unit. Do it together to end the lesson.

Digital Classroom

Presentation Plus: Unit 7

Audio 75

Digital Flashcards

Practice Extra

Extra Resources

- **Teacher Resources:** Unit 7, Downloadable Activity Book Teaching Notes
- **Teacher Resources:** Unit 7, Downloadable Activity Book Audio Script
- **Teacher Resources:** Unit 7, *Extension worksheet 2*
- **Teacher Resources:** Unit 7, *Video, Suzy's room*
- **T112 – Extension activity 1:** *Role play*
- **T112 – Extension activity 2:** *Animal quiz*

1 **Why does Key think the man isn't Robin Motors? Say 5 things.**

How do animals stay safe?

1 76 **Listen and read. Which animal is bad for birds?**

Grasshoppers are green, yellow and brown. They use camouflage, so animals can't see them in the grass. They can jump with their big legs to escape from other animals.

Hummingbirds are very small. They've got bright colours. They can fly very fast, so other animals can't catch them.

Monarch butterflies have got orange and black wings. They can fly. They're poisonous to birds.

Sea turtles are green, brown or black. They live in the sea. They can swim. They've got hard shells, so other animals can't eat them.

2 **Read again and complete the chart.**

animal	colours	How do they stay safe?
grasshoppers	green, yellow and 1 ________	use camouflage. They can jump.
monarch 2 ________	orange and 3 ________	They're 4 ________ to birds.
hummingbirds	bright colours	They can fly very 5 ________.
sea turtles	green, brown or black	They've got hard 6 ________.

3 **Work in pairs. Say and guess.**

It's got big legs.

A grasshopper!

DIDYOUKNOW...?

Octopuses can change colour to have better camouflage.

Science: animals staying safe |  learning to learn

Objectives

To learn about how animals stay safe.

Target language

- **Key language:** language from the unit
- **Additional language:** *bird, bright, butterfly, camouflage, escape, grasshopper, hard, hummingbird, octopus, poisonous, sea turtle, shell, wings*
- **Revision:** *catch, fly, jump, legs, swim*

Warmer

- Ask *What's your favourite animal?* Brainstorm animal names and write them on the board. Say, e.g. *Tell me an animal that's (bigger than a dolphin / has got big teeth / can fly).* Pupils suggest an animal on the board which meets the criteria.
- You are now ready to watch the ▶ Video.

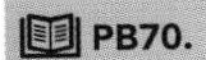

PB70.

How do animals stay safe?

- Tell pupils that they're going to learn more about animals in this lesson.
- Watch the ▶ Video and answer the questions in the ▶ Video.

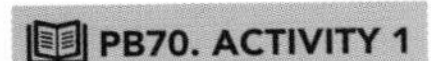

PB70. ACTIVITY 1

Listen and read. Which animal is bad for birds?

- Show Activity 1 on the whiteboard. Focus pupils on the pictures. Ask them if they know the names of the animals. Say *Open your Pupil's Books at page 70, please.* Ask *What can the animals do?* Pupils skim read the text to find the answer.

Extra support Pupils underline the actions that the animals can do (*jump, fly very fast, fly, swim*).

- Ask a pupil to read the question in the rubric aloud.
- Play the 🔊 Audio while pupils follow along in their books. Check with the class. Encourage pupils to explain their answers.

Key: Monarch butterflies are bad for birds.

🔊 76
As in Pupil's Book

PB70. ACTIVITY 2

Read again and complete the chart.

- Focus pupils on the chart and the headings in Activity 2. Pupils complete the chart with information from the text. Do the first one together as an example. Monitor pupils' progress. Check answers as a class.

Key: **1** brown, **2** butterflies, **3** black, **4** poisonous, **5** fast, **6** shells

PB70. ACTIVITY 3

Work in pairs. Say and guess.

- Focus pupils on Activity 3. Read the instruction aloud and ask two pupils to read the example aloud. In small groups, pupils describe and guess the animals.

Did you know ...?

- Invite a volunteer to read the information in the box aloud. Ask pupils if this fact surprises them.
- Point to the photo and say *This is an octopus. It's got eight arms.*

AB70. Answer key, see page T102

Ending the lesson

- Review what pupils have learnt about in this lesson. If time, play Word shark with the animal names from this lesson. Draw some waves on the board with a man swimming away. Underneath draw the letters for the word they have to guess. Every time pupils get a letter wrong, add a shark fin to the waves so that the shark is nearer the man.

Digital Classroom

Presentation Plus: Unit 7

Digital Flashcards

Audio 76

Practice Extra

Extra Resources

- **Teacher Resources:** Unit 7, Downloadable Activity Book Teaching Notes
- **T112 – Consolidation activity:** *Guessing game*
- **T112 – Extension activity:** *Butterfly art*

Objectives

To write a description of an imaginary animal.

Target language

- **Key language:** language from the unit
- **Additional language:** *hippo, octopus, scare away, starfish, teeth*
- **Revision:** *parrot, sea, shark, swim, zebra*

Warmer

- Write *How do animals stay safe?* on the board. Review the names of the animals from the previous lesson and the ways they stay safe.

PB71. ACTIVITY 4

Read the description of the imaginary animal. What can you say about the animal?

- Show Activity 4 on the whiteboard. Focus pupils on the drawing. Ask *Is this a real animal?* Ask which animals it looks like.
- Read the instruction and question in the rubric aloud. Give pupils time to read the text. Help with vocabulary if needed, but encourage pupils to use context to understand any unfamiliar words. Use the drawing to support meaning when possible.
- Say *Open your Pupil's Books at page 71, please.* In pairs, pupils discuss the question in pairs.

Extra support Ask questions to prompt the discussion, e.g. *Do you think the hippoctopus is a friendly animal? Why or why not?*

Project

- Remember to download your project notes from *Cambridge One*.

PB71. ACTIVITY 5

Circle the adjectives in Activity 4.

- Focus pupils on the sentences in the box. Point out the underlined words. Explain that we use adjectives to add information about a noun (a word for a person, place or thing). We can use adjectives after *be* and before nouns.
- Pupils circle the adjectives in Activity 4. They check answers with a partner.
- Monitor the activity and review as a class.

Key: pink, orange, big

Note: Some pupils may circle *fast*, thinking it is an adjective. If they do, explain that *fast* describes the verb *swim* and is an adverb here, not an adjective.

PB71. ACTIVITY 6

Combine two animals and invent a name. What features has it got?

- Write *zebra + parrot =* on the board. Ask a pupil to read the example sentences aloud.
- Elicit the name of the imaginary animal (zebrot) and write it on the board.
- Tell pupils they are going to make some other fun animal name combinations and descriptions.
- Use the example on the board to walk pupils through the steps of combining animals to make a name. Remind them that it is for fun, and that there are no wrong answers. In small groups, pupils brainstorm ideas and write a list of possible animal names. Then they choose one of the animals, draw a picture of it, and write about its features. Monitor and help as needed.

Extra support Write useful words for describing animals on the board, e.g. *wings, feet, teeth, horns, tail.*

- Elicit groups' imaginary animal names and write them on the board. Encourage the class to guess the animals in the combination.

Ending the lesson

- Sing *Head, shoulders, knees and toes* with the class. Then change the words to *Horns, claws, teeth and wings.* Encourage pupils to pretend to have those animal parts as they sing.

Digital Classroom

Presentation Plus: Unit 7

Digital Flashcards

Practice Extra

Extra Resources

- **Teacher Resources:** Unit 7, Downloadable Activity Book Teaching Notes
- **Teacher Resources:** Unit 7, *Project notes*
- **PB88–95 – A1 Movers Exam folder**
- **T112 – Consolidation activity:** *Ball toss*
- **T112 – Extension activity:** *Word sort*

7

4 Read the description of the imaginary animal. What can you say about the animal?

This is a 'hippoctopus.' It's part hippo, part octopus. It lives in the sea. It's pink and orange. It's got big teeth to scare away sharks. It eats starfish. It can swim fast.

5 Circle the adjectives in Activity 4.

Learning to write:

Adjectives

It is pink and orange.
It's got bright colours.

Ready to write:

Go to Activity Book page 70.

6 Combine two animals and invent a name. What features has it got?

It's part zebra, part parrot. It's a zebrot!
It's got the colourful wings of a parrot.

Project

Eleraffe

It's an elephant and a giraffe. It has giraffe legs.

Write a fact file for an imaginary animal.

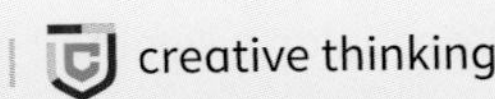

Science: animals staying safe | creative thinking

8 Weather report

1 Ask and answer. Look and check.

1 Who's got a pet?
2 Where's Meera on holiday?
3 Who's on holiday in the countryside?
4 Where's Lenny on holiday?

2 Look and say the name.

It's windy.

Simon and Stella!

3 77 Listen and say 'yes' or 'no'.

1 

4 

5 

6 

Objectives

To understand and talk about the weather.

Target language

- **Key language:** *weather, weather report, cloudy, cold, dry, hot, rain, rainbow, raining, rainy, snow, snowing*
- **Additional language:** *very, no (wind), really*
- **Revision:** characters, comparative adjectives, *can, beach, jungle, mountains, picnic, snowman*

Materials

- **Flashcards:** weather (109–115) and word cards

Warmer

- Write the date on the board. Ask *What's the date today?* Pupils respond, e.g. *It's Friday the 14th of May.* Say *Good.* Point to the window. Say *Is it hot today? Is it cold? What's the weather like?* Teach/Elicit the sentence for the weather today, e.g. *It's raining.* Pupils repeat. Explain that a weather report is a television or radio broadcast about the weather.

Presentation

- Write the question *What's the weather like?* in the centre of the board. Pre-teach/Elicit other words to describe the weather using the weather flashcards (*cloudy, hot, cold, sunny, dry, raining, rainy, snowing, snowy, windy, rainbow*). Check understanding and concept each time and stick the flashcards on the board to make a mind map, together with the word cards (or write the words).

PB72. ACTIVITY 1

Ask and answer. Look and check.

- Show Activity 1 on the whiteboard. Focus pupils on the pictures. Elicit one word to describe each one, e.g. *Raining.* Ask a pupil to read the activity instruction aloud and others to take turns to read the four questions. Pupils compare their predictions in pairs, looking for clues in the pictures but not in the postcard texts.
- Say *Open your Pupil's Books at page 72, please.* Pupils read the postcards quickly and silently to find the answers to Activity 1. They check in pairs. Check with the class. Pupils take turns to read the postcards aloud around the class. Check understanding of vocabulary, especially the new weather words. Ask pupils which their favourite postcard picture / type of holiday is.

Key: **1** Suzy. **2** In the mountains. **3** Simon and Stella. **4** At the beach.

PB72. ACTIVITY 2

Look and say the name.

- Read the instruction for Activity 2 aloud. Ask two pupils to read the example speech bubbles. In pairs, pupils take turns to say the weather and reply with the children who mention that weather in their postcard in Activity 1.

PB72. ACTIVITY 3

Listen and say 'yes' or 'no'.

- Focus pupils on the pictures in Activity 3 and on the activity instruction. Check pupils understand what to do. Remind them to whisper *yes* or *no* to their partner the first time they listen. Play the first one as an example. Play the rest of the **Audio**. Pupils listen and whisper. Play the **Audio** again. Check after each one.

Extra challenge Pupils correct the incorrect sentences.

Key: **1** No, **2** Yes, **3** No, **4** Yes, **5** No, **6** Yes

77

1 It's cloudy.
2 It's snowing!
3 It's raining.
4 Look! It's a rainbow.
5 It's very sunny.
6 It's really windy today.

Practice

- Pupils continue the game in pairs. They take turns. Pupil A says a sentence about the pictures. Pupil B says *yes* or *no* and corrects the incorrect sentences.

Ending the lesson

- Write some of the weather words as anagrams on the board for pupils to solve. They work in pairs. They write the words on paper. Pairs swap their papers with another pair. Check with the class by eliciting the words and the spelling each time.

Digital Classroom

Presentation Plus: Unit 8
 **Digital Flashcards**
 **Audio 77**
 **Practice Extra**

Extra Resources

- **Teacher Resources:** Unit 8, Downloadable Activity Book Teaching Notes
- **Teacher Resources:** Unit 8, *Reinforcement worksheet 1*
- **T112 – Consolidation activity:** *Sort the words*

Objectives

To talk about the weather.

Target language

- **Key language:** *It's (snowing, cold, wet, windy). There's no sun. What's the weather like (at the beach)?*
- **Revision:** weather, *country*, adjectives, *island*, *city*, *jungle*, *mountains*, *forest*, *beach*, *lake*, *fields*

Materials

- **Flashcards:** weather (103–109)
- Photocopiable 8, one for each pupil

Warmer

- Review the weather flashcards. Stick the flashcards on the board. Number them. Call out the numbers at random, e.g. *Number 2*. Pupils write a sentence, e.g. *It's snowing*. Pupils swap papers to correct.
- Check with the class. **Note:** There may be more than one possible correct answer, e.g. *It's raining. / It's rainy.*
- Point to the window. Say *What's the weather like today?* Pupils respond. A pupil comes and writes it on the board under the date, e.g. *It's hot and sunny*. Teach other weather words if necessary, e.g. *foggy*.

PB73. ACTIVITY 1

Listen and match.

- Show Activity 1 on the whiteboard. Focus them on the large picture. Elicit what they can see (island, mountains, etc.). Elicit the weather in the icons at the top of the page. Direct them to the activity instruction and the example answer. Check understanding.
- Say *Open your Pupil's Books at page 73, please*. Pupils write numbers 2 to 6 in their notebooks. Play the Audio. Pupils write the letters next to the numbers in their notebooks in pencil. They check in pairs. Check with the class. Elicit a sentence for each one, as well as the match, e.g. *2 raining, It's raining in the forest.*

Key: **2** raining, **3** cloudy, **4** sunny, **5** windy, **6** rainbow

78

Woman: It's time for today's weather report.
Thomas: Hello. Here in the mountains, it's snowing.
The birds aren't singing in the forest today because it's raining.
There's no sun on the island today. It's very cloudy.
At the lake, it's hot and sunny, so a lot of children are swimming.
It's a bad day for a picnic at the beach. It's very windy.
If you go to the fields, you can see a rainbow.
Have a good day, wherever you are.
Woman: Thank you, Thomas. Next, we are …

PB73. ACTIVITY 2

Listen and complete.

- Focus pupils on Activity 2. Pupils listen to the Audio, which is sentences about the weather report in Activity 1, and complete the sentences.

Key: **1** snowing, **2** raining, **3** cloudy, **4** hot, sunny, **5** windy, **6** rainbow

79

1 It's snowing in the mountains.
2 In the forest it's raining.
3 It's cloudy on the island.
4 It's hot and sunny at the lake.
5 At the beach it's very windy.
6 You can see a rainbow near the fields.

PB73. ACTIVITY 3

Ask and answer.

- Focus pupils on Activity 3. Elicit the places in pictures a to e (*beach*, *mountains*, *city*, *forest*, *country*). Focus on the speech bubbles. Pupils read them aloud. Elicit the picture for the example question and answer (a).

Extra support Underline the words in the example that will change (at the beach, windy).

- Pupils work in pairs. They take turns to ask and answer about the pictures. They choose pictures at random. Check by doing the activity in open pairs. Check for correct phrases, e.g. *at the beach*, *in the mountains*.

Key: **b** What's the weather like in the mountains? It's snowing. **c** What's the weather like in the city? It's cloudy. **d** What's the weather like in the forest? It's raining. **e** What's the weather like in the country? It's sunny.

- Use Photocopiable 8 from the Teacher Resources.

AB73. Answer key, see page T102

Ending the lesson

- Make six groups. Allocate a type of weather to each group. Start a chain by chanting *What's the weather like today?* Invite a group to reply. They chant, e.g. *It's cloudy, it's cloudy*. This group then repeats the question for another group to answer. Encourage pupils to ask groups randomly around the class. Direct the questioning if appropriate.

Digital Classroom

Presentation Plus: Unit 8
Digital Flashcards
Audio 78–79
Practice Extra

Extra Resources

- **Teacher Resources:** Unit 8, Downloadable Activity Book Teaching Notes
- **Teacher Resources:** Unit 8, Downloadable Activity Book Audio Script
- **T112 – Consolidation activity 1:** *Our weather*
- **T112 – Consolidation activity 2:** *Matching game*

Listen and match.

1 – snowing

windy

1 snowing

raining

sunny

rainbow

cloudy

2 79 Listen and complete.

1 It's ________ in the mountains.
2 In the forest it's ________ .
3 It's ________ on the island.
4 It's ________ and ________ at the lake.
5 At the beach it's very ________ .
6 You can see a ________ near the fields.

Ask and answer.

What's the weather like at the beach?

It's windy.

Language: *What's the weather like? It's (windy).*

1 80 Look, think and answer. Listen and check.

1 Who's Alex talking to?
2 Who's Alex with?
3 Where's Alex today?
4 Is the weather cold today?

2 81 Listen and say 'yesterday' or 'today'.

3 Ask and answer.

Where were you yesterday evening?

I was at the sports centre.

STUDY

It **was** wet and windy yesterday.
They **were** out yesterday.
It**'s** hot and sunny today.
They **are** at home today.

Objectives

To talk about the past using *was* and *were*.

Target language

- **Key language:** past simple affirmative and negative: *was, wasn't, were, weren't; sweater, scarf*
- **Additional language:** *at home, wet, yesterday*
- **Revision:** weather, present continuous, clothes, *today, country, have fun, cool*

Warmer

- Review clothes. Demonstrate the activity. Two pupils stand facing each other for 30 seconds. They stand back to back and take it in turns to describe their partner's clothes, e.g. *You're wearing blue jeans.* Pupils repeat in pairs.

Presentation

- Point to the day and date on the board. Say *What day is it today?* Pupils respond, e.g. *It's Thursday.* Say *What's the weather like today?* Pupils respond. Elicit and write the days of the week on the board. Say, e.g. *Today's Thursday. It's (cloudy). We're in school. Yesterday was Wednesday. It was (raining). We were in school.*
- Ask *What was the weather like?* for other days.

PB74. ACTIVITY 1

Look, think and answer. Listen and check.

- Show Activity 1 on the whiteboard. Elicit who they can see (Alex, Alex's aunt and Simon). Teach *sweater* and *scarf.*
- Say *Open your Pupil's Books at page 74, please.* Pupils compare their predictions in pairs.
- Play the **Audio**. Pupils listen and check. They check in pairs. Play the **Audio** again. Check with the class.
- Watch the **Video**.

Key: **1** He's talking to Simon. **2** He's with his aunt. **3** He's in the country. **4** No, it isn't cold.

80

Alex: Hello?
Simon: Hello, Alex. Where are you?
Alex: Simon, hi! I'm at my aunt's house in the country.
Simon: The country. Cool. Are you having fun?
Alex: Yeah, it's great. Yesterday I was out all day. In the morning the weather was really bad. It was wet, cloudy and windy.
Simon: What was the weather like in the afternoon?
Alex: It was better in the afternoon, but it was cold. I've got a new sweater and scarf.
Simon: That's nice.
Alex: Yeah. They were a present from my aunt, but it isn't cold today and now I'm really hot.

PB74. ACTIVITY 2

Listen and say 'yesterday' or 'today'.

- Focus pupils on Activity 2 and on the *Study* Box. Elicit which sentences are about the present and which are about the past.
- Direct pupils to the instruction for Activity 2. Play the first one as an example. Elicit the answer (yesterday). Play the rest of the **Audio**. Pause after each one for pupils to whisper the answer to their partner. Play the **Audio** again. Check.

Key: Yesterday, Today, Yesterday, Today, Yesterday, Today, Yesterday

81

In the morning the weather was really bad.
He's at his aunt's house.
It was wet, cloudy and windy.
It isn't cold.
He was out all day.
He's really hot.
The weather was better in the afternoon.

PB74. ACTIVITY 3

Ask and answer.

- Focus pupils on Activity 3. Read the instruction aloud and ask two pupils to read the example. Elicit other times of day which can be used with *yesterday* (*morning, afternoon*).

Extra support Elicit the names of different places first.

- In pairs, pupils ask and answer about where their partner was at different times of the day yesterday.

AB74. Answer key, see pages T102–3

Ending the lesson

- Review use of the past simple by asking pupils about the **Audio** from the beginning of the lesson, e.g. *Where was Alex yesterday?* Pupils answer using full sentences.

Digital Classroom

Presentation Plus: Unit 8
Audio 80–81
Digital Flashcards
Practice Extra

Extra Resources

- **Teacher Resources:** Unit 8, Downloadable Activity Book Teaching Notes
- **Teacher Resources:** Unit 8, *Reinforcement worksheet 2*
- **Teacher Resources:** Unit 8, *Extension worksheet 1*
- **AB87 and PB87 – Grammar reference 8**
- **T112 – Extension activity 1:** *How many sentences?*
- **T112 – Extension activity 2:** *Secret messages*

Objectives

To have more practice using *was* and *were* and to sing a song.

Target language

- **Key language:** *coat, hat, gloves, scarf, sweater, swim shorts, T-shirt*
- **Additional language:** *much better, wasn't any sun, weren't many children, wasn't much fun*
- **Revision:** past simple affirmative and negative: *was, wasn't, were, weren't*; clothes, weather, prepositions, *park, home, Grandpa*

Warmer

- Review the past with pupils. Make statements. Pupils write *T* (true) or *F* (false) in their notebooks for each one. Check with the class and elicit the corrections for the false ones. Use *was, wasn't, were, weren't*, e.g. *1 It wasn't sunny yesterday. 2 We were in the mountains yesterday morning. 3 There weren't any pupils in the school yesterday. 4 It was Monday yesterday.*

Song

PB75. ACTIVITY 1

Read and complete. Listen and check.

- Show Activity 1 on the whiteboard. Focus them on the two pictures. Tell them the text is in the past. Elicit what they can see (people, place, objects, weather). Elicit pupils' responses to the pictures, e.g. *Was it a nice day? Were they happy in the park? Do you like weather like this?* Focus pupils on the words in the box and on the activity instructions. Check understanding of *coat*.
- Say *Open your Pupil's Books at page 75, please.* Pupils look at the Song and substitute the right word for each picture. They check in pairs.
- Play the Audio. Pupils listen and check their answers. Play the Audio in verses and elicit the lines from pupils. Check understanding of vocabulary as you go.

Key: Hat, windy, coat, cold, snow, scarf, sweater, Hat, windy

82
As in Pupil's Book

PB75. ACTIVITY 2

Listen and sing. Do karaoke.

- Play the Audio again in sections. Pupils join in with the Song.
- Play the Audio right through for pupils to sing. Practise the Song with the class.

Extra challenge Encourage pupils to suggest actions for some of the adjectives in the Song.

82
As in Pupil's Book

- Say *Do karaoke.* Pupils listen to the karaoke version. They sing the Song as a class.

83
Karaoke version of the song

PB75. ACTIVITY 3

Make sentences.

- Focus pupils on the pictures in Activity 3. Ask two pupils to read out the sentences in the speech bubbles. Elicit which pictures they are about (1 b, 2 a). Focus pupils on the use of *in* (for clothes). Elicit other sentences from pupils around the class. Pupils work in pairs. They take turns to say sentences and to identify the pictures. Pupils can write the sentences in their notebooks. After checking, ask pupils to rephrase the answers in single sentences with *because*, e.g. *He was in a T-shirt because it was hot and sunny.*

Extra support Before making full sentences, pupils can decide in pairs which picture(s) each of the words in the word box belongs to.

Key: 3 c It was wet and rainy. She was in a coat and a hat.

AB75. Answer key, see page T103

Ending the lesson

- Sing the Song again as a whole class to end the lesson.

Digital Classroom

Presentation Plus: Unit 8

Digital Flashcards

Audio 82–83

Practice Extra

Extra Resources

- **Teacher Resources:** Unit 8, Downloadable Activity Book Teaching Notes
- **Teacher Resources:** Unit 8, *Song worksheet*
- **T112 – Consolidation activity 1:** *Weather snakes*
- **T112–3 – Consolidation activity 2:** *Living language*

1 82 Read and complete. Listen and check.

coat cold hat scarf snow sweater windy

___ , coat, sweater and scarf,
It was cold and ___ in the park, cold and windy …
It was grey and cloudy,
There wasn't any sun,
There weren't many children, it wasn't much fun.
Hat, ___ , sweater and scarf,
It was ___ and windy in the park, cold and windy …
There wasn't a rainbow,
There wasn't any ___ ,
Grandpa and I were ready to go.
Hat, coat, sweater and ___ ,
It was cold and windy in the park, cold and windy …
Back at home,
It was much better,
With a hot drink, and my big red ___ .
___ , coat, sweater and scarf,
It was cold and ___ in the park, cold and windy …
Windy in the park …

2 83 Listen and sing. Do karaoke.

3 Make sentences.

It was hot and sunny. He was in a T-shirt and swim shorts.

It was cold and windy. His gloves were grey and his scarf was blue.

sunny rainy snowy dry wet hot cold swim shorts T-shirt gloves coat scarf

1 

2 

3 

a 

b 

c 

Lock's sounds and spelling

1 84 **Watch the video. Watch again and practise.**

2 **Listen and write.**

In the sunny sky, bees dance and parrots fly.
A giraffe's over there sitting on a red chair.
He watches the bear paint frogs with no hair.

3 **Work in pairs. Say and guess.**

Show what you know

The __________ paints _______ on a _______ day.

Sounds and spelling: *y, ee, r, s, ff, ere, air, es, ear, ai, f*

Unit 8 Weather report
Pupil's Book p.76

Objectives

To review sounds from the previous units in context and with a focus on spelling patterns.

Target language

- **Key language:** review of sounds: *y, ee, f, es, r, ear, ay, i*
- **Revision:** actions, weather, places, animals

Warmer

- Ask pupils what weather words they remember and write those on the board. Tell pupils to guess what the weather was like and where you were. Say *Yesterday I was in a T-shirt and sunglasses* and pupils call out their guess, e.g. *It was sunny/ dry and you were at the beach / the park.*
- In groups of four, pupils describe what they were wearing yesterday for the others to guess the weather and location.

Presentation

PB76. ACTIVITY 1

Watch the video. Watch again and practise.

- Write these animals on the board: *bees, parrots, giraffes, bears, frogs.* Ask pupils to work in pairs and tell each other what they know about these animals and then feed back as a whole class. Encourage pupils to think about habitats, habits, food preferences and abilities.
- Watch the ▶ **Video**. Ask pupils what animals were in the ▶ **Video** (bees, parrots, a giraffe, a bear and a painting of frogs) and what they were doing (flying, playing, painting). Ask pupils where they were and what the weather was like.

▶ 84

Voice: sky /aɪ/ bees /iː/ parrots /r/ fly /f/
Lock & Key: In the sunny sky, bees dance and parrots fly.
Voice: giraffe's /s/ there /eə/ red /r/ chair /eə/
Lock & Key: A giraffe's over there sitting on a red chair.
Voice: watches /ɪz/ bear /eə/ paint /eɪ/ frogs /f/ hair /eə/
Lock & Key: He watches the bear paint frogs with no hair.
Lock & Voice: In the sunny sky, bees dance and parrots fly. A giraffe's over there sitting on a red chair. He watches the bear paint frogs with no hair.
Lock: Come on, everyone. One, two, three … let's say it with Key!
Lock, Key & Voice: In the sunny sky, bees dance and parrots fly. A giraffe's over there sitting on a red chair. He watches the bear paint frogs with no hair.
Lock: I say, well done, Key!

- Watch the ▶ **Video** again. Say the first line from the ▶ **Video** and ask pupils if they can hear any sounds that are the same, to elicit /aɪ/ (*sky, fly*) and /eə/ (*there, chair, bear, hair*). In pairs, pupils say the sentences and find more matching sounds. Call out a sound and pupils tell you the words from the sentences.

PB76. ACTIVITY 2

Listen and write.

- Show Activity 2 on the whiteboard. Pupils close their books. Say *sky* for pupils to write the word in their notebooks.
- Ask pupils what animals were in the sky, to elicit *bees* and *parrots* for pupils to write. Ask pupils what the actions were, to elicit *dance* and *fly*. Ask which animal is 'over there' (giraffe) and what it's sitting on (a red chair). Ask which animal it's watching (bear), what the bear is painting (frogs), and what the frogs haven't got (hair). Pupils write each of the words and phrases you elicit. In pairs, they compare the words they've written and try to reconstruct the rhyme from the key words they have. Then they check in their Pupil's Books.

PB76. ACTIVITY 3

Work in pairs. Say and guess.

- Focus pupils on Activity 3. Ask pupils to look at the map showing different places and weather. Ask pupils what weather they can see. Read out the speech bubbles with a pupil.
- In pairs, one pupil imagines and says what they were wearing and doing, and their partner guesses where they were and what the weather was like.

Show what you know

- Focus on the *Show what you know* Box. Pupils complete the sentence with the missing words and practise saying it.

Key: giraffe, bears, windy

AB76. Answer key, see page T103

Ending the lesson

- Put pupils in groups. Tell them you'll say a sound and each group has to think of a word with that sound. Say sounds from today's lesson and invite groups to say a word.

Digital Classroom

Presentation Plus: Unit 8
Audio 84
Digital Flashcards
Practice Extra

Extra Resources

- **Teacher Resources:** Unit 8, Downloadable Activity Book Teaching Notes
- **T113 – Consolidation activity:** *Guessing game*
- **T113 – Extension activity:** *Chain game*

Objectives

To read a story and review language from the unit.

Target language

- **Key language:** language from the unit
- **Additional language:** *At what time …?*
- **Revision:** telling the time, *police station, Let's go …, ask some questions*

Warmer

- Write *Lock and Key* in the centre of the board. Elicit what pupils remember about the story so far and about the characters. Ask them if the detectives have any special things they say, e.g. *No problem*, and who says it. Elicit what happened in the previous episode and the name of the car thief (Robin Motors).

Story

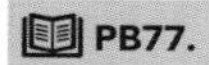

Watch the video.

- Say *Open your Pupil's Books at page 77, please.* Elicit which episode this is (nine). Set the pre-watching questions: *Where's Robin Motors? What's the weather like? Where was Robin Motors last Thursday morning?* Watch the ▶ **Video**. Pupils answer the questions and check in pairs. Check with the class (at the police station; it's raining; at the police station).
- Watch the ▶ **Video** with the class. Pupils listen and repeat. Encourage them to say the words with intonation and feeling. They answer the questions and check in pairs.
- Check comprehension by pointing to the pictures on the whiteboard and asking questions, e.g. *Where are they?* (in the detective agency). *Are they hot or cold?* (cold). *What does Lock ask Robin Motors?* (*Where were you last Thursday morning?*)

🔊 ▶ 85

Lock: Key! The police have got Robin Motors! Let's go to the police station to ask him some questions.
Key: I don't think it was him, Lock.
Key: Are you cold, Lock? No problem. We can go in the car.
Lock: But we haven't got a car now … and it's raining!
Lock: So, Mr Motors. Where were you last Thursday morning?
Robin: Thursday morning? At what time?
Key: At eleven o'clock.
Lock: You were in Baker Street at eleven o'clock last Thursday morning
Robin: No, I wasn't.
Key: Oh yes you were.
Lock: YOU WERE IN MY CAR LAST THURSDAY MORNING!
Police officer: No, Mr Lock … He was here at the police station.
Robin: That was my brother, Nick Motors.
Key: I was right! It wasn't Robin Motors!

PB77. ACTIVITY 1

Work in pairs. Describe the pictures.

- Ask a pupil to read the instructions aloud. Focus attention on the example speech bubble. Give pupils time to describe each picture in pairs. Check answers as a class.

Extra challenge Say or write a sentence with *is* or *are* about each picture, e.g. *Lock's cold and wet.* Write *Yesterday …* on the board and ask pupils to put the sentences into the past.

AB77. Answer key, see page T103

Ending the lesson

- Ask pupils which chant or song they'd like to do again from the unit. Do it together to end the lesson.

Digital Classroom

Presentation Plus: Unit 8
Audio 85
Digital Flashcards
Practice Extra

Extra Resources

- **Teacher Resources:** Unit 8, Downloadable Activity Book Teaching Notes
- **Teacher Resources:** Unit 8, *Extension worksheet 2*
- **Teacher Resources:** Unit 8, *Video, Suzy's room*
- **T113 – Extension activity 1:** *Role play*
- **T113 – Extension activity 2:** *What was the weather like?*

Lock & Key!

85

1 Work in pairs. Describe the pictures.

In picture 1, Lock's happy.

What does nature sound like?

1 86 **Listen. What do the instruments sound like?**

animals birds rain thunder

a

______

b

______

c

______

d

______

2 87 **Read and match. Listen and write 'wind' or 'percussion'.**

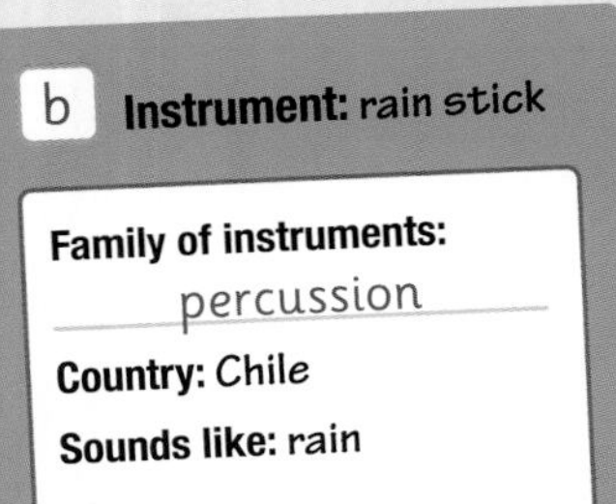

b **Instrument:** rain stick

Family of instruments: percussion

Country: Chile

Sounds like: rain

☐ **Instrument:** vuvuzela

Family of instruments: ______

Country: South Africa

Sounds like: elephants

☐ **Instrument:** thunder drum

Family of instruments: ______

Country: Indonesia

Sounds like: thunder

☐ **Instrument:** didgeridoo

Family of instruments: ______

Country: Australia

Sounds like: Australian birds

3 **Work in pairs. Ask and answer.**

What country is the vuvuzela from?

South Africa.

DID YOU KNOW...?

A sea organ is a musical instrument that you don't need to play. Waves make the music.

Unit 8 Weather report
Pupil's Book p.78

Objectives
To learn how instruments can recreate sounds in nature.

Target language
- **Key language:** language from the unit
- **Additional language:** *didgeridoo, drum, insects, musical instrument, percussion, rain stick, sea organ, sounds like, thunder, vuvuzela, wind, waves*
- **Revision:** *rain*

Materials
- **Warmer:** A recording of nature sounds
- **Did you know ...?:** A photo or video of a sea organ (optional)

Warmer
- Play a nature sounds recording as pupils come into the classroom. Encourage them to comment on what they hear. Brainstorm other nature sounds and write them on the board, e.g. *the wind, the rain, thunder, ocean waves, birds, whales.*
- You are now ready to watch the ▶ Video.

PB78.

What does nature sound like?
- Tell pupils that they're going to learn about musical instruments and nature sounds in this lesson.
- Watch the ▶ Video and answer the questions in the ▶ Video.

PB78. ACTIVITY 1

Listen. What do the instruments sound like?
- Show Activity 1 on the whiteboard and focus pupils on the instruments in the pictures. Play the Audio for pupils to listen to the instruments.
- Say *Open your Pupil's Books at page 78, please.* Ask the question in the rubric. Point out the options in the word box. Play the Audio. Pupils write their answers. They check in pairs, then check as a class.

Extra support Write *sounds like* on the board. Clarify meaning with gestures and pupils' L1 if necessary.

86

a [sound of vuvuzela]
b [sound of rain stick]
c [sound of didgeridoo]
d [sound of thunder drum]

Key: a birds, **b** rain, **c** animals, **d** thunder

PB78. ACTIVITY 2

Read and match. Listen and write 'wind' or 'percussion'.
- Focus pupils on the instrument fact files in Activity 2. Say *These are the instruments from Activity 1.* Ask pupils if they have ever seen or heard these instruments in person.
- Ask *What type of information is in each fact file?* Ask pupils what instruments their country is famous for.
- Discuss the differences between wind and percussion instruments: *With wind instruments, you use your breath to make the sound. With percussion, you hit something to make the sound.*
- Pupils read the incomplete fact files and match them to the pictures in Activity 1. Check answers as a class.
- Play the Audio. Pupils listen and complete each fact file with *wind* or *percussion*. Check answers.
- Ask *Which instrument do you prefer?* Pupils discuss in pairs. Then invite volunteers to share their opinion with the class.

Key: a wind, d percussion, c wind

87

As Pupil's Book and key

PB78. ACTIVITY 3

Work in pairs. Ask and answer.
- Focus pupils on Activity 3. Ask two volunteers to read the example out loud. In pairs, pupils take turns asking and answering questions about the instruments in this lesson.

Extra support Elicit more examples of questions pupils can ask as a class before they start working in pairs.

Did you know ...?
- Focus pupils on the photo and invite a volunteer to read the information in the box out loud. If possible, show a photo or video of a sea organ.

AB78. Answer key, see pages T103

Ending the lesson
- Talk about the different instruments pupils learnt about today. Pupils report on the lesson in their notebooks. They draw a picture of some instruments or objects that can make nature sounds.

Digital Classroom

Presentation Plus: Unit 8

Digital Flashcards

Audio 86–87

Practice Extra

Extra Resources
- **Teacher Resources:** Unit 8, Downloadable Activity Book Teaching Notes
- **T113 – Extension activity:** *Musical instruments*

Unit 8 Weather report
Pupil's Book p.79

Objectives
To write an invitation to an event.

Target language
- **Key language:** language from the unit
- **Additional language:** *let us know, see you, message*
- **Revision:** *concert, garden, hear, musical instruments, rain, sounds like, thunder*

Materials
- **Warmer:** Sticky notes with the days of the week and months written on

Warmer
- Before class, write the names of the days of the week on sticky notes (one day per note), and stick them under pupils' desks. Do the same with the months.
- At the start of the lesson, tell pupils to look under their desks for a sticky note. Pupils with notes should find others with either days of the week or months, and then put themselves in order.
- Say the days of the week and the months together with the class to check.
- Put pupils into pairs to discuss their favourite day of the week and their favourite month. Invite volunteers to share their opinions with the class.

PB79. ACTIVITY 4

Read the invitation. What is the event? What do you need to know about it?
- Show Activity 4 on the whiteboard. Focus pupils on the invitation. Ask *When do people give invitations?* and elicit suggestions. Point out the exclamation marks. Say *It looks exciting!*
- Say *Open your Pupil's Books at page 79, please.* Give pupils time to read the text. Help with vocabulary if needed, but encourage pupils to use context to understand any unfamiliar words.
- Ask a pupil to read the questions in the instructions aloud. They answer in pairs. Check with the class.

Project
- Remember to download your project notes from *Cambridge One.*

Extra challenge Ask *Do you want to go to Kyle's event? Why or why not?* Pupils discuss in pairs.

Key: It's a nature sounds concert. You need to know when and where it is.

PB79. ACTIVITY 5

Underline the key information with the correct colours.
- Focus pupils on Activity 5. Explain that the date, time and place are key information in invitations. People need to know what the event is, where to find it and when it takes place. Read out the question words in the box. Pupils underline the key information in Activity 5 with the correct colour. Monitor the activity and review as a class.
- Ask pupils to write three questions about the nature sounds concert. Tell them to use *What …? Where …?* and *When …?* in their questions.
- In pairs, pupils ask and answer the questions.

Key: Green: nature sounds concert; pink: Kyle's garden; blue: Saturday, 14th May, 4 p.m.

PB79. ACTIVITY 6

In groups, list musical instruments you have or can make. Who's going to play each instrument?
- Focus pupils on Activity 6. Brainstorm things pupils have at home which they could use to make wind and percussion instruments, such as spoons, large sheets of paper, aluminium foil.
- Explain to pupils that they are going to make a list of musical instruments they have or can make. In pairs, they complete the table in their notebooks.
- Elicit pupils' ideas and write them on the board.

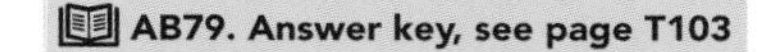
AB79. Answer key, see page T103

Ending the lesson
- Ask pupils what other events people give out invitations for, such as birthday parties, costume parties, holiday parties, graduation. Write their suggestions on the board. Conduct a class vote of pupils' favourite type of event.

Digital Classroom

Presentation Plus: Unit 8

Practice Extra

Digital Flashcards

Extra Resources
- **Teacher Resources:** Unit 8, Downloadable Activity Book Teaching Notes
- **Teacher Resources:** Unit 8, *Project notes*
- **PB88–95 – A1 Movers Exam folder**
- **T113 – Consolidation activity 1:** *Board slap*
- **T113 – Consolidation activity 2:** *Date, time or place?*

4 **Read the invitation. What is the event? What do you need to know about it?**

You're invited!

Come to our nature sounds concert! You can hear musical instruments that sound like thunder and rain. Make your own instruments, too!

Date: Saturday, 14th May

Time: 4 pm

Place: Kyle's garden

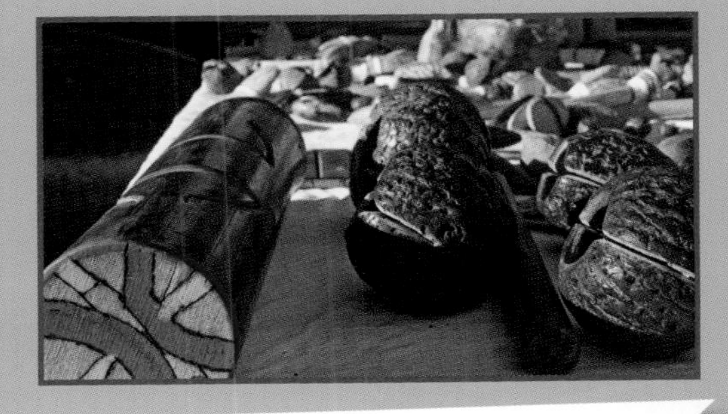

RSVP: Please message us on 0786547112 to let us know you're coming. See you on Saturday!

Kyle and friends

5 **Underline the key information with the correct colours.**

What? Where? When?

Learning to write:

Key information

What? Where? When?

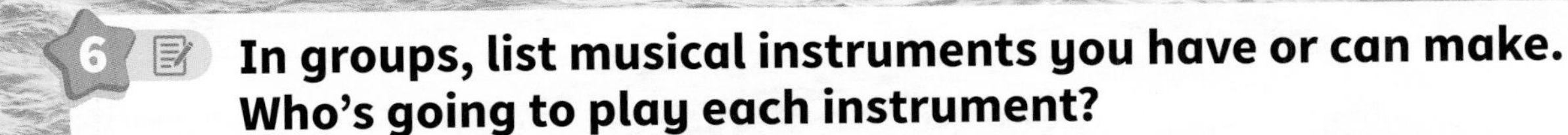

6 **In groups, list musical instruments you have or can make. Who's going to play each instrument?**

Name	Instrument

Ready to write:

Go to Activity Book page 78.

Project

Plan a musical event and make a poster.

Review Units 7 and 8

Instructions

1 Play in pairs.
2 Choose:
- weather and clothes
- animals
- in town
- in the countryside

3 Write the topic and the 7 words in your notebook.

1 Play the game.

START

1 2 3 4 5 6 7 8 9 10 11 12 13 14 15 16 17 18 19 20 21 22 23 24 25 26 27 28

Objectives

To review language from Units 7 and 8 and play a game.

Target language

- **Key language:** vocabulary and language from Units 7 and 8
- **Revision:** weather, wild animals, *city*, *country*, language for games, adjectives

Materials

- Dice and four different coloured counters
- **Warmer:** Four large pieces of paper with *weather* written on one, *wild animals* on another, *city* on another and *country* on another
- **Flashcards:** city (53–62), country (71–78), wild animals (91–99), weather (103–109)

Warmer

- Display the four pieces of paper with the topics written on them around the room. Mix up the flashcards from Units 4, 6, 7 and 8 and hand one to each pupil in the class. Pupils stand up and stick their card on the correct piece of paper. Fast finishers come and collect another card from you.
- Pupils sit down again. Ask volunteers to read the words in each category. Check if the words are in the correct place with the class.
  Note: If you do not have flashcards, call out words from the different topics at random.
- Pupils all point to the piece of paper with the appropriate topic. Volunteers write the words on the paper.

PB80. ACTIVITY 1

Play the game.

- Show Activity 1 on the whiteboard. Elicit what pupils can see (a game). Ask what number the game looks like (8). Say *Can you remember some of the language we use in games?* Elicit *Whose turn is it? Pass the dice. I'm red. What does … mean? You've won. That's not fair.* Remind pupils to use English. Say *You speak* (their mother tongue)*, you miss a turn!* Check understanding of *miss a turn*.
- Say *Open your Pupil's Books at page 80, please.* Focus pupils on the Instructions box. Read the instructions aloud and check comprehension of the topics.

Extra support Elicit which words on the board belong to each category (weather and clothes: rainy, windy, snowy, cloudy, rainbow, scarf, sweater; animals: panda, lion, kangaroo, shark, bat, penguin, parrot; in town: café, bus station, cinema, hospital, supermarket, swimming pool, sports centre; country: river, lake, forest, plants/grass, leaves/plants, mountains, waterfalls).

- Check pupils know how to play and demonstrate the game. They play in groups of four. Each pupil has one group of words to collect, e.g. *animals*. They write their topic in their notebook, find the seven words for their topic in the game and write them in their notebooks as well. Pupils take it in turns to throw the dice and go around the board. When they land on a word from their word group, e.g. *parrot*, they must say it and then tick it in their notebooks.
- As a further follow-up activity, play a spelling game, with pupils using target words and language from Units 7 and 8, e.g. *penguin, brilliant, huge*. Elicit the beginning of each word, e.g. say *Give me a 'p'* (class repeat), *Give me an 'e'* (class repeat).
- Pupils make groups of four. They clear their desks and place one book in the centre. Hand out a dice and four different coloured counters to each group. They throw the dice to see who starts. Play moves from Start to square 28. The first pupil in each group to collect all their seven words is the winner.

AB80. Answer key, see page T103

Ending the lesson

- Do a spelling chant to finish the lesson, e.g.
  Teacher: *Give me a 'c'.*
  Pupils: *c*
  Teacher: *Give me an 'l'.*
  Pupils: *l*
  Teacher: *Give me an 'o'.*
  Pupils: *o*
  Teacher: *Give me a 'u'.*
  Pupils: *u*
  Teacher: *Give me a 'd'.*
  Pupils: *d*
  Teacher: *Give me a 'y'.*
  Pupils: *y*
  Teacher: *What have you got?*
  Pupils: *Cloudy!*
- Pupils can take turns to lead other chants.

Digital Classroom

 **Presentation Plus:** Unit 8
 **Practice Extra**

Extra Resources

- **Teacher Resources:** Unit 8, Downloadable Activity Book Teaching Notes
- **T111 – Consolidation activity:** *Sing a song*

Objectives

To review language from Units 7 and 8 and do a listening activity.

Target language

- **Key language:** vocabulary and language from Units 7 and 8, *crying*
- **Revision:** vocabulary and language from Units 7 and 8

Warmer

- Play a game of I can see … Say, e.g. *I can see someone. This pupil's wearing green socks.* Pupils take turns to guess. Vary the game by describing objects as well as pupils.

PB81. ACTIVITY 2

Listen and draw lines. There is one example.

- Show Activity 2 on the whiteboard. Focus pupils on the picture and elicit some of the actions the children are doing. Teach *crying* using the picture of the little boy who's lost the balloon.
- Say *Open your Pupil's Books at page 81, please.* Play the Audio. Pupils listen and write the names and the letters in their notebooks. They check in pairs. Play the Audio again. Check with the class. **Note:** An exam task would have six items not five.

Key: Anna d, Beth e, Daisy a, Abdul b, Zak c

88

Listen and draw lines. There is one example.
Woman: Hello. What are you all doing today?
Boy: We're playing in the park.
Woman: What's that boy's name? I don't know him.
Boy: That's Jack.
Woman: Why's he jumping on one leg?
Boy: Oh, he's hopping because he's playing a game.

1 **Woman:** What's Anna doing?
Boy: Anna? She's over there. She's skipping with Beth.
Woman: Oh, yes. I can see her. She's wearing a long purple scarf and black gloves.
Boy: That's right, and the one with the red leggings and big green sweater is Beth.

2 **Woman:** Look at Daisy. She's having fun. She's flying her kite.
Boy: Yes, but it's very windy and her hair's in her eyes.

3 **Woman:** Who's climbing the tree?
Boy: That's Abdul. He's better at climbing than me.

4 **Woman:** What's the matter with that little boy in the red sweater and green boots?
Boy: He's crying because he can't catch his balloon.
Woman: Do you know him?
Boy: Yes, he's Jack's younger brother. His name's Zak.
Woman: Let's go and say hello.
Boy: OK.

PB81.

Quiz

- Say *Now let's do a quiz.* Focus pupils on the questions. Pupils look back through Units 7 and 8 and find the answers. They discuss them in groups of four. Check with the class.

Extra challenge Pairs write two more quiz questions with a page reference for each for another pair to answer.

Key: **1** Whale, dolphin and shark. **2** A penguin. **3** They go to a café in town. **4** In the mountains. **5** It was cold and windy. Grandpa was wearing a hat, coat, sweater and scarf. **6** Pupils say the sounds for the spellings *y, ee, r, s, ff, ere, air, es, ear, ai, f*. **7** He was at the police station. **8** A sea organ.

AB81. Answer key, **see page T103**

Ending the lesson

- Pupils work in groups of four. They need one, 'Do you remember?' (Activity Book page 81 activity 1). Two pupils (A) use a book (or paper) to cover the words from Unit 7. The other two pupils (B) take turns to say what each picture is and to spell the word. 'A's look and check. They reverse roles for Unit 8.
- Ask pupils which lessons, topics and/or activities were their favourites. If this is your last class, say *Goodbye. See you next year!*

Digital Classroom

Presentation Plus: Unit 8

Digital Flashcards

Audio 88

Practice Extra

Extra Resources

- **Teacher Resources:** Unit 8, Downloadable Activity Book Teaching Notes
- **T113 – Consolidation activity:** *Play a game*

2 🎧 88 Listen and draw lines. There is one example.

Daisy ____ Anna ____ Beth ____

Jack f Abdul ____ Zak ____

Quiz

1 Which 3 animals are in the sea? (p 64)

2 This bird can swim but it can't fly. What is it? (p 65)

3 Where do Lock and Key go for a cold drink? (p 69)

4 Where was Meera on holiday? (p 72)

5 What was the weather like at the park and what was Grandpa wearing? (p 75)

6 Say all the different sounds on page 76.

7 Where was Robin Motors last Thursday morning? (p 77)

8 What instrument is played by the waves in the sea? (p 78)

Units 1&2 Values Give and share

1 89 Look and complete. Listen and check.

1 The boys' clothes are too ________ .
2 Ana can eat the ________ they planted.
3 The children are painting the ________ .
4 The children are putting ________ into the boxes.

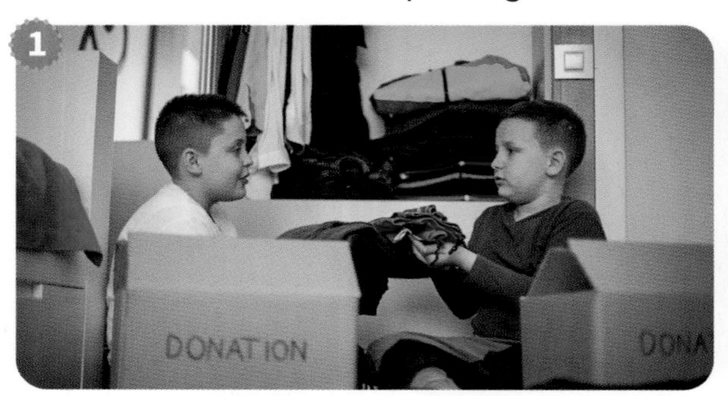

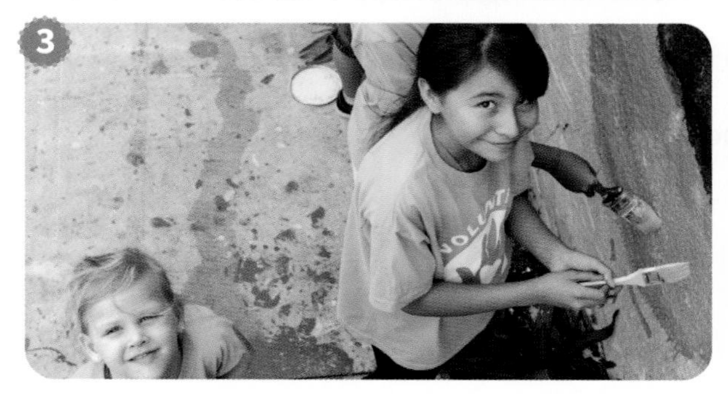

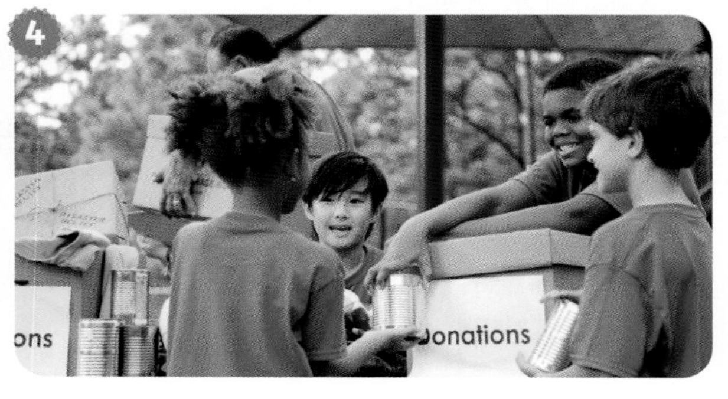

2 Read and correct.

1 They share toys with other people.
2 The children are planting flowers in the community garden.
3 The children are painting the wall red.
4 The children are putting the food in the cupboard.
5 The boys want to keep their clothes.
6 One person eats the food from the community garden.

3 Think and discuss. What do you share?

I share a computer with my brother.

Objectives

To listen to a story and to talk about giving and sharing.

Target language

- **Key language:** *give, share, small for (someone)*
- **Additional language:** *box, community garden, Great idea!, plant, ready*
- **Revision:** clothes, fruit, vegetables, *wall*

Materials

- **Warmer:** Some old books or toys in a cardboard box

Warmer

- Show the class the old books/toys you have brought. Say *Look. These are my (books). Are they new or old?* Pupils respond *Old.* Say *I don't need them. What do I do with them?* Teach *bin.*

PB82. ACTIVITY 1

Look and complete. Listen and check.

- Say *Open your Pupil's Books at page 82, please.* Focus pupils on the pictures. Elicit what they can see (clothes, children, plants, paint, etc.). Teach/Elicit *box.* Pupils work in pairs to complete the sentences, either in pencil or orally. Do not confirm answers.
- Play the **Audio**. Pupils listen and check their answers to Activity 1. Talk briefly in L1 about giving and sharing. Remind pupils that Values lessons are about doing the right thing. Ask pupils what they do with their old toys, books and clothes.

Key: **1** small, **2** vegetables, **3** wall, **4** food

89

1 **Boy 1:** Look, Max, these clothes are too small for us. Let's put them in the donation box so that other children can have them.
Boy 2: Great idea! I have some clothes that I want to give to other children, too.

2 **Girl:** Look at the vegetables. They're ready to eat.
Boy: It's great to plant fruit and vegetables.
Girl: Can you put these onions in your basket, please?

3 **Girl 1:** This wall looks fantastic blue.
Girl 2: Yes, I love our new wall. It's great to help keep our town looking nice.

4 **Boy 1:** Look at all this food.
Boy 2: Let's put it in the donation boxes and give it to people who need it.
Girl: Can you take this, please?

PB82. ACTIVITY 2

Read and correct.

- Focus pupils on Activity 2. Pupils work in pairs. They read the sentences, discuss them and write a correct version in their notebooks. Demonstrate by writing the first sentence on the board. Elicit the correct sentence and underline the word pupils need to change (toys). Write the corrected sentence on the board (*They share clothes with other people.*). Monitor and help pairs as necessary.

Key: **2** The children are planting fruit and vegetables in the community garden. **3** The children are painting the wall blue. **4** The children are putting the food in the boxes. **5** The boys want to give their clothes to other children. **6** People eat the food from the community garden.

PB82. ACTIVITY 3

Think and discuss. What do you share?

- Focus pupils on Activity 3. Pupils discuss the question in small groups. Invite groups to share their ideas with the class.

AB82. Answer key, see page T103

Ending the lesson

- Write the following responses on the board: *Yes, but they're small for me. / Yes, that's a great idea. / Yes, please. / You can play with mine.* Say *Can I give my toys to the hospital, Mum?* and elicit the correct response from the ones on the board (Yes, that's a great idea.). Repeat the question. The class reply in chorus with the correct response. Ask more questions to practise the other responses.

Digital Classroom

Presentation Plus: Units 1 & 2 Values

Audio 89

Digital Flashcards

Practice Extra

Extra Resources

- **Teacher Resources:** Units 1 & 2 Values, Downloadable Activity Book Teaching Notes
- **T111 – Extension activity:** *Have one of mine*

Objectives

To talk about respecting their environment and to complete rules for behaviour in public.

Target language

- **Key language:** *love your city, throw rubbish, park (a car), sign, Sorry*
- **Additional language:** *seat, elderly, break*
- **Revision:** city, prepositions, imperatives, *can* (permission), *ground, bin, flowers, train, bus, play football, clean, beautiful*

Warmer

- Sit at the front of the class with your feet on your desk. Ask your pupils *Is this OK? Can I put my feet on the desk?* Elicit *No. / You can't. / Don't put your feet on the desk.* Throw some rubbish on the classroom floor. Ask the class *What about this? Can I throw rubbish in the classroom?* Elicit *No. You can't/mustn't throw rubbish.* Say *Different places have different rules.* Tell pupils in L1 that they are going to talk about how to behave in different places in this lesson.

PB83. ACTIVITY 1

Look and think. Say 'yes' or 'no'. Listen and check.

- Show Activity 1 on the whiteboard. Focus on the lesson title and review the meaning of *Values* and *Love your city*. Direct pupils to the pictures. Elicit what they can see (e.g. signs, park, seats). Read the activity instructions aloud and choose pupils to read the sentences. Check comprehension. Elicit the answer for sentence 1 from the class (no).
- Say *Open your Pupil's Books at page 83, please.* Pupils work in pairs to talk about the rest of the sentences. Monitor and encourage them to speak in English but do not confirm answers.
- Tell pupils to listen carefully. Play the Audio. Pupils listen and check their answers. Check with the class. Play the Audio again and check comprehension. Ask, e.g. *Where must you put rubbish? What is the girl doing? What must the boy do? Where must they park?* Talk briefly in L1 about respecting your city and looking after public property. Ask pupils if there are problems with graffiti and litter in their city/hometown.

Key: **1** No, **2** No, **3** No, **4** No

90

1 **Fred:** Mmm. That chocolate was good, but I'm still hungry!
Jill: Fred! Don't throw your rubbish on the ground!
Fred: Where can I put it?
Jill: Look, there's a bin in front of you.
Fred: Oh, yes. Thanks, Jill!
Jill: No problem!

2 **Woman:** Hey, we can't park here. Look at the sign.
Man: Oh, yes. The sign says 'No parking'.
Woman: Uff! Where can we park?
Man: Oh look, there's a car park. Let's park there.

3 **Boy:** Peter, look, you can't sit on that seat. It's for elderly people. Look at the sign on the seat.
Peter: Oh, I'm sorry. Where can I sit?
Boy: You can sit over there. Those seats are for everyone.
Peter: That's a good idea. Thanks!

4 **Boy:** What are you doing?
Girl: I'm running here in the flowers.
Boy: But it's not good for the flowers. Look, the sign says 'Stay out of the flowers'.
Girl: Oh yes – sorry.

PB83. ACTIVITY 2

Read and match.

- Focus pupils on Activity 2. Pupils read and join the sentence halves. They check in pairs and then check with the class.

Key: **2** c, **3** f, **4** a, **5** e, **6** d

PB83. ACTIVITY 3

Think and discuss. What can you do to help your town?

- Focus pupils on Activity 3. Pupils discuss the question in small groups. Invite each group to choose one of their ideas to share with the class. Discuss each group's suggestion as a class.

AB83. Answer key, see page T103

Ending the lesson

- Mime one of the inappropriate behaviours from the lesson (e.g. throwing rubbish on the ground). Pupils tell you *You mustn't throw rubbish on the ground! / Don't throw rubbish on the ground. / Put your rubbish in the bin.* Repeat with different types of behaviour (e.g. putting your feet on the desk, writing on the wall, playing football in the classroom, writing on the desk).

Digital Classroom

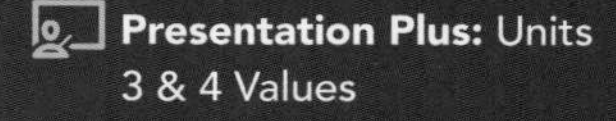
Presentation Plus: Units 3 & 4 Values

Audio 90

Digital Flashcards

Practice Extra

Extra Resources

- **Teacher Resources:** Units 3 & 4 Values, Downloadable Activity Book Teaching Notes
- **T113 – Extension activity 1:** *Act it out*
- **T113 – Extension activity 2:** *Make a poster*

Units 3&4 Values Love your city

1 90 Look and think. Say 'yes' or 'no'. Listen and check.

1 In the street, it's OK to throw rubbish on the ground.
2 It's OK to park your car next to a 'No parking' sign.
3 On the train, it's OK not to give your seat to an elderly person who needs to sit down.
4 In a park, it's OK to play football next to the flowers.

2 Read and match.

1 – b

1 Don't break flowers …
2 You can put your …
3 You can park …
4 On trains and buses don't …
5 Don't park next to …
6 You can help to make your …

a … sit in seats that are for elderly people.
b … and trees in the park.
c … rubbish in the bin.
d … town clean and beautiful.
e … the no parking sign.
f … in the car park.

3 Think and discuss. What can you do to help your town?

I can have a picnic in the park and put my rubbish in the bin.

Units 5&6 Values Fair play

1 🎧 91 Look, read and match. Listen and check.

1 You mustn't be angry when you don't win.
2 In sport you must help other players.
3 In sport it is good to learn new skills.
4 When you play sport you need to know the rules.

2 Read and correct.

1 We mustn't be friendly to the other players.
2 You must never follow the rules of the game.
3 When we play sport it's always important to win.
4 Don't help other players.
5 It isn't important to enjoy playing sport.
6 We must be angry when we don't win.

3 Think and discuss. Is it important to play or to win? Why?

I think it's important to play, because I can learn new things.

Objectives

To listen to examples of fair play and to talk about rules for playing fairly.

Target language

- **Key language:** *fair play, team, player, alright, Excellent / Nice / Great game, Well done!*
- **Additional language:** *yellow card, follow the rules, Shall I get the teacher? It's OK*
- **Revision:** sports, parts of the body, imperatives, rules, *angry, win, good at, touch, important, My leg hurts. Can I help you? must/mustn't*

Materials

- **Warmer:** Clip from a video of the end of a football or tennis match, where players are shaking hands

Warmer

- Play a clip from a video of sports people shaking hands. Elicit who pupils think the winner(s) is/are. Elicit what the losing player(s) is/are saying (see if pupils can remember *Well done!*). Write *Fair play* on the board and elicit a translation.

PB84. ACTIVITY 1

Look, read and match. Listen and check.

- Say *Open your Pupil's Books at page 84, please.* Elicit the names of the sports (baseball, football). Use picture 1 to teach *team* and *player.*
- Pupils discuss answers in pairs. Do not confirm answers.
- Play the Audio. Pupils listen and check.

Key: 3, 4, 2, 1

91

1 **Teacher:** Excellent game, everyone. Lucy's team wins 5–3.
Vicky: Nice game, Lucy. Well done!
Lucy: Thanks, Vicky. Your team's very good, too!
Vicky: It was a great game. Let's get a photo of our teams!

2 **Jim:** Ow! My leg.
Zara: Are you OK, Jim?
Jim: No, my leg hurts.
Zara: Can I help you? Shall I get the teacher?
Jim: Yes, please. Thanks, Zara.

3 **Teacher:** OK, Jack. You're in Fred's team.
Jack: I don't like baseball. I'm not very good at it.
Fred: That's OK, Jack. We can help you.
Teacher: Look, hold the bat like this.
Fred & Teacher: Yes! That's right. Go, Jack!

4 **Referee:** Paul! You mustn't touch the ball with your hands. Yellow card for you!
Paul: That's not fair! Yellow card.
Referee: That's the rules.
Paul: You're right. I'm sorry.
Referee: That's alright, but you must follow the rules of the game.

PB84. ACTIVITY 2

Read and correct.

- Focus pupils on Activity 2. Pupils work in pairs to read and discuss.

Key: **1** We must be friendly to the other players. **2** You must always follow the rules of the game. **3** When we play sport it isn't always important to win. **4** You must help other players. / Help other players. **5** It's important to enjoy playing sport. **6** We mustn't be angry when we don't win.

PB84. ACTIVITY 3

Think and discuss. Is it important to play or to win? Why?

- Focus pupils on Activity 3. Pupils discuss the question in small groups. Invite groups to share their ideas with the class.

AB84. Answer key, see page T103

Ending the lesson

- Divide the class into two 'teams'. Tell them they have just finished a football match. Tell one team they are the winners and the other team they are the losers. Elicit appropriate phrases from the lesson for each team, e.g. Losers: *You win. Well done! Excellent game! You're a great player.* Winners: *Thank you. Nice match. You're good at football, too.* Pupils walk around, shaking hands and saying the phrases. Swap roles.

Digital Classroom

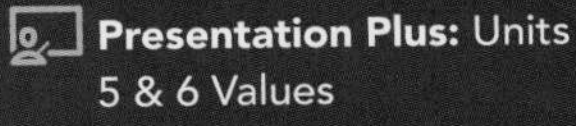

Presentation Plus: Units 5 & 6 Values

Audio 91

Digital Flashcards

Practice Extra

Extra Resources

- **Teacher Resources:** Units 5 & 6 Values, Downloadable Activity Book Teaching Notes
- **T113 – Extension activity:** *Act it out*
- **T114 – Consolidation activity:** *What do you say?*

Objectives

To listen to examples of and to talk about ways of helping the environment.

Target language

- **Key language:** *help the world, turn off, go shopping, catch a bus*
- **Additional language:** *use, It's better to …, all the time, bring, electricity, later, lights*
- **Revision:** *always, never, mustn't, need to, water, clean, bag, ride a bike, drive, walk, go to work*

Materials

- **Warmer:** Picture/Photograph of the world

Warmer

- Draw a simple picture of the world on the board or show a picture/photograph. Elicit *world*. Write the phrase *Help the world* on the board and elicit a translation. Tell pupils they will be thinking and talking about ways of helping the world in today's lesson.

PB85. ACTIVITY 1

Look and think. Say 'yes' or 'no'. Listen and check.

- Show Activity 1 on the whiteboard. Focus on the lesson title and review the meaning of *Help the world*. Direct pupils to the four pictures. Elicit what they can see and help with language as necessary (e.g. *clean your teeth, shopping, bags, turn off, electricity*). Read the activity instructions aloud and choose pupils to read the sentences. Check comprehension.
- Elicit the answer for sentence 1 from the class (yes).
- Say *Open your Pupil's Books at page 85, please.* Pupils work in pairs to talk about the rest of the sentences. Monitor and encourage them to speak in English but do not confirm answers.
- Tell pupils to listen carefully. Play the Audio. Pupils listen and check their answers. Check with the class. Play the Audio again and check comprehension. Ask, e.g. *Is it good to use the car all the time? Why does the girl turn off the tap? Does the woman want bags in picture 3? Why not? What is the boy doing in picture 4? Why?* Talk briefly in L1 about making small changes to daily habits to help our world. Ask pupils if they do any of the things in the pictures or if they help in different ways.

Key: **1** Yes, **2** Yes, **3** No, **4** No

92

1 **Mum:** Shall I drive you to school this morning?
Girl: Thanks, Mum, but we want to walk to school. It's better to walk than to drive.
Girls: Yes! Let's walk to school!
Mum: Yes, you're right. It's not good to use the car all the time. Today I can go to work on the bus, too.
Girls: Yay! Let's run!

2 **Dad:** Yasmin! You must turn off the water when you clean your teeth.
Yasmin: You're right. We mustn't use a lot of water. I forgot.
Dad: That's OK.

3 **Woman:** Would you like a bag?
Mum: No, thank you. We've got two bags. My daughter always brings them from home. Well done, Anna!
Anna: Thanks, Mum.

4 **Tom:** Come on, Jack. Let's go!
Jack: Wait a minute, Tom. We need to turn off the computer first.
Tom: No, that's alright. We can turn it off later.
Jack: No. Let's turn it off now. When we aren't using computers and lights, we need to turn them off. They use a lot of electricity.

PB85. ACTIVITY 2

Read and match.

- Focus pupils on Activity 2. Read the activity instruction aloud and point out the example. Check comprehension of *light* (in number 5). Pupils work in pairs to match the rest of the sentence halves. Check with the class.

Key: **2** f, **3** b, **4** e, **5** c, **6** a

PB85. ACTIVITY 3

Think and discuss. What can you do to help the world?

- Focus pupils on Activity 3. Pupils discuss the question in small groups. Invite groups to share their ideas with the class. Brainstorm ideas on the board.

AB85. Answer key, see page T103

Ending the lesson

- Mime an action from the lesson. Pupils show 'thumbs up' if it helps the world and 'thumbs down' if it doesn't help the world. Elicit a phrase to describe what you are doing after each mime. Example mimes: turning off the television, turning on a tap and spending a long time washing your hands, driving a car, walking, asking a cashier for a bag at the supermarket, turning off a light switch, travelling on a bus / an underground train.

Digital Classroom

Presentation Plus: Units 7 & 8 Values

Audio 92

Digital Flashcards

Practice Extra

Extra Resources

- **Teacher Resources:** Units 7 & 8 Values, Downloadable Activity Book Teaching Notes
- **T114 – Extension activity 1:** *Act it out*
- **T114 – Extension activity 2:** *Class poster*

Units 7&8 Values Help the world

1 🎧 92 Look and think. Say 'yes' or 'no'. Listen and check.

1 If you live near your school you can sometimes walk there.
2 When you clean your teeth you can turn the water off.
3 You mustn't take bags with you when you go shopping.
4 You never need to turn computers or televisions off.

1

2

3

4

2 Read and match.

1 – d

1 Turn off the computer when …
2 Don't always use the car, catch …
3 When you clean your teeth, …
4 Take bags with you …
5 Turn off the light …
6 When you live near your school, …

a … you can walk there.
b … turn off the water.
c … when you go out of the room.
d … you aren't using it.
e … when you go shopping.
f … a bus or ride a bike.

3 Think and discuss. What can you do to help the world?

I walk or ride my bike to school.

The doll is next to the ball. The book is on the floor. The bike is in front of the table. The helicopter is under the table. The game is between the doll and the camera. The kite is behind the bike.	
What are you doing? What's Daisy doing? What's Peter doing? What are Paul and Jane doing?	I'm riding my bike. She's reading. He's flying a kite. They're playing hockey.
Is Pete flying a kite?	Yes, he is. No, he isn't.

Who's Simon? Who's Suzy? Who are Grandma and Grandpa Star?	He's Stella's brother. She's Stella's sister. They're Stella's grandparents.

I He / She	like / love / enjoy don't like / love / enjoy likes / loves / enjoys doesn't like / love / enjoy	riding my bike. reading about science.
I He / She	want wants	to ride my bike. to read about science.

Do you like taking photos? Do you want to take a photo? Does he / she enjoy playing football? Does he / she want to play football?	Yes, I do. No, I don't. Yes, he / she does. No, he / she doesn't.

Has your house got a basement?	My house hasn't got a basement. My house has got three bedrooms.

What do you do before school? What does he / she do before school?	I have breakfast. He / She has breakfast.
How often do you play in the park? How often does he / she play in the park?	I never / sometimes / always play in the park. I play in the park every day. He / She never / sometimes / always plays in the park. He / She plays in the park every day.

Where do you go to play basketball?	You go to the sports centre to play basketball.
Must I / Simon / Suzy go to school?	Yes, you / he / she must.

What's the matter?	I've / You've / He's / She's / We've / They've got a headache. My head hurts.
He must stay in bed. He mustn't go to the park. We must be quiet in the library. We mustn't eat in the library.	

I'm hungry. I'm cold.	Shall I make breakfast? Shall I close the window?

weak → weaker thin → thinner naughty → naughtier good → better bad → worse	Parrots are weaker than bears. Dolphins are thinner than whales. Monkeys are naughtier than lions. Sharks are better at swimming than elephants. Pandas are worse at jumping than kangaroos.

What's the weather like?	It's sunny.	
I / He / She / It You / We / They	was / wasn't were / weren't	at the park yesterday. at the beach yesterday.
Where were you / they on Saturday? Where was he / she / it on Sunday?		
It There There	was / wasn't was / wasn't were / weren't	cold and windy yesterday. a lot of snow yesterday. a lot of children yesterday.

Activity Book

AB86. ACTIVITY 0. *Match the sentences.*

Key: 1 c, 2 d, 3 b, 4 a

AB86. ACTIVITY 1. *Read and circle the best answer.*

Key: 1 likes, 2 enjoy, 3 wants, 4 want

AB86. ACTIVITY 2. *Look and complete.*

Key: 1 Has, 2 hasn't, 3 got, 4 it's got

AB86. ACTIVITY 3. *Match the sentences.*

Key: 1 d, 2 c, 3 a, 4 b

AB87. ACTIVITY 4. *Read and order the words. Make sentences.*

Key: 1 Where do you go to buy food? 2 Where do you go to fly a kite? 3 Where do you go to see a doctor?

AB87. ACTIVITY 5. *Look and complete.*

Key: 1 Must, 2 must, 3 Can, 4 mustn't

AB87. ACTIVITY 6. *Match the sentences.*

Key: 1 b, 2 c, 3 a

AB87. ACTIVITY 7. *Complete the sentences.*

Key: 1 quicker, 2 smaller, 3 dirtier, 4 better

AB87. ACTIVITY 8. *Look and complete the sentences.*

Key: 1 was, 2 wasn't, 3 weren't, 4 were

Movers Listening

1 93 **Describe the pictures. Listen. Circle the correct picture. There is one example.**

2 94 **Listen and draw lines. There is one example.**

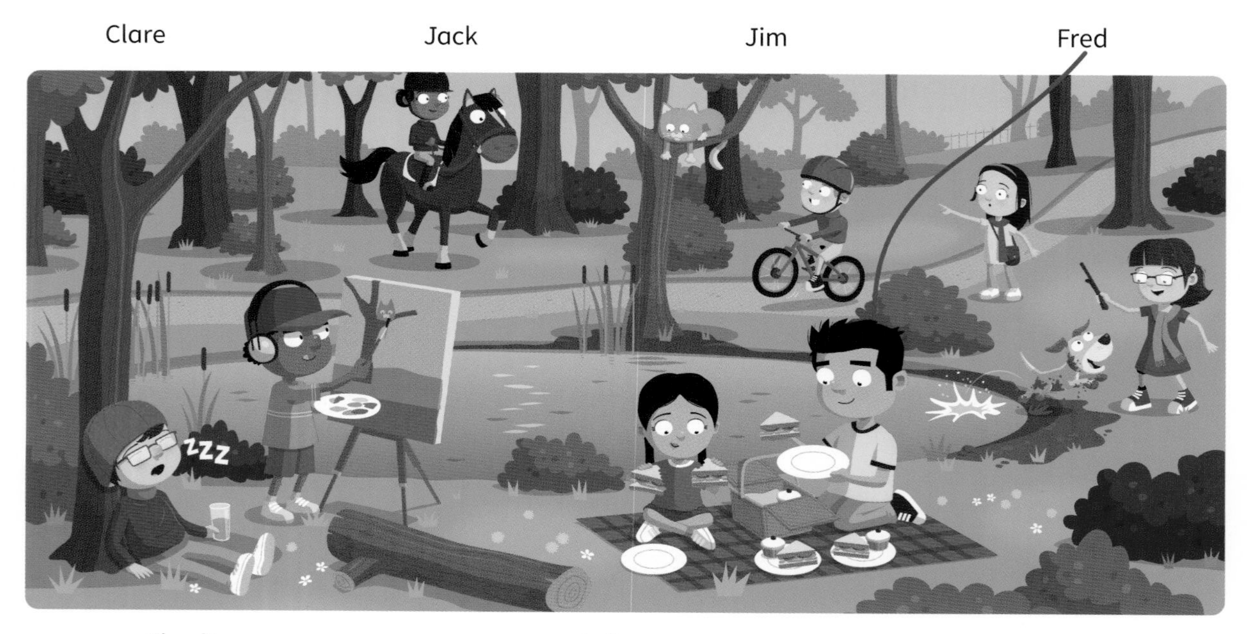

A1 Movers Exam folder
Movers Listening

Objectives
To complete a practice task for Part 1 of the Movers Listening exam.

Target language
- **Key language:** names, activities, clothes, adjectives, physical appearance, food, prepositions

EXAM SKILLS
- Listening for specific information (names and descriptions)

EXAM TIPS
- Pupils draw straight lines between a name and the person in the picture. It doesn't matter if the lines cross over each other or cross over other people in the picture as long as it is clear which person each line leads to.
- The names on the **Audio** do not follow the order of the names around the picture.
- Pupils only draw lines from the names they hear in the instructions. There is one extra name, which pupils will not connect to a person in the picture.
- Pupils listen to all the information about a particular person in the picture before drawing their line. Sometimes there is extra information at the end of the dialogue.

Warmer
- Write a list of the names from the Movers test in two columns, as follows:

	1	2
a	Jack	Jane
b	Lily	Sally
c	Clare	Mary
d	Peter	Paul
e	Jane	Jim
f	Zoe	Daisy
g	Julia	Jane
h	Charlie	Clare
i	Sally	Zoe
j	Vicky	Lily
k	Jim	Jack

- Call out a letter and one name in each pair, e.g. *h Charlie*. Pupils listen and look at the table. If the name appears in the first column, they hold up one finger. If it appears in the second column, they hold up two fingers. Repeat with other names from the list.

PB88. ACTIVITY 1

Describe the pictures. Listen. Circle the correct picture. There is one example.
- Show Activity 1 on the whiteboard. In pairs, pupils describe the silhouettes and talk about what each child is doing, wearing, etc. Invite volunteers to share their descriptions.
- With Pupil's Books still closed, play the **Audio**. Pupils listen and write down the four names they hear in their notebooks. Check answers and spelling.
- Say *Open your Pupil's Books at page 88, please*. Play the **Audio** a second time. Pupils listen and circle the correct pictures. Remind them to listen to the whole dialogue before circling. Check answers with the class.

Key: **1** c, **2** a, **3** b, **4** a

93

Audio scripts for the Exam folder can be downloaded from *Teacher Resources*.

PB88. ACTIVITY 2

Listen and draw lines. There is one example.
- Explain that Activity 2 is similar to the Part 1 Listening task in the Movers test.
- Ask pupils how many names they can see around the illustration (seven) and how many they will match (six). Go through the Exam tips opposite with the class.
- Play the example and pause. Clarify any doubts. Continue playing the **Audio**. Pupils listen and carry out the task.
- Circulate and check pupils are drawing clear lines.
- Check answers by inviting volunteers to come to the front and draw lines on the whiteboard from the names to the people in the picture. Alternatively, play the **Audio** and stop after each description and elicit the name. Ask questions to confirm the person in the picture, e.g. *Where is he/she?*
- Exploit the picture by reviewing descriptions and actions.

Key: **2** Julia – girl eating sandwiches, **3** Sally – girl with wet dog, **4** Jack – boy in sweater sleeping under tree, **5** Clare – girl riding horse, **6** Charlie – boy with blue cap painting picture

94

Audio scripts for the Exam folder can be downloaded from *Teacher Resources*.

Ending the lesson
- Ask pupils how they felt about the task. They can show how confident they feel about the task type with a thumbs up or thumbs down or tilting their hands back and forth (to indicate *so-so*).

Digital Classroom

Presentation Plus: Movers Exam folder

Practice Extra

Audio 93–94

Extra Resources
- **Teacher Resources:** Downloadable Exam folder Audio Script
- **T114 – Extension activity:** *Mime and guess*

Objectives

To complete a practice task for Part 4 of the Movers Listening exam.

Target language

- **Key language:** physical descriptions, food, animals, illnesses, actions, clothes, times

EXAM SKILLS

- Listening for key words and specific information
- Listening to a complete description and ignoring distractors

EXAM TIPS

- Pupils look at the pictures carefully and notice details before listening.
- Pupils tick only one box of three.
- Pupils need to be aware that there are distractors that provide similar information but don't answer the question.
- Pupils listen to the whole dialogue before they choose which picture to tick, as sometimes there is also more information at the end.

Warmer

- Play Categories. Draw a grid on the board with seven rows and seven columns. In the first column, starting with row 2, write the following categories: *animals, clothes, illnesses, places, toys, weather*. Pupils copy the table in their notebooks.
- Play the first round together. Write *S* at the top of the second column. Together brainstorm one vocabulary item per category beginning with *S*. If there is no word for that category beginning with the letter, pupils place an X (e.g. *snake, scarf, stomach-ache, supermarket, X, snow*).
- Divide the class into groups of three or four. Write a letter, e.g. *C*, at the top of the third column. Give groups one minute to write a vocabulary item for each category.
- Check answers and write examples on the grid on the board. Each group scores one point for each word.
- Repeat the procedure with four more letters (e.g. *C: cat, coat, cough, cinema, computer, cloudy; H: hippo, hat, headache, hospital, helicopter, hot; B: bear, boots, backache, bank, bike, X; T: tiger, trousers, temperature, town, train, X; R: rabbit, X, X, river, robot, rainy*).

PB89. ACTIVITY 1

Listen. Draw the missing information. There is one example.

- Show Activity 1 on the whiteboard and focus pupils on the pictures. In pairs, they look at each picture and talk about what they can add to make the picture different, e.g. the clown: change to a red/pink mouth, blue hair, straight hair; the houses and flat: add a balcony / tree / garden; colour the doors different colours; the picnic: add different food / drink / grass / a bird; the beach: add shells / a jellyfish / bananas in the tree.
- Invite pairs to share their ideas as a class.
- Play the **Audio** for each picture. Pupils listen and colour or add the detail. Allow a minute for pupils to add the changes to each picture.
- Check answers with the class by eliciting the new descriptions.
- Play the **Audio** again, pausing after each dialogue or specific sentences to highlight the use of distractors, e.g. *My house has only got one balcony* in dialogue 2, and the importance of listening until the end of the dialogues, e.g. *No, that's an island* in dialogue 4.

Key: **2** a garden and tall tree next to the small house, **3** three bananas and a watermelon, **4** two shells on the beach and a dolphin in the sea

95

Audio scripts for the Exam folder can be downloaded from *Teacher Resources.*

PB89. ACTIVITY 2

Listen and tick (✓) the box. There is one example.

- Explain that Activity 2 is similar to the Part 4 Listening task in the Movers test.
- Go through the Exam tips opposite with the class.
- Play the example and pause. Make sure pupils understand why the answer is the lion.
- Pupils listen and tick the correct boxes.
- Check answers with the class. Repeat any dialogues pupils found particularly difficult.

Key: 1 C, **2** A, **3** C, **4** B, **5** A

96

Audio scripts for the Exam folder can be downloaded from *Teacher Resources.*

Ending the lesson

- Ask pupils how they felt about the task. They can show how confident they feel about the task type with a thumbs up, thumbs down, or tilting their hands back and forth (to indicate *so-so*). Elicit any other comments about what they found easy or difficult, and use pupils' feedback to plan more listening practice.

Digital Classroom

Presentation Plus: Movers Exam folder

Practice Extra

Audio 95–96

Extra Resources

- **Teacher Resources:** Downloadable Exam folder Audio Script
- **T114 – Extension activity:** *False descriptions*

Movers Listening

1 95 **Listen. Draw the missing information. There is one example.**

1

2

3

4

2 96 **Listen and tick (✓) the box. There is one example.**

Example

What is the story about?

A  B ☐ C ☐

1 What is the matter with Clare today?

A ☐ B ☐ C ☐

2 What is Zoe's brother doing?

A ☐ B ☐ C ☐

3 Who is Paul's science teacher?

A ☐ B ☐ C ☐

4 Where were Charlie's socks?

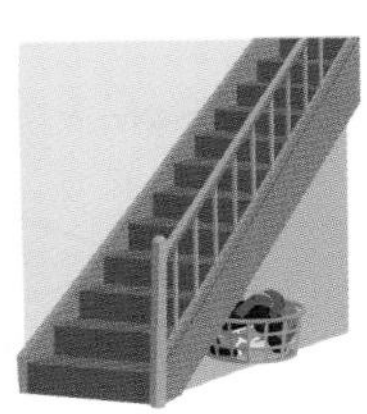

A ☐ B ☐ C ☐

5 What time must Jane get up?

A ☐ B ☐ C 

1 **Colour each thing a different colour. Talk to your partner. What's different? Tick (✓).**

blanket ☐ towel ☐ flower ☐ one bird ☐ one cloud ☐ sandwich ☐

2 97 **Listen and colour and write. There is one example.**

Objectives

To complete a practice task for Part 5 of the Movers Listening exam.

Target language

- **Key language:** colours, food, animals, objects, prepositions, *colour*, *write*

EXAM SKILLS

- Listening for specific information (words, colours and prepositions)

EXAM TIPS

- Pupils prepare these colours: black, blue, brown, green, grey, orange, pink, purple, red, yellow.
- There are six dialogues. One is the example. Pupils colour only the objects they are told to colour. They also write one word. The word is from the Starters or Movers wordlist and has a connection to the picture in some way.
- Pupils listen carefully for prepositional phrases which describe where something is (e.g. *the fish next to the girl*; *the parrot in front of the cloud*).
- Pupils do not need to colour very neatly. The important thing is that it is clear which items they have coloured and in which colours.

Warmer

- Pupils lay out their coloured crayons on their desks.
- Spell out each colour word quickly (e.g. *B-L-U-E*). Pupils must wait until you have spelt out the whole word before calling out the colour and holding it up.
- Play Simon says with colours. Say, e.g. *Simon says touch an object that is blue*. If pupils touch a colour without hearing the words *Simon says*, they must sit down. If you have a large group, pupils point to the object instead of touching it.

PB90. ACTIVITY 1

Colour each thing a different colour. Talk to your partner. What's different? Tick (✓).

- Show Activity 1 on the whiteboard and ask pupils to describe the picture.
- Ask *Where's the ...?* for each object/animal to review the prepositions *above, below, in, on, next to, under, in front of, between*.
- Individually, pupils colour each item indicated in the list below the picture a different colour. They can use their imagination and colour the items a colour they would not normally be, e.g. a blue sandwich.
- Put pupils into pairs and tell them not to let their partner see their picture. Focus pupils on the example speech bubbles and check understanding of the task. They compare their pictures by describing the items they've coloured. They tick the box for each item that they've coloured in a different colour.
- Remind pupils they can ask for repetition if necessary (*Sorry, can you repeat that?*)

PB90. ACTIVITY 2

Listen and colour and write. There is one example.

- Explain that Activity 2 is similar to the Part 5 Listening task in the Movers test.
- Describe what the test involves. Refer to the tips and reminders opposite. Suggest that the first time they listen, they place a dot of the correct colour on each object. When they listen the second time, they can add more colour. Remind them that they will also need to write a word.
- Play the Audio. Pupils listen and follow the instructions. Circulate and check pupils are not spending too long on colouring.
- Pupils compare their picture with a partner. Then check with the class. Point to each item and elicit the colour. Ask a volunteer to write the word they wrote on the whiteboard.

Key: **1** Colour blanket in front of bear – yellow, **2** Colour fish next to the girl – pink, **3** Colour parrot flying in front of cloud – green, **4** Write 'park' on the rock above the bear's head, **5** Colour the girl's shirt – orange

97

Audio scripts for the Exam folder can be downloaded from *Teacher Resources*.

Ending the lesson

- Ask pupils how they felt about the task. They can show how confident they feel about the task type with a thumbs up, thumbs down, or tilting their hands back and forth (to indicate *so-so*). Elicit any other comments about what they found easy or difficult and use pupils' feedback to plan more listening practice.

Digital Classroom

Presentation Plus: Movers Exam folder

Practice Extra

Audio 97

Extra Resources

- **Teacher Resources:** Downloadable Exam folder Audio Script
- **T114 – Extension activity:** *Chain game*

A1 Movers Exam folder
Movers Reading and Writing

Objectives
To complete a practice task for Part 1 of the Movers Reading and Writing exam.

Target language
- **Key language:** places, parts of the house, *whale, rainbow, breakfast, grass, people, this, here*

Materials
- Nine flashcards

EXAM SKILLS
- Developing careful reading skills
- Becoming familiar with the structures and vocabulary commonly used in defining things

EXAM TIPS
- Pupils need to be familiar with the use of *you* for general reference, relative pronouns (*This is a person who … / a place where … You wear this when …*) and the infinitive to express purpose (*You use these to go up and down*).
- Pupils should practise accurate copying. They should copy the whole option and not add anything extra. This means they write the article if there is one and do not add one if there isn't.
- Pupils should always check they have spelt the word correctly.

Warmer
- Draw a 3 x 3 grid on the board. Choose nine flashcards and place one in each square. As you do, elicit the name of the item and write it below the flashcard.
- Explain that you will give an oral definition for eight of the nine words. After each definition you will count to three. Pupils can then say the word together.
- Give the definitions and elicit the word. Invite a volunteer to take down the flashcard for that word.
- There will be one card left. Pairs write a definition for this last word. Volunteers read out their definition. Write a few definitions on the board. As a class, decide which definition would be best or how to improve them.
- Review the definitions for each flashcard. Write them on the board and highlight the typical structures used in defining things. (See Exam tips above.)

PB91. ACTIVITY 1

Read. Cross out the word. There is one example.
- Focus pupils on Activity 1 and check understanding of the task. They read each definition and cross out the word being described. Explain that there are nine words and only seven definitions, so there will be two words left over at the end.
- Check answers by reading out each definition and inviting pupils to call out the word. Ask which two words didn't have a definition (a whale, breakfast).

Key: stairs, a market, a rainbow, a city, a cinema, a park

PB91. ACTIVITY 2

Write a definition for the two missing words.
- Focus pupils on Activity 1. In pairs, they write a definition of the words *a whale* and *breakfast*.
- Ask volunteers to read out their definitions. Write one or two on the board and use the opportunity to highlight again typical defining features.

Key: (Possible answers) a whale – It's the biggest animal in the sea. breakfast – You eat this in the morning.

Ending the lesson
- Ask pupils how they felt about the task. They can show how confident they feel about the task type with a thumbs up, thumbs down, or tilting their hands back and forth (to indicate *so-so*). Elicit any other comments about what they found easy or difficult and use pupils' feedback to plan more reading and writing practice.

Digital Classroom

Presentation Plus: Movers Exam folder

Practice Extra

Extra Resources
- **T114 – Extension activity:** *Matching game*

Movers Reading and Writing

1 Read. Cross out the word. There is one example.

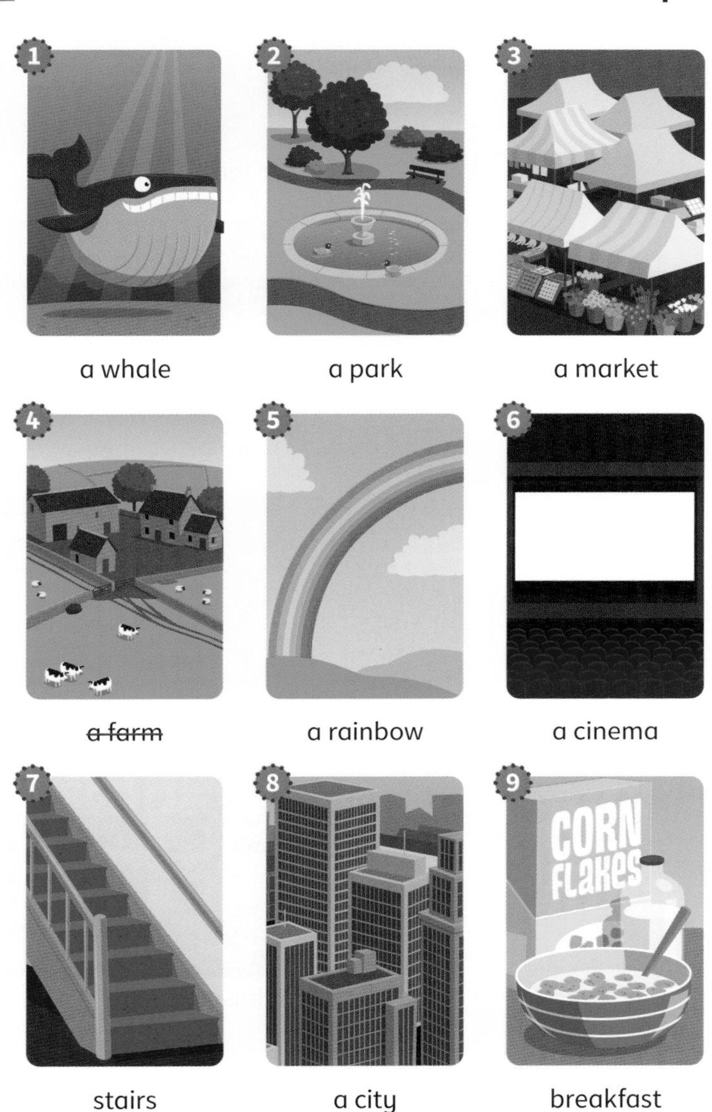

a whale — a park — a market — ~~a farm~~ — a rainbow — a cinema — stairs — a city — breakfast

Chickens often live here.
a farm

You go up and down these when you're inside a house.

People can go here to buy food.

You sometimes see this when it's rainy *and* sunny.

It's a busy place with lots of people, buses and cars.

People go here to see a film.

Children play and have fun here.

2 Write a definition for the two missing words.

3 Look and read. Choose the correct words and write them on the lines. There is one example.

a station

a forest

a basement

grass

~~a village~~

a lift

a roof

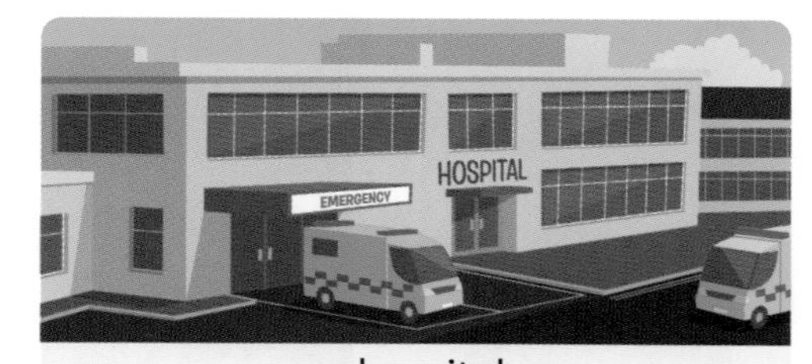

a hospital

Example

This is a quiet place to live in the countryside. ___a village___

Questions

1 People often go here when they aren't well. ______
2 This is on top of your house to keep it warm and dry. ______
3 People wait here to catch a train. ______
4 This machine takes you up and down a tall building. ______
5 This grows in fields and sheep love to eat it. ______

Objectives

- **To provide exam practice for Movers Reading and Writing Part 1 and task type.**
- **To provide practice reading and matching words to their definitions.**
- **To familiarise pupils with the structures and vocabulary commonly used in defining thing.**

Target language

- **Key language:** places in town, parts of a house, *a forest*, *grass*

EXAM SKILLS

- Developing careful reading skills
- Becoming familiar with the structures and vocabulary commonly used in defining things

EXAM TIPS

- Pupils need to be familiar with the use of *you* for general reference, relative pronouns (*This is a person who … / a place where … You wear this when …*) and the infinitive to express purpose (*You use these to go up and down*).
- Pupils should practise accurate copying. They should copy the whole option and not add anything extra. This means they write the article if there is one and do not add one if there isn't.
- Pupils should always check they have spelt the word correctly.

Warmer

- Play a spelling bee game with the class. Spell out a word from the Movers word list, e.g. *H-E-L-I-C-O-P-T-E-R*. As you are spelling the word, pupils try to guess what the word is. When they think they know, they put up their hand and say the word. This can also be played in smaller groups.

PB92. ACTIVITY 3

Look and read. Choose the correct words and write them on the lines. There is one example.

- Explain that Activity 3 is similar to the Part 1 Reading and Writing task in the Movers test.
- Describe what the test involves. Refer to the Exam tips and reminders opposite. Ask *Which word doesn't have 'a' or 'an' in front of it?* (grass). Remind pupils that they must not write *a* or *an* if the word doesn't have it.
- Read the example aloud.
- Circulate and check pupils are copying words correctly and neatly.
- Check answers by reading out each definition and inviting pupils to say the word.

Key: **1** a hospital, **2** a roof, **3** a station, **4** a lift, **5** grass

Ending the lesson

- Ask pupils how they felt about the task. They can show how confident they feel about the task type with a thumbs up, thumbs down, or tilting their hands back and forth (to indicate *so-so*). Elicit any other comments about what they found easy or difficult and use pupils' feedback to plan more reading and writing practice.

Digital Classroom

Presentation Plus: Movers Exam folder

Practice Extra

Extra Resources

- **T114 – Extension activity:** *What's the word?*

Objectives

To complete a practice task for Part 4 of the Movers Reading and Writing exam.

Target language

- **Key language:** animals, actions, comparatives, conjunctions, relative pronouns

EXAM SKILLS

- Becoming aware of grammatical forms that can help pupils with word choices
- Reading holistically to gain a sense of the text and its meaning

EXAM TIPS

- Pupils select one word out of three options to complete the sentence.
- They should read the whole text first to get the general gist and sense.
- They should read carefully to make the best word choice, which could be a verb, an adjective, a noun, a preposition or a pronoun.
- Use opportunities to sensitise pupils to singular/plural nouns and verb endings, pronouns, nouns beginning with a vowel, review articles and quantifiers, and prepositions.
- Pupils should check they have copied the word they need from the correct set of options.

Warmer

- Write the subject of the first sentence from Activity 1 on the board (*Penguins …*). Elicit ideas for sentences as a class, e.g. *Penguins … like cold weather / are black and white / can swim / can't fly / are bigger than parrots / don't live on a farm.*
- Now write the subject of sentence 2 (*Kangaroos …*). In small groups, pupils have one minute to write a sentence in their notebooks or on a mini whiteboard.
- Elicit pupils' sentences and write some on the board. Use the opportunity to draw attention to grammatical structures.

PB93. ACTIVITY 1

Read and match. Draw the lines. There is one example.

- Write the example sentence on the board with the word *but* missing: *Penguins can't fly ______ they can swim.* Prompt pupils to make suggestions as a class for the missing word.
- Say *Open your Pupil's Books at page 93, please.* Pupils read the sentences and match the sentence parts.
- Check answers with the class. Read each sentence starter and pause for pupils to supply the rest of the sentence.

Key: **2** Kangaroos can jump. **3** Plants need the sun and water to grow. **4** I drink water because I'm thirsty. **5** An island has got water all around it. **6** Pandas are black and white.

PB93. ACTIVITY 2

Read the text. Choose the right words and write them on the lines. There is one example.

- Explain that Activity 2 is similar to the Part 4 Reading and Writing task in the Movers test.
- Describe what the test involves. Refer to the tips opposite.
- Ask pupils to read each whole sentence first and then think about the word(s) for each space.
- Pupils work individually to complete the test. Circulate and check they are on task.
- Pupils compare answers in pairs. Then read the text aloud, pausing to elicit the answers. Clarify any doubts pupils may have.

Key: **1** a lot of, **2** hop, **3** are, **4** swim, **5** taller

Ending the lesson

- Ask pupils how they felt about the task. They can show how confident they feel about the task type with a thumbs up, thumbs down, or tilting their hands back and forth (to indicate *so-so*). Elicit any other comments about what they found easy or difficult and use pupils' feedback to plan more reading and writing practice.

Digital Classroom

Presentation Plus: Movers Exam folder

Practice Extra

Extra Resources

- **T114 – Extension activity:** *Sentence puzzles*

Movers Reading and Writing

1 Read and match. Draw the lines. There is one example.

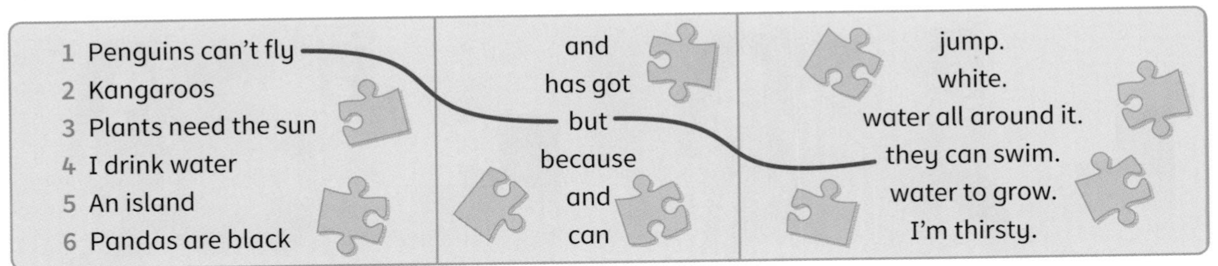

1 Penguins can't fly	and	jump.
2 Kangaroos	has got	white.
3 Plants need the sun	but	water all around it.
4 I drink water	because	they can swim.
5 An island	and	water to grow.
6 Pandas are black	can	I'm thirsty.

2 Read the text. Choose the right words and write them on the lines. There is one example.

Kangaroos

It isn't easy to see kangaroos (example): ___because___ they only live in a country called Australia. They eat grass, but they don't need (1) ______________ water.

Kangaroos are different from other animals because they cannot run or walk. They (2) ______________ . They (3) ______________ one of the only animals in the world that moves around in this way.

Their two strong legs, huge feet and long tail help them jump. They can also (4) ______________ very well.

Did you know that when kangaroos stand up, they are (5) ______________ than a person?

Example:	then	(because)	but
1	many	a	a lot of
2	hop	hops	hopping
3	is	are	was
4	swim	swam	swimming
5	tall	taller	more tall

Movers Speaking

1 Look. Find the differences. Complete the sentences. There is one example.

Example: The bed is pink in this picture, but in this one it's orange.

1 In this picture the girl has got brown hair, but here she has ______________.
2 The jacket is red, but this one's ______________.
3 Here you can see a dolphin, but here there's a ______________.
4 There's a cupboard behind the door, but here there's a ______________.
5 Here the girl is holding a book, but here she's got ______________.

2 Look. Find the differences. Talk about the pictures.

Objectives

To complete a practice task for Part 1 of the Movers Speaking exam.

Target language

- **Key language:** objects, colours, prepositions, weather, numbers, actions, *there's / there are*, present continuous, *here, in this picture, in this one*

EXAM SKILLS

- Responding to greetings and stating their name and age with confidence
- Giving clear descriptions
- Making basic comparisons

EXAM TIPS

- Pupils will be asked their name and how old they are.
- They will need to identify four differences between two pictures. These will be related to colour, size, number, position, appearance and activity.
- Pupils should practise describing differences between two pictures and using sentence stems such as *In this picture ... but in this picture ...; Here ... but here ...; It's / There is ... in this picture, but it's / there is ... in this one.* Although these are ideal structures to use, simpler responses are also acceptable, such as *Here three cows, here four cows; This is red, this is green.*

Warmer

- Give pupils one minute to move around the classroom, saying *Hello, what's your name?* and *How old are you?* to as many classmates as possible.
- Explain that answering the questions *What's your name?* and *How old are you?* is an important part of the Speaking test.

PB94. ACTIVITY 1

Look. Find the differences. Complete the sentences. There is one example.

- Say *Open your Pupil's Books at page 94, please.* Divide the class into two groups. One group looks at the first picture and covers the second picture. The other group looks at the second picture and covers the first. They look for 15 seconds and notice as much detail as possible. They then close their books. In their group, pupils tell a partner what they remember. Monitor and help with vocabulary as necessary.
- Divide the board into two columns. Write the sentence starter *In this picture,* as a heading for each column. Elicit what each group noticed, e.g. *There is a mother and daughter. / The girl is sitting on the floor. / The girl has got brown hair.*
- Rub out sentences that are the same. Encourage pupils to help you match up sentences with the same subject but which are different, e.g. *the bed is pink / the bed is orange.*
- Ask questions about the scene to elicit more information if necessary, e.g. *What colour is the ...? What's the girl doing? What's behind the ...?*
- Write a big *but* between the two columns to show how we can talk about differences: *In this picture ... but in this picture ...* Also introduce use of *Here ... but here ...* Review use of *there is/are/isn't/aren't.*
- Pupils open their books and look at both pictures. They talk about the differences using structures highlighted on the board.
- Pupils read and complete the sentences below the pictures.
- Check answers. Volunteers read out a sentence each. Highlight how it's not necessary to repeat *in this picture* each time, and also the use of *in this one.* Pupils underline these useful structures in each sentence (*here / in this picture / in this one*).

Key: **1** blonde hair, **2** green, **3** panda, **4** bookcase, **5** cars

---

PB94. ACTIVITY 2

Look. Find the differences. Talk about the pictures.

- Explain that Activities 1 and 2 provide practice for Part 1 of the Speaking task in the Movers test.
- Explain what the test involves. Refer to the Exam tips opposite if necessary.
- In pairs, pupils talk about the differences between the pictures. They then draw a third picture with four more differences to the pictures in the test, e.g. three sheep not rabbits. They talk about the differences between their picture and their partner's.
- While pupils are working in pairs, circulate and carry out the Speaking test with each pair. Make a note of each pupil's performance in the test.

Key: (Possible answers) In this picture there's a tractor and a farmer. Here there isn't a farmer. Here the boy is wearing a blue sweater, but here he's wearing an orange one. Here the boy is wearing a scarf, but here he isn't. There are three rabbits in this picture. In this picture there are four rabbits. Here it's cloudy, but here it's sunny. Here the boy is writing. Here he is taking a photo.

Ending the lesson

- Ask pupils how they felt about the task. They can show how confident they feel about the task type with a thumbs up, thumbs down, or tilting their hands back and forth (to indicate *so-so*). Elicit any other comments about what they found easy or difficult and use pupils' feedback to plan more speaking practice.

Digital Classroom

 **Presentation Plus:** Movers Exam folder

 **Practice Extra**

Extra Resources

- **T114 – Extension activity:** *Comparing bedrooms*

Objectives

To complete a practice task for Part 2 of the Movers Speaking exam.

Target language

- **Key language:** actions, feelings, places, objects, present continuous, *has got*

Materials

- A photo or picture of a busy scene

EXAM SKILLS

- Telling a simple story

EXAM TIPS

- Pupils have a moment to look at the pictures before they start to speak. Any names of characters will be shown on the story.
- Pupils say a sentence or two about each picture without necessarily developing these comments into a narrative.
- Pupils shouldn't worry if they can't follow the narrative of the story.
- The examiner will prompt the pupil by asking questions if they need help.
- Structures that will be most helpful for pupils for this task are: *There is/are*; present tense of *be* and *have (got)*; modals *can/can't*; *must/mustn't* and the present continuous tense for actions. Pupils should also be able to describe simple feelings, e.g. *The boy is/isn't happy. The girl is sad/ surprised.*

Warmer

- Show a scene with a lot of activity. This could be a photo, poster or one of the pictures from the Pupil's Book.
- Say true and false sentences about the picture using the present continuous, *have got, there is/are, can/can't, must/ mustn't.* Pupils change seats with their partner if the sentence you say is true or stay in their seat if the sentence is false.

PB95. ACTIVITY 1

Look. Tell the story with your partner. Read and number. There is one example.

- Explain that in Part 2 of the Speaking test, pupils will tell a story. There will be four pictures. The examiner will say the title and describe the first picture. Pupils will then describe the other three pictures.
- Ask pupils what the title is (*A dolphin helps*). Focus on the first picture and elicit the names of everything in the picture (*family, boy, girl, mum, dad, car, beach, ball, sun*). Write the words on the board and then prompt pupils to give you sentences, e.g. *There is a family. Dad is driving. The girl has got a ball.* Tell pupils that they can also use words like *happy, sad* or *surprised* to describe how people are feeling.
- Pupils tell the story in pairs. Circulate and help as necessary.
- Pupils work individually to number the sentences and then check with a partner. Check with the class.
- Ask questions about each picture and elicit full answers, e.g. Picture 1: *Who's driving?* (Dad's driving). *Who's got the ball?* (the girl's got the ball).

Key: 1, 4, 2, 2, 4, 3, 2, 4

PB95. ACTIVITY 2

Look and listen. Then continue the story.

- Prompt pupils to tell you what the Movers Speaking Part 2 task involves. Refer to the Exam tips opposite if necessary.
- Ask pupils to look at the pictures on page 95. Say *These pictures tell a story. It's called Picnic time by the river. Look at the first picture. The children are having a picnic by the river. They're eating sandwiches. Their dad's fishing. Two parrots are watching them.*
- Play the first part of the story. Say *Now look at the pictures. How do you think the story continues?* In groups, pupils can talk about the pictures and continue the story. Say *Now you tell the story.*
- Pairs take turns talking about each picture. Make a note of each pupil's performance in the test.
- Review the story as a class and play the **Audio** of example answers. Address any issues that you noticed and praise pupils on their good descriptions and speaking.

Key: (Possible answer) Picture 2: The children are looking at a big fish in the river. The girl is pointing to the fish. Dad is standing up and looking at the fish too. They are surprised. Picture 3: Everyone is looking at the two parrots. The parrots are flying. They've got the sandwiches. The fish is swimming in the river. Picture 4: The sandwiches are falling. The fish is jumping. The fish is eating the sandwich. Dad and the children are happy and laughing. The parrots are sad.

98

Audio scripts for the Exam folder can be downloaded from *Teacher Resources.*

Ending the lesson

- Ask pupils how they felt about the task. They can show how confident they feel about the task type with a thumbs up, thumbs down, or tilting their hands back and forth (to indicate *so-so*). Elicit any other comments about what they found easy or difficult and use pupils' feedback to plan more speaking practice.

Digital Classroom

Presentation Plus: Movers Exam folder

Practice Extra

Audio 98

Extra Resources

- **Teacher Resources:** Downloadable Exam folder Audio Script
- **T114 – Extension activity:** *Story-telling*

Movers Speaking

1 Look. Tell the story with your partner. Read and number. There is one example.

A dolphin helps

Example: The girl is crying. 3

The family are driving to the beach. ☐

A dolphin has got the ball. ☐

The children are playing with a ball. ☐

Mum is eating a sandwich. ☐

The girl is sitting on her dad's shoulders. ☐

The boy can't get the ball. ☐

Dad is taking a photo. ☐

The family are watching the dolphin. ☐

2 98 Look and listen. Then continue the story.

Picnic time by the river

Unit 0

AB4. ACTIVITY 1

Read and complete the sentences.

Key: a nine, sister. b I'm, reading, comic.

AB5. ACTIVITY 2

Listen and write.

Key: 2 11 lorries, 3 17 games, 4 12 cameras, 5 19 trains, 6 16 computers, 7 20 dolls, 8 15 bikes

AB6. ACTIVITY 1

Match and write.

Key: 2 Lenny, 3 Alex, 4 Stella, 5 Meera, 6 Suzy

AB6. ACTIVITY 2

Now answer the questions.

Key: 2 No, she isn't. 3 No, he isn't. 4 No, she isn't. 5 Yes, she is. 6 Yes, he is.

AB6. ACTIVITY 3

Read and match.

Key: 2 d, 3 b, 4 a, 5 c

AB7. ACTIVITY 1

Read, write and colour.

Key: Children's names (left to right, top row first): Beth, Fred, Sally; Paul, Jane, Vicky, Zak
Pupils should colour the picture as follows: purple ball, brown dog near Beth, orange kite, yellow T-shirt and blue jeans for Jane, green camera, grey dog on the bench next to Zak.

AB7. ACTIVITY 2

Look at the picture. Correct the sentences.

Key: 2 No. Vicky's got a camera. 3 No. Paul and Jane are playing hockey. 4 No. Sally's got a bike. 5 No. Zak and Beth have got dogs. 6 No. The dog's getting the ball.

AB8. ACTIVITY 1

Say and write.

Key: /aɪ/ spider, nine, five, drive, bike, kite, like; /eɪ/ late, play, paint, grey, train, plane

AB8. ACTIVITY 2

Complete the words with the letters.

Key: 2 Eight girls are painting. 3 We've got a bike and a grey car. 4 I like eating sandwiches and cake. 5 Can you play the piano?

AB8. ACTIVITY 3

Read and complete the table.

Key:

Name	Peter	Daisy
Ride a bike	✓	✓
Swim	✗	✓
Play the piano	✓	✓
Play badminton	✓	✗

AB9. ACTIVITY 1

Listen and join.

Key: 4, 10, 2, 8, 15, 5, 19, 13, 17, 9, 4, 16, 18, 3, 11, 1

AB9. ACTIVITY 2

Complete and answer.

Key: Pupils' own answers.

Unit 1

AB10. ACTIVITY 1

Listen and match.

Key: Simon c, Grandma and Grandpa Star b, (Mr and Mrs Star e,) Aunt May a, Uncle Fred f, Stella and Suzy d

AB10. ACTIVITY 2

Look at Activity 1 and complete the sentences.

Key: 2 grandson, 3 granddaughters, 4 daughter, 5 son, 6 uncle, 7 parents, 8 aunt

AB11. ACTIVITY 1

Who is speaking? Read and write 'a' or 'b'.

Key: 2 a, 3 b, 4 a, 5 b

AB11. ACTIVITY 2

Read and complete the sentences.

Key: 2 uncle, 3 sleeping, 4 aunt, 5 good, 6 grandparents, 7 dining room, 8 parents

AB12. ACTIVITY 1

Read and circle the best answer.

Key: 2 b, 3 a, 4 b, 5 a, 6 a

AB12. ACTIVITY 2

Look and match the sentences.

Key: 2 b, 3 f, 4 d, 5 a, 6 c

AB13. ACTIVITY 1

Find and write the words.

Key: 2 naughty, 3 quiet, 4 beard, 5 funny, 6 curly, 7 straight, 8 fair

AB14. ACTIVITY 1

Look and write.

Key: 2 baker, 3 burgers, 4 computer

AB14. ACTIVITY 2

Write the missing letters.

Key: All of the missing letters are *er*

AB14. ACTIVITY 3

Look and circle 'true' or false'.

Key: **2** false, **3** false, **4** true, **5** false, **6** false

AB15. ACTIVITY 1

Listen and colour and write. There is one example.

Key: **1** Colour the boy's shoes brown. **2** Write 'comic' next to the comic. **3** Colour the dog red. **4** Colour the big bike green. **5** Colour the grandmother's jacket yellow.

AB16. ACTIVITIES 1, 2 & 3

Key: Pupils' own answers.

AB17. ACTIVITY 1

Listen and colour and write. There is one example.

Key: **1** Colour the hair of the naughty girl next to the tree yellow. **2** Colour the grandmother's hair blue. **3** Colour the curly hair of the girl on the bike red. **4** Write 'Test' on the paper the boy is holding. **5** Colour the straight hair of the man black.

AB17. ACTIVITY 2

Write the answers.

Key: He's got straight black hair, a black beard and a moustache. **2** He's wearing a big dirty hat and an old jacket. **3** Lock and Key are in the park. **4** The pet thief. **5** She is wearing a jacket and a hat like the pet thief. **6** Because Key takes her cat and she is not a pet thief.

Unit 2

AB18. ACTIVITY 1

Match. Write the words.

Key: **2** lift, live, **3** basement, balcony, **4** downstairs, door, **5** street, stairs

AB18. ACTIVITY 2

Complete the crossword.

Key: **Across: 4** flat, **5** town, **7** basement, **8** village, **9** floor
Down: 2 upstairs, **3** street, **6** home, **7** balcony

AB19. ACTIVITY 1

Read and complete.

Key: **2** street, **3** floors, **4** upstairs, **5** downstairs, **6** balcony

AB19. ACTIVITY 2

Write about your home. Draw or take a photo.

Key: Pupils' own answers.

AB20. ACTIVITY 1

Look at the photos. Read and circle. Write number '1' or '2' in the box.

Key: **2** carrying (1), **3** carrying (1), **4** smiling (1), **5** on (2), **6** coming in (2)

AB20. ACTIVITY 2

Read and complete. Match.

Key: **2** lift b, **3** pen g, **4** wardrobe f, **5** camera e, **6** lorry h, **7** laptop c, **8** downstairs a

AB21. ACTIVITY 1

Match the words and numbers.

Key: **1** ninety, **2** eighteen, **3** forty, **4** seventeen, **5** fifty, **6** sixty, **8** thirteen

AB21. ACTIVITY 2

Read and colour.

Key: 93 green, 94 purple, 95 red, 83 grey, 84 pink, 85 brown, 73 blue, 74 orange, 75 yellow

AB22. ACTIVITY 1

Look and write the missing letters.

Key: city, thirteen, twenty, sheep, country, seventeen, seventy, three, thirty, tree, street

AB22. ACTIVITY 2

Read and write the house numbers.

Key: 13, 20, 17, 18, 40, 3

AB23. ACTIVITY 1

Read the text and choose the best answer.

Key: **1** C, **2** B, **3** A, **4** B, **5** C, **6** B

AB24. ACTIVITY 1

Match the words and the contractions.

Key: **2** e, **3** b, **4** a, **5** d

AB24. ACTIVITY 2

Reread the description on Pupil's Book page 25. Complete the table.

Key: **2** bed, **3** toys, **4** cat

AB24. ACTIVITIES 3 & 4

Key: Pupils' own answers.

AB25. ACTIVITY 1

Read and complete the table.

Key:

	city	village	flat	house	garden	balcony	basement
Jack	✓	✗	✓	✗	✗	✓	✓
Sally	✓	✗	✓	✗	✗	✓	✗
Paul	✓	✗	✗	✓	✓	✗	✗
Mary	✗	✓	✗	✓	✓	✗	✓

AB25. ACTIVITY 2

Write the answers.

Key: 1 They're in Mrs Potts' house. 2 Because she thinks it's got a monster. 3 He's scared. 4 Lock and Key see something and they're scared. 5 Because they think that the cat is a monster. 6 Because she's got her cat.

AB26. ACTIVITY 1

Listen and write the numbers.

Key: 2 43, 3 42, 4 70, 5 37, 6 50

AB26. ACTIVITY 2

Read and match.

Key: 2 c, 3 e, 4 b, 5 d

AB27. ACTIVITY 3

Circle the odd one out and say.

Key: 2 balcony, 3 monster, 4 basement, 5 thirty, 6 street, 7 climb, 8 lift, 9 shop, 10 listen

AB27. ACTIVITY 4

Complete the crossword using the words from Activity 3. Use the code to write the message.

Key: Across: balcony, monster, street, listen
Down: shop, lift, basement, climb, down, forty
Message: Well done!

Unit 3

AB28. ACTIVITY 1

Read and number the sentences.

Key: 2 b, 3 a, 4 i, 5 g, 6 h, 7 e, 8 d, 9 c

AB28. ACTIVITY 2

Look and read and write.

Key: 1 dressed, 2 boy, 3 He's having a shower. 4 It's seven o'clock. 5&6 e.g. The boy gets up at seven o'clock. The woman with curly hair is saying goodbye.

AB29. ACTIVITY 1

Look and match.

Key: Eleven o'clock a, Seven o'clock f, Six o'clock c, Three o'clock e, One o'clock b

AB29. ACTIVITY 2

Write 'before' or 'after'.

Key: 2 before, 3 after, 4 before, 5 after, 6 before

Now write two more sentences.

Key: Pupils' own answers.

AB30. ACTIVITY 3

Talk to your friend. Is your routine the same or different?

Key: Pupils' own answers.

AB30. ACTIVITY 1

Find and write the words.

Key: Tuesday, Wednesday, Thursday, Friday, Saturday, Sunday

AB30. ACTIVITY 2

Look, read and write.

Key: Thursday, Tuesday, Saturday, Friday, (Monday), Wednesday, Sunday

AB31. ACTIVITIES 1, 2 & 3

Key: Pupils' own answers.

AB32. ACTIVITY 1

Say and write.

Key: -s: gets up, puts on, eats;
-es: brushes, washes, dances, watches

AB32. ACTIVITY 2

Read and match.

Key: 2 washes her hands, 3 dances, 4 catches the bus, 5 wakes up, 6 puts on clothes, 7 starts school, 8 plays, 9 brushes his hair

AB33. ACTIVITY 1

What food does Lily have in these places? Listen and write a letter in each box. There is one example.

Key: ice cream B, cake C, sweets D, banana E, sandwich A

AB34. ACTIVITY 1

Look and complete the times.

Key: 1 three, 2 past, 3 o'clock, 4 half past, 5 ten, 6 past eight

AB34. ACTIVITY 2

Reread the blog on Pupil's Book page 35. Which activity does Sally do?

Key: wash

AB34. ACTIVITIES 3, 4, 5 & 6

Key: Pupils' own answers.

AB35. ACTIVITY 1

Read and complete the story.

Key: 2 shower, 3 kitchen, 4 jacket, 5 bus, 6 school, 7 four o'clock, 8 computer, 9 bed, 10 nine o'clock

AB35. ACTIVITY 2

Write the answers.

Key: 1 They work a lot and get up before you and me. 2 They never get up before ten o'clock. 3 Because it's nine o'clock. They're in bed. 4 clever and quiet, 5 no, 6 No, he doesn't, because they get up late.

Unit 4

AB36. ACTIVITY 1

Sort and write the words.

Key: 2 town, 3 hospital, 4 supermarket, 5 cinema, 6 bus station, 7 building, 8 village, 9 car park, 10 hotel, 11 school, 12 library

AB36. ACTIVITY 2

Look at the code. Write the secret message.

Key: There's a swimming pool next to the cinema.

AB37. ACTIVITY 1

Look, read and write. Match.

Key: **2** hotel, **3** sports centre, **4** bank, **5** cinema, **6** bus station, **7** swimming pool, **8** market; 4, 7, 2, 5, 1, 8, 6, 3

AB37. ACTIVITY 2

Complete the picture. Answer the questions.

Key: **1** car park, **2** The bus station is next to the library / car park. **3** The cinema is next to the sports centre / opposite the market. **4** The car park is opposite the library / between the market and the bus station. **5** The sports centre is opposite the market / between the cinema and the library. **6** The library is opposite the car park / between the sports centre and the bus station.

AB38. ACTIVITY 1

Read and circle the best answer.

Key: **2** b, **3** c, **4** c, **5** c, **6** a, **7** b, **8** a

AB38. ACTIVITY 2

Read and match.

Key: Pupils draw lines: from kite to top of cupboard, from T-shirt to in cupboard, from crayons to on desk, from shoes to under bed, from toy box to between bed and bookcase

AB39. ACTIVITY 1

Read and tick (✓). Listen and check.

Key: Pupils' own answers.

AB39. ACTIVITY 2

Write. What must/mustn't you do in these places?

Key: (Possible answers) In the library I mustn't speak loudly. In school I mustn't run. At school I must respect my teachers. At home I must help my parents.

AB40. ACTIVITY 1

Complete with 'ere', 'air' or 'ear' and number the pictures.

Key: **1** hair, **2** Where, chair, bear, **3** pears, **4** There, bear, chair; 2, 4, 3

AB40. ACTIVITY 2

Look and write.

Key:

-ere	*-air*	*-ear*
where there	hair chair	pear bear

1 chair, pear, **2** bear, chair, **3** There, pears, chair, **4** pear, hair, pear, hair, **5** Where, bear, **6** There, chair, bear

AB41. ACTIVITY 1

Read the story. Choose a word from the box. Write the correct word next to numbers 1–5. There is one example.

Key: **1** park, **2** dog, **3** walk, **4** supermarket, **5** book, **6** Jack's week

AB42. ACTIVITY 1

Circle the nouns. Use red for people, green for places, and blue for things.

Key: (red) superhero, (green) New York City, USA, (blue) Brooklyn Superhero Supply Company, shop, costumes, masks, capes, kit, robot, message, ink

AB42. ACTIVITY 2

Reread the adverts on Pupil's Book page 43. Complete the table.

Key:

Shop name	Moving **1** Books	**2** C + M ice cream
Location	different places	**3** in a van
What can you buy?	**4** books	ice cream
Why is the shop special?	It can go to different **5** places	**6** it drives to your street or your school

AB42. ACTIVITIES 3 & 4

Key: Pupils' own answers.

AB43. ACTIVITY 1

Put the words in groups

Key: Actions: have lunch, get up, catch, play, wash
Places: cinema, shop, hospital, library, café
Home: basement, stairs, balcony, lift, downstairs
Family: uncle, daughter, parent, grandson, aunt

AB43. ACTIVITY 2

Write the answers.

Key: **1** They're looking for work. **2** He is thinking the woman is Lottie Cash, the bank robber. **3** Because it's a lovely day for shopping in the city. **4** They're going to go to the bank to stop the bank robber. **5** Key shouts at Mrs Potts' friend. Mrs Potts hits him with her bag. **6** Because her friend is not Lottie Cash.

AB44. ACTIVITY 1

Read and order the words. Make sentences.

Key: **2** Tom never wakes up before 7 o'clock. **3** Mary never rides her bike at the weekend. **4** We always wash our hands before dinner. **5** Jim and Peter never do their homework in the evening. **6** They always read on Sunday mornings.

AB44. ACTIVITY 2

Find the words.

Key: always, swim, market, town, never, read, daughter, robot, tell, library, yes, station, need, dinner

AB44. ACTIVITY 2

Now answer the questions.

Key: There are five town words. They are: cinema, market, town, library, station.

AB45. ACTIVITY 3

Circle the odd one out and say.

Key: **2** shower, **3** afternoon, **4** bedtime, **5** funfair, **6** stairs, **7** teacher, **8** children, **9** Tuesday, **10** never

AB45. ACTIVITY 4

Complete the crossword using the words from Activity 3. Use the code to write the message.

Key: **Across:** feet, Tuesday, children, never, shower
Down: bedtime, stairs, afternoon, teacher, funfair
Message: Correct!

Unit 5

AB46. ACTIVITY 1

Look and write the words.

Key: **2** eye, **3** tooth, **4** shoulder, **5** stomach, **6** leg, **7** foot, **8** hair, **9** ear, **10** nose, **11** mouth, **12** back, **13** arm, **14** hand

AB46. ACTIVITY 2

Complete the sentences.

Key: **2** toothache, **3** headache, **4** temperature, **5** stomach-ache, **6** cough

AB47. ACTIVITY 1

Read and circle.

Key: **2** tooth, **3** foot, **4** leg, **5** arm, **6** hand

AB47. ACTIVITY 2

Look at Activity 1. Write.

Key:
2 What's the matter? My leg hurts. I can't ride my bike.
3 What's the matter? My tooth hurts. I can't eat.
4 What's the matter? My hand hurts. I can't catch the ball.
5 What's the matter? My foot hurts. I can't kick the ball.
6 What's the matter? My arm hurts. I can't play tennis.

AB48. ACTIVITY 1

Listen and write the number.

Key: a 3, b 6, c 2, d 5, e l, f 4

AB48. ACTIVITY 2

Choose a place and write the rules.

Key: Pupils' own answers.

AB49. ACTIVITY 1

Look and match.

Key: **2** pick up a big bag, **3** listen to music, **4** play computer games, **5** eat cakes, biscuits or chocolate, **6** go swimming

AB49. ACTIVITY 2

Now write sentences.

Key: **2** When you've got a backache you mustn't pick up a big bag.
3 When you've got an earache you mustn't listen to music.
4 When you've got a headache you mustn't play computer games.
5 When you've got a toothache you mustn't eat cakes, biscuits or chocolate.
6 When you've got a cold you mustn't go swimming.

AB50. ACTIVITY 1

Look, circle and write. Use ''s' and ''ve'.

Key: **2** He's, **3** We've, **4** She's, **5** I've, **6** She's

AB50. ACTIVITY 2

Match and write.

Key: (Possible answers) **2** I've got a cough. I must go to the doctor.
3 She's got a toothache. She mustn't eat sweets.
4 They've got a stomach-ache. They mustn't eat burgers. They must go to bed.

AB51. ACTIVITY 1

Look and read and write.

Key: **1** T-shirt, **2** hospital, **3** He's talking on his phone. **4** They're on a table. **5&6** e.g. The old man has got a backache. The girl is reading.

AB52. ACTIVITY 1

Look and write the affirmative or negative imperatives.

Key: **1** Don't run, **2** Don't use, **3** Write, **4** raise, **5** don't eat

AB52. ACTIVITY 2

Reread the leaflet on Pupil's Book page 53. Complete the table.

Key: **1** cold, **2** fast, **3** count, **4** Eat (a spoon of)
Pupils' own answers.

AB52. ACTIVITIES 3 & 4

Key: Pupils' own answers.

AB53. ACTIVITY 1

Read and order the words. Make sentences.

Key: **2** We mustn't sleep in class. **3** Vicky must stay in bed because she's got a temperature. **4** Daisy mustn't carry big bags because she's got a backache. **5** We must clean our teeth with toothpaste. **6** What's the matter with Jack?

AB53. ACTIVITY 2

Write the answers.

Key: **1** She wants them to look after her painting. **2** He's got a toothache. **3** Because he likes all the cakes. **4** He's got an apple cake, a carrot cake, a lemon cake and a chocolate cake. **5** He's got a stomach-ache. **6** A thief has got the painting.

Unit 6

AB54. ACTIVITY 1

Look at the picture. Sort and write the words.

Key: 2 field, 3 forest, 4 plant, 5 lake, 6 leaf, 7 grass, 8 waterfall, 9 rock

AB54. ACTIVITY 2

Read the text. Write 'yes' or 'no'.

Key: 2 No, 3 Yes, 4 No, 5 Yes, 6 No, 7 No, 8 Yes

AB55. ACTIVITIES 1 & 2

Key: Pupils' own answers.

AB56. ACTIVITY 1

Find the pairs and number the pictures.

Key: 2 loud – 9 quiet, 3 strong – 10 weak, 4 hungry – 8 thirsty, 5 fat – 6 thin
(clockwise) 1, 10, 7, 9, 5, 4, 6, 2, 3, 8

AB56. ACTIVITY 2

Look and read. Then number and write the questions.

Key: 2 Shall I get a chair? 3 Shall I get you an ice cream? 4 Shall I make lunch? 5 Shall I get you a drink?

AB57. ACTIVITY 1

Put the words in groups.

Key: People: hungry, thin, strong, thirsty, fat
People and places: good, hot, loud, cold, quiet, bad

AB57. ACTIVITY 2

Look and read. Correct the sentences.

Key: 2 No. It's loud. 3 No. He's very strong. 4 No. It's very bad. 5 No. She's hungry. 6 No. It's cold.

AB58. ACTIVITY 1

Write the words. Match.

Key: 2 river, 3 forest, 4 grass, 5 bread, 6 river, 7 crocodile, 8 four hungry rats, 9 three thirsty parrots

AB58. ACTIVITY 2

Match the sentence halves.

Key: 2 d, 3 a, 4 e, 5 f, 6 b

AB59. ACTIVITY 1

Look and read. Choose the correct words and write them on the lines. There is one example.

Key: 1 grass, 2 a picnic, 3 a forest, 4 a tree, 5 a field, 6 a leaf

AB60. ACTIVITY 1

Read and circle the words that need a capital letter.

Key: Tokyo, Japan, Milly, Ambar

AB60. ACTIVITY 2

Reread the emails on Pupil's Book page 61. Complete and write notes for you.

Key:

Ruby	Metin
4 riding horses	2 Istanbul 3 skateboarding 5 pollution

AB60. ACTIVITIES 3 & 4

Key: Pupils' own answers.

AB61. ACTIVITY 1

Listen, colour and write.

Key: Pupils colour: the flower under the tree red, the apple on the blanket yellow, the hair of the boy next to the river black, and the duck in the river orange. They write 'blanket' below the blanket.

AB61. ACTIVITY 2

Write the answers.

Key: 1 They're going to the countryside. 2 In picture there is nothing. 3 She's taking a photo of the lake. 4 Because he thinks she's cold. 5 Because he thinks Lock is hungry. 6 Because Lock doesn't want his food and Mrs Potts doesn't want his blanket, so he is angry.

AB62. ACTIVITIES 1 & 2

Key: Pupils' own answers.

AB63. ACTIVITY 3

Circle the odd one out.

Key: 2 hungry, 3 hurts, 4 stomach, 5 field, 6 leaf, 7 fat, 8 picnic, 9 grass, 10 blanket

AB63. ACTIVITY 4

Complete the crossword using the words from Activity 3. Use the code to write the message.

Key: **Across:** grass, hurts, picnic, leaf, blanket
Down: hungry, stomach, fat, shoulder, field
Message: Nice try!

Unit 7

AB64. ACTIVITY 1

Put these animals in alphabetical order.

Key: 2 bear, 3 dolphin, 4 jellyfish, 5 kangaroo, 6 panda, 7 parrot, 8 shark, 9 whale

AB64. ACTIVITY 2

Follow the animals. Answer.

Key: bear, panda, kangaroo, lion, whale, giraffe, elephant, dolphin, jellyfish, shark, monkey, parrot, hippo, mouse, bat, tiger, fish: 17; library, hospital, cinema, market; funny, clean, strong, hungry, thirsty, clever, long, huge, naughty

AB65. ACTIVITY 1

Look at the animals. Read and correct.

Key: **1** This animal has got four legs and a lot of hair on its head. It eats meat and sleeps a lot. It's a big cat. **2** This big brown animal lives in Australia. It's got two long, strong legs and two short, thin arms. It can jump. It carries its baby in a bag next to its stomach. **3** This small black or brown animal can fly but it isn't a bird. It eats fruit and insects. It sleeps in the day and wakes up and flies at night.

AB65. ACTIVITY 2

Write about your favourite wild animal.

Key: Pupils' own answers.

AB66. ACTIVITY 1

Read and circle.

Key: **2** longer, **3** louder, **4** quicker, **5** taller, **6** stronger

AB66. ACTIVITY 2

Look at the picture. Read and write 'yes' or 'no'.

Key: **2** Yes, **3** Yes, **4** No, **5** Yes, **6** No

AB67. ACTIVITY 1

Read and match. Write the words in the table.

Key: **2** e, **3** k, **4** c, **5** a, **6** h, **7** d, **8** l, **9** b, **10** f, **11** g, **12** i
longer: cleaner, weaker, quieter; bigger: thinner, hotter, better, fatter; happier: easier, dirtier, hungrier; different!: worse, better

AB67. ACTIVITY 2

Colour and write.

Key: Pupils' own answers.

AB68. ACTIVITY 1

Think and complete the words.

Key: food, forest, elephant, field, faster, giraffe, cough, fish, laugh, frog, dolphin

AB68. ACTIVITY 2

Look, read and write 'yes' or 'no'.

Key: **b** Yes, **c** No, **d** Yes, **e** No, **f** No, **g** No

AB69. ACTIVITY 1

Listen and write. There is one example.

Key: **1** 15, **2** Sea animals, **3** Shark, **4** Fish and dolphins, **5** Sea World

AB70. ACTIVITY 1

Circle the adjectives.

Key: **2** big, **3** orange, black, **4** bright

AB70. ACTIVITY 2

Reread the imaginary animal description on Pupil's Book page 71. Complete the chart.

Key: **2** pink, **3** orange, **4** teeth; Pupils' own answers.

AB70. ACTIVITIES 3 AND 4

Key: Pupils' own answers.

AB71. ACTIVITY 1

Sort and write the words.

Key: **2** bigger, **3** dirtier, **4** easier, **5** older, **6** quieter, **7** smaller, **8** stronger, **9** worse, **10** fatter

AB71. ACTIVITY 2

Now find the words.

Key:

r	d	u	j	m	o	l	d	e	r
b	i	g	g	e	r	r	t	g	e
m	r	x	w	p	m	j	i	q	a
s	t	r	o	n	g	e	r	u	s
e	i	e	r	t	q	f	a	i	i
b	e	i	s	p	w	p	v	e	e
x	r	o	e	u	m	i	a	t	r
s	m	a	l	l	e	r	b	e	o
s	j	q	f	a	t	t	e	r	n
b	e	t	t	e	r	a	q	b	s

AB71. ACTIVITY 3

Write the answers.

Key: **1** They're tired and thirsty. **2** To get a cold drink. **3** Robin Motors is a car thief. He's got curly brown hair. **4** Because the man is uglier than Robin Motors. **5** The man's nose is bigger and his hair is longer. Robin Motors is taller and thinner. **6** Robin Motors takes Lock and Key's car.

Unit 8

AB72. ACTIVITY 1

Match. Write the words.

Key: **2** the sun, **3** rain, **4** snow, **5** a rainbow, **6** a cloud

AB72. ACTIVITY 2

Read and circle the correct word.

Key: **2** rainbow, **3** cloudy, **4** snow, **5** raining, **6** sunny, **7** raining, **8** dry, **9** raining, **10** snowing

AB73. ACTIVITY 1

Listen and draw the weather.

Key: **1** e windy in mountains, **2** a raining on beach, **3** d cloudy in forest, **4** c, d sunny and windy in city, **5** b snowing and cold in countryside, **6** f hot and sunny at lake

AB73. ACTIVITY 2

Now complete the sentences.

Key: **2** it's sunny and windy. **3** it's cloudy. **4** it's (hot and) sunny. **5** it's snowing (and very cold). **6** it's raining.

AB74. ACTIVITY 1

Read and complete the sentences.

Key: **2** were, **3** was, **4** brilliant, **5** wasn't, **6** scarf, **7** sweater, **8** gloves, **9** weren't

AB74. ACTIVITY 2

Look at the code. Write the secret message.

Key: We were in the jungle last week. It wasn't wet and windy and we weren't cold. It was fun.

AB75. ACTIVITY 1

Choose two more times and write answers for you. Then ask and answer.

Key: Pupils' own answers.

AB75. ACTIVITY 2

Write about your weekend.

Key: Pupils' own answers.

AB76. ACTIVITY 1

Circle the correct letters and complete the words.

Key: **2** y, **3** f, **4** ee, **5** air, **6** gh

AB76. ACTIVITY 2

Read and complete.

Key: **2** bees, **3** sheep, **4** jumps, **5** going, **6** elephant, **7** stomach-ache, **8** mustn't

AB77. ACTIVITY 1

Read the text. Choose the right words and write them on the lines.

Key: **1** are, **2** a, **3** because, **4** many, **5** don't

AB78. ACTIVITY 1

Complete the table.

Key: What? column: a concert, a game night;
Where? column: at my house, at the park, at a restaurant;
When? column: after school, at 7 p.m., on Saturday

AB78. ACTIVITY 2

Reread the invitation on Pupil's Book page 79. Complete the table.

Key: **2** Saturday, **3** 4 p.m., **4** garden

AB78. ACTIVITIES 3 & 4

Key: Pupils' own answers.

AB79. ACTIVITY 1

Write about your day. Draw a picture.

Key: Pupils' own answers.

AB79. ACTIVITY 2

Write the answers.

Key: **1** Because he wants to ask Robin Motors some questions. **2** Because they haven't got a car. **3** In Baker Street. **4** Because their car was in Baker Street. / Because they think he was in their car. **5** Because Robin Motors was at the police station. **6** Because Key was right. / Because the man at the café wasn't Robin Motors.

AB80. ACTIVITY 1

Read, colour and draw.

Key: Pupils colour: the thinner bear grey, the longer snake green, the shorter snake yellow, the smaller bat black, the bigger bat grey, the louder parrot red, the quieter parrot yellow, the bigger whale blue, the smaller whale black and white, the happier jellyfish pink, the sadder jellyfish purple.
Pupils draw: a man in the boat, wearing a coat and a scarf, looking at the fruit in the trees.

AB81. ACTIVITY 2

Circle the odd one out and say.

Key: **2** rainbow, **3** beach, **4** dry, **5** bear, **6** hat, **7** dirty, **8** weather, **9** teacher, **10** raining
2 Kangaroo, shark and lion are animals.
3 Wind, snow and rain are weather.
4 Scarf, sweater and coat are clothes.
5 Parrot, bat and bird can fly.
6 Wet, cold and dry are weather adjectives.
7 Sunny, windy and cloudy are weather words.
8 Weaker, better and hotter are comparative adjectives.
9 Easier, worse and thinner are comparative adjectives.
10 Countryside, mountains and beach are places.

AB81. ACTIVITY 3

Complete the crossword using the words from Activity 2. Use the code to write the message.

Key: **Across:** dry, bear, teacher, beach, dirty
Down: rainbow, panda, weather, hat, raining
Message: Goodbye!

AB82. ACTIVITY 1

Listen and number.

Key: a 3, b 4, c 1, d 2, e 5

AB82. ACTIVITIES 2 & 3

Key: Pupils' own answers.

AB83. ACTIVITIES 1 & 2

Read and choose. Match.

Key: 2, 1, 5, 3, 4
1 window, **2** park, **3** help, **4** don't step, **5** can't

AB83. ACTIVITY 3

Key: Pupils' own answers.

AB84. ACTIVITY 1

Listen and number.

Key: a 1, b 3, c 2, d 4

AB84. ACTIVITY 2

Complete. Choose the right answer.

Key: **1** like/b, **2** hurts/b, **3** like/a, **4** help/a

AB85. ACTIVITY 1

Read and match.

Key: a 3, b 5, c 2, e 4, f 6

Unit 0

Page 4

- **Extension activity: *What's it called?***

Teach the following chant to the class. First they perform as a whole class and then in two groups, one group asking and the other responding. Then divide pupils into groups. They create their own versions of the chant, substituting key words. They perform for the class: one pupil giving the information and the rest of the group asking the questions.

I've got a sister.
What's she called?
She's called Emma and she's ten.

I've got a horse.
What's it called?
It's called Blacky and it's white.

- **Consolidation activity: *Who's who?***

Materials: Two strips of paper for each pupil

Hand out two strips of paper to each pupil. They write and complete the third sentence from Activity Book Activity 2 (*I've got a …*) on one strip and the fifth (*I like …*) on the other strip. Put pupils into groups of four. They place the strips face down on the table and mix them around. Pupils take it in turns to turn over a strip, read it aloud and guess whose it is. Each pupil gets a point for a correct guess. When they have guessed for all the sentences, make new groups of four and repeat. Remind them of the classroom language, e.g. *Yes, that's right. / That's me. / Wrong!*

Page 5

- **Consolidation activity 1: *Find the number***

Materials: Two rolled-up newspapers

Write the numbers *eleven* to *twenty* in words at random over the board. Divide the class into two or three teams, depending on the size of the class. They line up one behind the other facing the board. Give a rolled-up newspaper to pupils at the front of each team. Call a number, e.g. *Fifteen*. Pupils run to hit the correct word. Award a point to the pupil who hits the right word first. The pupils go to the back of the line. Hand the newspapers to the pupils at the front of the line and continue until all the pupils have had a turn. The team with the most points is the winner.

- **Consolidation activity 2: *Spell it***

Materials: Alphabet cards from Teacher's Resource Book

Pupils close their books. Hand out copies of the alphabet cards from *Kid's Box Teacher's Resource Book 3*, page 80 (one copy per pupil). Pupils cut along the dotted lines to make cards. Divide the class into pairs. Pairs put together their alphabet cards so they have two of each letter. Spell out the word *C-A-M-E-R-A*. Pupils work with their partner to arrange the alphabet cards to make the word on their desks. Monitor. Elicit spelling and write *camera* on the board for pupils to check. Pupils mix up their cards. Spell out *kite*, *monster* and *doll* for pupils to make the three words with their cards in the same way. Pairs compare their words with other pairs. Check with the class. Pupils mix up their cards. Repeat with *bike* and *lorry*. Then repeat for *helicopter*, and finally *game*, *train* and *computer*.

Note: It is important for pupils to mix up their cards between the groups/pairs of words, as they only have two of each letter of the alphabet in their set of cards (so they can't arrange the letters for, e.g. *computer* and *helicopter* at the same time, as they would need three letter 'e's).

If you do not wish to use the alphabet cards, pupils do a similar activity with paper and pen. They close their books and work individually. They write numbers 1–10 down the side of the page. Spell out ten words from the lesson, e.g. *1 D-O-L-L, 2 G-A-M-E*. Spell each word once. Pupils check their words in groups. Elicit one answer from each group. They must spell the word back to you. Other groups can help if the group makes a mistake.

Page 6

- **Consolidation activity: *Making patterns***

Write the following words on the board at random: *jumping, reading, sitting, drinking, listening, eating, playing, writing, talking, kicking, hitting, painting, riding, doing, showing*. Above each word, write its infinitive. Quickly check understanding of the words. Draw three columns on the board. At the top of one, write *write / writing*. At the top of another, write *jump / jumping*. At the top of the third, write *sit / sitting*. Put pupils into groups of three. They draw the columns in their notebooks and then place the other words in the right columns. Monitor pupils as they are working. Check with the class and elicit what's different about the spelling of each group of words.

- **Extension activity: *Jumbled questions***

Materials: A big piece of paper with the following written large enough for all pupils to read:

1. juice 's drinking She orange .
2. doing What Suzy is ?
3. a riding He bike is .
4. Lenny eating 's What ?
5. friend your playing baseball Is ?
6. isn't No, she .
7. is Meera a book reading .
8. 's Simon tennis playing .
9. is he Yes, .
10. teacher your is doing What ?

Display the large piece of paper with the jumbled questions and statements. Pupils work in pairs to unjumble them and write them correctly on a piece of paper. Give a time limit, e.g. five minutes. Pairs swap papers with other pairs. Correct as a class. Pupils correct each other's work. Make sure pupils read contractions (or not) correctly. Elicit an answer to question 10.

Key: **1** She's drinking orange juice. **2** What is Suzy doing? **3** He is riding a bike. **4** What's Lenny eating? **5** Is your friend playing baseball? **6** No, she isn't. **7** Meera is reading a book. **8** Simon's playing tennis. **9** Yes, he is. **10** What is your teacher doing?

Page 7

- **Consolidation activity: *Magic pocket***

Show pupils your bag or your pocket. Say, e.g. *Listen. In my magic pocket I've got a red ball, a yellow pencil, a green ruler, a small book and a fat doll.* Pause. Tell pupils not to write anything down. Say *What have I got in my magic pocket?* Elicit the objects. They don't have to be in the right order. Pupils work in pairs and write a list of five things in their magic pocket/bag. They take turns to say them to the class and for the class to remember.

- **Extension activity: *Put them in order***

Pupils work in pairs. Elicit the toys from the lesson and other toys pupils know. Write them on a mind map on the board, with *Toys* in the centre. Pupils work in pairs. They copy down the toys in their notebooks, writing them in alphabetical order. Before they start, check they remember how to sequence, e.g. *ball, bike*. Check with the class by eliciting and then writing the correct list down the side of the board.

Page 8

- **Extension activity: *Sound cards***

Materials: Small pieces of card

Write words from the lesson with /aɪ/ and /eɪ/ on the board. Give pupils small pieces of card and ask them to write each of the words on a piece of card. On the other side they should draw either a circle or a triangle to match the sound of the word (circle for words with the /aɪ/ sound and triangle for words with the /eɪ/ sound. In pairs, they stack their cards word up in front of them. They take turns to present their first word on the top of their stack to their partner, who says the word and the sound. Then they turn the card over to check – circle for /aɪ/ and triangle for /eɪ/. Pairs continue in turns until their stack is finished.

Page 9

- **Extension activity: *Role play***

Make groups of four. Elicit from pupils who the four 'characters' in the story are (answerphone, cat owner, Lock, Key). Pupils decide roles in their groups. Play the **Audio** again. Pause after each frame. Pupils repeat their section in role. Encourage pupils to say their lines with feeling. Pupils continue to practise the role play in their groups. Confident pupils can perform their role plays for the class.

- **Consolidation activity: *Spelling race***

Materials: 12 words from the unit written on a large piece of paper, each in jumbled letter order

Display the large piece of paper with the 12 jumbled words from the unit. In pairs, pupils race to unjumble the words and write them correctly on a piece of paper. Pairs swap papers. Check by eliciting the spelling for each word as you write it on the board. Pairs check and mark another pair's work. The pairs with the most correct words are the winners.

Unit 1

Page 10

- **Extension activity: *Family game***

Pupils draw their own family trees. Pupils work individually and write four statements about their family trees for others to respond to, e.g. *She's my aunt's daughter*. Working in groups of four, they take turns to place their family tree on the table and read out their statements. The other pupils individually write the answers. They get one point for each correct answer. When all four pupils have had a turn, the pupil with the most correct answers is the winner of the group.

- **Consolidation activity: *True or false***

Materials: A long piece of tape

You will need space for this activity. Draw a line or place a piece of tape across the centre of the room. Pupils stand on one side of the line. When you say a sentence which is true, they don't move. If it's false, they jump to the other side of the line. Pupils who make a mistake are out. Continue until you have a small group of winners. Ideas for sentences: *A helicopter can fly. A bus hasn't got wheels. Planes can't fly. A bike has got two wheels. Stella's mum is Mrs Star. Simon's Grandpa Star's granddaughter. Simon hasn't got an uncle.*

Page 11

- **Consolidation activity: *Questions and answers***

Pupils write the questions and answers from Pupil's Book Activity 3 in their notebooks.

- **Extension activity: *Chant***

Teach the following chant to pupils. They make an enclosing motion with their arms when chanting *We're all family.* Divide the class into four groups. Each group chants a verse. Groups swap verses. Repeat.

Uncles, aunts,
Parents, children,
We're all family.
Yes, we are.
We've got grandparents,
One, two, three, four.
We've got grandparents,
Yes, we have.

Sons and daughters,
Mums and dads,
We're all family.
Yes, we are.
They've got grandchildren,
One, two, three, four.
They've got grandchildren,
Yes, they have.

Page 12

- **Consolidation activity: *Catch and say***

Materials: Scrunched-up balls of paper (one for each group)

Demonstrate the activity first. Say, e.g. *I've got an apple*. Pupil A says, e.g. *I want to eat it!* Pupil A makes another statement, e.g. *I've got a camera.* Pupil B says, e.g. *I want to take a photo!* Make groups of 6–8 pupils. Each group stands in a circle. Give a scrunched-up ball of paper to one pupil in each group. This pupil starts. He/She makes a statement using *I've got* and throws the ball to another pupil in the group. This pupil responds making a statement with *I want to*. The same pupil then makes another statement using *I've got* and throws the ball to another pupil in the circle. The game continues in the same way.

Page 13

- **Consolidation activity: *Spelling game***

Draw a 3 x 3 grid on the board and stick a different coloured square in each one. Pupils close their books. Make two teams: A and B. Team A choose a colour. They must spell it correctly. If they do, remove the colour and place a X in the square. If they don't, leave the colour in the square. Repeat for team B, but draw a O in the square for them. The first team to get a line of X or O is the winner.

Page 14

- **Consolidation activity: *Plate mingle***

Materials: A4 paper or paper plate (one sheet/plate for each pupil)

Draw a big plate/circle on the board (draw a knife and fork either side for clarity or bring in a plate). Draw (or show) your favourite food on the plate and say *I love eating vegetables / I like eating salad / I enjoy eating ice cream*, for example. Give pupils a piece of A4 paper (or a paper plate) to draw a plate on and tell pupils to draw and label their favourite food. Once pupils have finished, ask them to mingle with their plates, showing, sharing and discussing. Tell pupils you'll watch the **Video** now to see what the family are eating.

- **Extension activity: *Stop!***

Pupils work in groups of four, using the picture from Activity Book Activity 3. Demonstrate the activity for the class. One pupil starts describing the picture and makes a deliberate mistake. The pupil in the group who hears it says *Stop!* and continues the description. He/She makes a deliberate mistake and another pupil calls *Stop!* The game continues. Pupils each get a point for calling *Stop!* when there is a mistake and lose a point for calling *Stop!* when there isn't. Check the winner(s) from each group.

Page 15

- **Extension activity: *Role play***

Make groups of three. Elicit from pupils who the three characters in the story are (Lock, Key, lady). Do the role play as for the page 9 Extension activity.

- **Consolidation activity: *Guess who***

Materials: Family flashcards

Hold one of the family flashcards so the class can't see it. Describe the person in the picture, e.g. *It's a man. He's got straight hair. He's got brown hair.* Pupils guess by putting up their hands. The pupil who guesses correctly comes to the front, chooses a family flashcard and describes it in the same way (hidden from the class). Repeat with all the family flashcards.

Page 16

- **Extension activity: *Measure the teacher***

Ask *How tall am I?* Have pupils guess your height in centimetres. Then help them to measure you. Stand with your back to the board and mark your height.

Encourage pupils to say how you can find the measurement with measuring tape or rulers. Point out the units of measurement on the ruler, metre stick or measuring tape. Show pupils how to measure from the floor to the mark to find your height.

Page 17

- **Extension activity 1:** ***Creating maths sentences***

Pupils write their own maths sentence using the chart in Pupil's Book Activity 4 as a guide. Then put pupils into pairs. They read their maths sentences aloud for their partner to write. Then they check their answers.

- **Extension activity 2:** ***Word train***

Materials: Measuring tools, e.g. rulers and tape measures
Give pupils time to measure other objects in the classroom. Mingle with pupils and ask about their findings.

Unit 2

Page 18

- **Consolidation activity 1:** ***Chain game***

Write *Country* on the board and elicit positive things about living there, e.g. *There are lots of trees. It's quiet. I can swim in the river.* Draw a circle around *Country* and build a mind map of the ideas. Do the same for *Town*. Accept and encourage ideas from pupils. Say *I like living in the country. It's quiet.* Invite a pupil to continue (using the prompts on the board), e.g. *I like living in the country. It's quiet and I can play in the garden.* Continue the chain by asking pupils at random. Pupils can't repeat the ideas. Start another chain about *Town* in the same way.

Pupils copy the mind maps into their notebooks.

- **Consolidation activity 2:** ***Match the word***

Materials: Home flashcards, Unit 2 word cards
Display the home flashcards on one side of the board, at a height pupils can reach. Elicit the words. Display the word cards for Unit 2 on the other side of the board, in random order. Call a volunteer to the board.

Say *Make a pair.* The pupil moves the correct word card next to one of the flashcards. Check with the class. Elicit the spelling. Repeat with the rest of the flashcards.

Page 19

- **Consolidation activity:** ***Letter chant***

Do a letter chant with the class, e.g.

Teacher: *Give me an 'f'* Pupils: *f*
Teacher: *Give me an 'l'* Pupils: *l*
Teacher: *Give me an 'o'* Pupils: *o*
Teacher: *Give me an 'o'* Pupils: *o*
Teacher: *Give me an 'r'* Pupils: *r*
Teacher: *What have you got?* Pupils: *floor*

Tell pupils to think of other words on the same topic. Give them time to prepare. Invite pupils in turn to the front to lead the chant. They can have the word written to help them.

- **Extension activity:** ***My house/flat***

Pupils work individually. They copy the picture of their house/flat from Activity Book Activity 2. They label their picture. Pupils work in pairs. Pupil A reads his/her text and Pupil B looks at A's picture to check. OR Pupils work in groups of four. They place the pictures face down on the table and mix them around. Pupils turn one over. They take turns to read their texts aloud for the others to guess which picture is theirs.

Page 20

- **Consolidation activity 1:** ***Meera says …***

Play a game of Meera says … to review colours. Say, e.g. *Meera says hold up a blue pen* (pupils hold up a blue pen). Say, e.g. *Point to a white sock* (pupils don't point). Continue reviewing the colours, as well as classroom objects.

- **Consolidation activity 2:** ***Word lines***

Eight pupils come to the front of the class. Whisper a word from the unit to each pupil. They stand in a line in alphabetical order. They say their words in order and the class checks. Repeat with different pupils and some (though not all) different words.

Page 21

- **Consolidation activity:** ***Whisper and write***

Make four teams. Teams line up facing the board. Whisper a different number between *11* and *100* to the pupils at the front of each team. Pupils whisper it back along the line and the pupil at the back comes and writes it on the board. Award one point for writing the number correctly (in words, not as a figure). Pupils from the front go to the back of the line. Repeat with different numbers.

Page 22

- **Consolidation activity:** ***Street number sums***

Materials: Sticky notes or small pieces of paper (one per pupil)
Give pupils a sticky note (or small piece of paper) each and tell them to write their house number on it. Ask pupils to stand up and arrange themselves in a line in order of the numbers from low to high as though they were a street. Say, e.g. *Who lives at 3 + 4?* and invite pupils to look and say. With large classes you can put pupils into groups for this task.

- **Extension activity:** ***ee and y words***

On a piece of paper, pupils write the letter *y* on one side at the top and the letters *ee* on the other side at the top. Underneath the *y* pupils write the /i/ sound words, and under the *ee* pupils write the /iː/ sound words. In pairs, pupils say a sound and their partner says a word from the list with that sound and then swap over roles.

Page 23

- **Extension activity 1:** ***Read and draw***

Pupils draw a picture of the monster in the basement, as Mrs Potts describes it. They add their own features and then write a description. Confident pupils read their descriptions to the class and show their pictures.

- **Extension activity 2:** ***Role play***

Make groups of three. Elicit from pupils who the three characters in the story are (Lock, Key, Mrs Potts). Do the role play as for the page 9 Extension activity.

Page 24

- **Consolidation activity:** ***Describe and guess***

Describe one of the types of homes, e.g. *It's in a big tree.* Encourage pupils to call out the type of home: *A tree house.* Do the same with other types of homes. In small groups, pupils describe and guess the homes.

- **Extension activity:** ***Draw and guess***

Pupils take turns drawing and guessing features from the text.

Page 25

- **Consolidation activity:** ***Chain game***

Say *Let's create a dream bedroom together.* Suggest one feature of the bedroom, e.g. *In our dream bedroom, there's a bed on stilts.* Invite a pupil to repeat what you've said and add an extra feature, e.g. *In our dream bedroom, there's a bed on stilts and a spiral staircase up to the bed.* Continue in the same way, with each pupil repeating the list and adding an extra feature each time. Encourage pupils to help each other when they get stuck or forget a feature in the list.

Review Units 1 and 2

Page 26

- **Consolidation activity:** ***Sing a song***

Sing one of the songs or chants from Units 1 and 2 with the class.

Page 27

- **Consolidation activity:** ***Play a game***

Play one of the team games from Units 1 and 2 with the class.

Unit 3

Page 28

- **Extension activity:** ***Clocks***

Materials: A paper plate, a butterfly clip and card for every pupil, one clock already made with the numbers on the clock face

Show pupils your clock. Set and reset the hands and elicit the time. Hand out the plates, clips and card. Pupils cut out the hands, write the numbers on the plate and attach the hands. In pairs, they take turns to set their clocks and say *What's the time?* Pupils write their names on their clocks. Put them in a safe place.

- **Consolidation activity:** ***Mime***

Pupils take turns to come and mime their daily routines. Pupils do the complete mime. Then the class says the actions in the right order, e.g. *Lara wakes up. Then she has a shower …* The pupil who mimed says *Wrong* if the class make a mistake.

Page 29

- **Consolidation activity 1:** ***What's the time, Mr Wolf?***

You'll need a large space for this activity. Demonstrate the activity. One pupil (Mr Wolf) stands at one end of the room, facing the wall. The other pupils line up at the other end of the room. They creep forward so Mr Wolf doesn't hear. The aim is to reach Mr Wolf. Mr Wolf keeps turning round. When he does, pupils freeze. A pupil asks *What's the time, Mr Wolf?* Mr Wolf responds, e.g. *It's eight o'clock* and turns back to the wall. One time Mr Wolf responds *It's dinner time!* and runs to catch one of the pupils. Repeat with a new Mr Wolf.

- **Consolidation activity 2:** ***Set the time***

Materials: Clocks from previous lesson Extension activity. If you didn't make them, you need: a paper plate, a butterfly clip and card (for the hands) for every pupil. One clock already made with the numbers on the clock face

Hand out the clocks from the previous lesson. If you didn't use them, see page 28 Extension activity for instructions on how to make them.

Put pupils into groups of four. Each pupil secretly writes a list of six different times. One pupil calls out the different times, and the others set the time on their clocks. The first pupil each time to do it correctly wins a point. At the end of the game, the pupil in each group with the most points is the winner.

Page 30

- **Extension activity:** ***About me***

Draw the following table on the board. Elicit more actions and days/times and add them to the table. Elicit example sentences from pupils and write them on the board.

I	always	watch TV	after school.
	sometimes	do my homework	before school.
	never	go to the park	on Sunday mornings.

In their notebooks, pupils write six true sentences about what they do. Monitor and support if necessary.

- **Consolidation activity:** ***How often?***

Materials: (Optional) Three large cards with the words *never*, *sometimes* and *always* written on them

You will need space for this activity. Pupils stand up. Point to one corner of the classroom and say *Never.* Point to another corner and say *Sometimes.* Point to a third corner and say *Always.* Alternatively, stick large cards with the words *never, sometimes, always* on the walls in the appropriate corners if you wish. Call out an activity, e.g. *I go swimming on Tuesdays.* Pupils run to the corner which is true for them. Repeat with other activities on different days of the week.

Page 31

- **Extension activity:** ***Team quiz***

Divide the class into two teams. Draw a 3 x 3 grid on the board and number the squares *1–9.* Teams take turns. Team A chooses a number. Read out the appropriate question below. If they answer correctly, put a X in the square. Team B chooses another number. Read out the appropriate question. Put a O in their square if they answer correctly. The first team to get a line is the winner.

Questions (answers in brackets for your reference):

1 *How many days are there in a week?* (seven)
2 *Which two days are the weekend?* (Saturday and Sunday)
3 *Which days do we have English?* (answer will depend on your pupils' timetable)
4 *Which day comes before Saturday?* (Friday)
5 *Which two days have got eight letters?* (Thursday and Saturday)
6 *Spell 'Thursday'.* (Pupils spell the word aloud)
7 *Which day has got seven letters?* (Tuesday)
8 *Which days do you have maths?* (answer will depend on your pupils' timetable)
9 *Which day comes after Wednesday?* (Thursday)

Page 32

- **Extension activity 1:** ***Sound action sentences***

Look at the pictures and sentences from Pupil's Book Activity 2 together. Divide the class into two groups. Tell one group they are the /s/ sound and the other group they are the /ɪz/ sound. Read out the sentences, stopping at each word with one of the target sounds for the appropriate group to say and do the hand or arm action, e.g. Say *Owl …* Group /ɪz/ says *dances* and does the hand gesture for /ɪz/.

- **Extension activity 2:** ***Animal routines***

Materials: A4 paper (one sheet per pupil)

Ask pupils to choose one of the animals and the routine they created for them. Give each pupil a piece of A4 paper and ask them to create, illustrate and write about their chosen animal to show, share and display in class.

Page 33

- **Extension activity 1: *Role play***

Make groups of three. Elicit from pupils who the three characters in the story are (Lock, Key, Johnny). Do the role play as for the page 9 Extension activity.

- **Extension activity 2: *Interview***

Pupils work in pairs. They write a list of questions they would ask Lock and Key if they could interview them. Elicit some examples and write them on the board, e.g. *Do you like your job? What's inside your detective box? Who is the pet thief? What time do you usually have lunch?* Pairs work with pairs. They use their questions to role-play an interview, with one pair asking questions and the other pair pretending to be Lock and Key. Then they swap roles.

Page 34

- **Consolidation activity: *Sally's day***

Say *Sally describes her everyday routine.* Elicit some of the activities she mentions and list them on the board: *wake up, wash, get dressed, have breakfast, work, tidy up, exercise, read, watch films, look at the Earth.* Ask *Is Sally's day unusual?* Encourage pupils to explain their answers.

- **Extension activity: *Astronaut role play***

Pupils role-play being astronauts on the Space Station. Remind them to imagine that everything there floats.

Page 35

- **Consolidation activity: *Find the lie***

Pupils write three sentences about their day with times. Two sentences are true and one is false. In pairs, pupils read their sentences out loud. Their partner guesses which sentence is not true.

Unit 4

Page 36

- **Consolidation activity 1: *Listen and draw***

Pupils each secretly draw a High Street with five shops on each side. They label the shops. In pairs, they take turns to describe their street for their partner to draw. They look and compare.

- **Consolidation activity 2: *Patterns***

Elicit the city vocabulary and write it at random over the board (*bank, bus station, café, car park, cinema, hospital, library, market, shop, sports centre, supermarket, swimming pool, park*). In pairs, pupils sort the words by number of syllables and write them in columns in their notebooks. Elicit from the class. Pupils clap the rhythm of the two-, three- and four-syllable words (to check correct word stress).

Key: one syllable: bank, shop, park; two syllables: café, car park, library, market; three syllables: bus station, cinema, hospital, sports centre, swimming pool; four syllables: supermarket

Page 37

- **Consolidation activity 1: *True or false***

Say sentences about places in town to the class. Some are true and some are false, e.g. *You go to the market to buy clothes* (true). *You go to the park to borrow a book* (false). Play True or false as for the page 10 Consolidation activity.

- **Consolidation activity 2: *Hot seats***

Divide the class into two or three teams, depending on class size. Place one chair for each team at the front of the class, with its back to the board. A pupil from each team comes to sit on the chair. They mustn't look at the board. Write a place/shop from the lesson on the board, e.g. *Bus station.* Teams call out clues to their team member without using the word on the board, e.g. *You go here to get home. You can catch something from here.* The first pupil to guess wins a point for their team. Repeat with other pupils and other words. **Note:** This can be a noisy game, but it's productive noise!

Page 38

- **Extension activity 1: *Role play***

Materials: A large sheet of paper with the audio script for Pupil's Book Activity 1

Display the large sheet of paper with the audio script for Pupil's Book Activity 1. Make groups of seven. Pupils decide who they are. Pupils repeat their roles in chorus. Groups then practise the role play together with actions. More confident groups can perform theirs for the class.

- **Extension activity 2: *Word search***

Pupils work in pairs. They choose ten new words from the unit so far. They draw a 12 × 12 grid. They write the words under the grid. Then they write the letters of the words in the grid (horizontally or vertically) and fill the grid in with random letters.

Put pairs together to form groups of four. Pairs swap word searches with other pairs. They circle the words and then say each word in a sentence.

Page 39

- **Extension activity: *Crazy school***

Pupils work in fours. They write a list of six rules, using *must*, for a crazy school. Monitor to help and check. They read their rules to the class. The class votes for the best crazy list.

Page 40

- **Consolidation activity 1: *Word tracing game***

Put pupils in pairs, A and B. Ask 'B's to close their books and turn their back on their partner. Ask 'A's to pick an /eə/ sound word from the ▶ **Video** and write it on Pupil B's back for B to guess and say. Then pairs swap roles.

- **Consolidation activity 2: *Sound mini-book***

Materials: A4 paper (one sheet per pupil)

Give pupils a piece of A4 paper each. With the piece of paper placed horizontally, make three vertical folds to create a mini-book with four inside pages. On the cover, they write the title: *-ere, -ear and -air words.* On the first inside page, pupils write the *-ere* words they know. On the second page, pupils write the *-ear* words. On the third page, pupils write the *-air* words. On the final page, pupils use the words to write their own rhyme or sentences. Invite volunteers to share their rhymes/sentences with the class.

Page 41

- **Extension activity: *Role play***

Make groups of four. Elicit from pupils who the four characters in the story are (Lock, Key, Mrs Potts, her friend). Do the role play as for the page 9 Extension activity.

- **Consolidation activity: *Mime game***

Pupils work in groups of four. They take it in turns to mime actions for different places in the city. The other pupils in the group guess. The pupil who mimed has to say what he/she was doing in the mime after their friends guess the right place. Encourage them to think of different mimes from the usual ones. Groups choose the best ideas from their group and mime them to the class.

Page 42

- **Extension activity:** ***Shop symbols***

Materials: Realia from shops pupils know of

Provide pupils with realia from shops they know of, e.g. a photo of a store front, a catalogue, an advert. Brainstorm types of shops and write them on the board. Draw a symbol for each type of shop, such as a book for a bookshop or a flower for a garden shop.

Page 43

- **Consolidation activity:** ***Odd word out***

Write two nouns and a verb or adjective on the board, e.g. *pets, toy, draw*. Ask if each word is a noun, and cross out the word that is not a noun (draw). Do the same with other words pupils know, writing two nouns and one verb or adjective each time, for pupils to identify which word is not a noun.

Review Units 3 and 4

Page 44

- **Consolidation activity:** ***Sing a song***

Sing one of the songs or do one of the chants from Units 3 and 4 with the class.

Page 45

- **Consolidation activity:** ***Play the game***

Materials: Envelopes of cards (Photocopiable activity 4a)

Hand out Photocopiable activity 4a (see *Teacher Resources*) to each pupil. If they have not played the game previously, they cut out the cards. They colour one small part of each card so they know which are theirs after the game.

If pupils played before, hand them out their envelopes of cards. Hold up each one in turn and elicit a sentence, e.g. *dirty shoes – You must clean your shoes.* Eight cards trigger a response with *must* (the untidy bed, hungry dog, dirty shoes, untidy desk, long hair, pile of letters, dirty plates, and jacket on the ground) and four with *can* (TV, park gates, ice cream, cinema). Make sure pupils know the difference between the sentence for each type of card (e.g. *bed – You must make your bed*, but *cinema – You can go to the cinema*). Pupils play in pairs. They put their cards face down on the table and mix them around. They take turns. One pupil turns over two cards and makes the sentence for each one. If the cards are the same, he/she keeps them. If not, he/she turns them face down again. At the end, the pupil with the most pairs is the winner.

If you do not wish to use the cards again, pupils stick them into their notebooks and write a sentence under each one. Monitor and check for accuracy and appropriacy.

Unit 5

Page 46

- **Extension activity:** ***Role play***

Materials: A large sheet of paper with the Pupil's Book Activity 2 dialogue

Divide the class into groups of three. Display the large sheet of paper with the Pupil's Book Activity 2 dialogue on the board. Pupils choose roles in their groups. Read the dialogue aloud with pupils in role. Pupils practise the dialogue, including miming the actions. More confident groups can change parts of the dialogue. Call for volunteers to perform their dialogues to the class.

- **Consolidation activity:** ***Label it***

Pupils draw a picture of themselves in their notebooks and label it with the words from Activity Book Activity 1.

Page 47

- **Extension activity 1:** ***Chant***

Teach the following chant to pupils. When they are confident with the words, make two groups: A and B. They do the chant as a dialogue and mime. Pupils swap roles. Substitute other illnesses. Pupils repeat the chant in small groups/pairs. Use this activity to review *hurts*.

A: *Hi. How are you?*
B: *I'm not well.*
A: *What's the matter?*
B: *I've got a stomach-ache.*
A: *Oh, poor you!*
B: *Yes, it hurts.*

- **Extension activity 2:** ***Draw and write***

Write one of the dialogues from Activity Book Activity 2 on the board. Erase words so it looks like this: *What's the matter? My _______ hurts. I can't _______ .*

Elicit various possibilities for the gaps so that the dialogue makes sense. Pupils choose how to complete the sentences, and draw a picture to illustrate the situation (using Activity Book Activity 2 pictures as a model). Fast finishers can write more dialogues.

Page 48

- **Extension activity:** ***Class rules***

Pupils develop their own class rules: two 'must', two 'mustn't'. They work in pairs and write four rules. Then pairs join pairs and they agree the best four. Elicit the rules from the groups, write them on the board and, as a class, agree the best six.

Page 49

- **Consolidation activity:** ***Do what I say …***

You need space for this game. Pupils stand up. Give instructions for pupils to follow, using imperatives / *mustn't*, e.g. *Walk slowly around the room. You mustn't touch anyone. Don't walk. You must stand still. Close your eyes. Touch your nose with one finger. Don't look! Open your eyes. Start hopping. You mustn't talk or laugh!*

- **Extension activity:** ***Consequences***

Materials: A4 paper (one sheet for each pupil)

Pupils work in groups of six. Hand out a piece of paper to each pupil. They make sure their friends don't see what they're writing. Tell pupils to write the person's name and where he/she is, e.g. *Jim's at school / on the bus / in bed / at home / in the cinema.* They fold the paper over to hide the writing and pass it to their left. Say *What's the matter?* They write on the new piece of folded paper, e.g. *He's got a cough*. They fold and pass the paper on again. Continue with the prompts: something he mustn't do, something he must do, something he can't do, how he feels. When pupils get their papers back, they open them and read the 'story' to their group. Elicit the best stories from groups.

Page 50

- **Consolidation activity:** ***Whisper and write***

Use the words for illnesses from the unit to play Whisper and write as for the page 21 Consolidation activity.

- **Extension activity:** ***Picture gallery***

Materials: A4 paper (one sheet per pupil)

Give each pupil a piece of paper. They each draw a person or group with an ailment. Stick the completed pictures up around the room. In pairs, pupils walk around the room, looking at the pictures and describing what they see, using *he's/she's/they've got* + illness.

Page 51

- **Extension activity: *Role play***

Make groups of four. Elicit from pupils who the four characters in the story are (Lock, Key, Miss Rich, the waiter). Do the role play as for the page 9 Extension activity.

- **Consolidation activity: *Play the game***

Materials: Envelopes of cards (Photocopiable activity 5)

Hand out Photocopiable activity 5 (see *Teacher Resources*) to each pupil. If you used it before, hand pupils their envelopes with their cards in. If you haven't used it before, tell pupils to cut out the cards. They make a dot or similar on the cards so they can identify their own at the end of the game. Elicit that the cards with words on are a different shape.

Demonstrate the game. Turn over a square card (with an illness on). Say a sentence, e.g. *I've got a cough.* A pupil turns over a triangular card. They make a sentence using the prompt word, e.g. *can – You can watch TV.* Check the examples for *can/can't* are permission, not ability. Keep the illness card and the word card. Repeat, with the pupil taking a square card and you taking a word card. Pupils play in pairs. They put all their cards face down on their desks and take turns to start. Monitor and help.

At the end of the game, elicit some of the pupils' sentences. If you do not wish to use the cards again, pupils stick the cards into their notebooks, writing some of the sentences and responses from their game.

Page 52

- **Consolidation activity: *Class survey***

Pupils role-play being ill and suggesting remedies from the text.

Page 53

- **Extension activity: *Silly remedies***

Materials: Dice (one per group)

Put pupils into small groups and give each group a die. Tell them they are going to make silly remedies. Write the numbers 1 to 6 on the board, and next to each number write:

1 *Jump up and down.*
2 *Count backwards. (10, 9, 8 …)*
3 *Spin in a circle.*
4 *Open and close your eyes three times.*
5 *Touch your tongue to your nose.*
6 *Dance!*

One pupil chooses an illness, e.g. sore throat. The next player says, *Help! I've got a sore throat.* The next player rolls the die and gives the advice on the board. The 'ill' player completes the task. Have them continue playing, until all pupils have tried a silly remedy. If you have time, groups can come up with their own six silly remedies and repeat the activity.

- **Consolidation activity: *Simon says***

Play Simon says with affirmative commands, e.g. *Close your eyes. Hop on one foot. Spin in a circle. Touch your nose.* Confident pupils can take a turn at being the caller. Make sure they use the imperative form of the verb when giving commands.

Unit 6

Page 54

- **Consolidation activity: *Spell it***

Materials: Country flashcards

Stick the country flashcards on the board. Letter them a–h. Pupils study the spellings of the words in their Pupil's Book for 30 seconds. They close their books. Say, e.g. *What's f?* Pupils respond. Ask them to spell it for you. Write the word under the picture. Repeat for the other pictures. Erase words that pupils found difficult and elicit the spellings again.

- **Extension activity: *Things I enjoy***

Brainstorm with pupils some of the things they enjoy/like/love doing in the country, using the key words from the lesson. Pupils write six sentences in their notebooks about themselves, e.g. *I enjoy going to the country for picnics. I love swimming in the river …*

Page 55

- **Consolidation activity: *True or false***

Say sentences about/from the story in the Pupil's Book and play *True or false* as for the page 10 Consolidation activity. Possible sentences: *Charlie, Lily and their grandmother are in the park. The blanket's between the river and the trees. They can't eat the bread. The ducks are eating the old bread.*

- **Extension activity: *Picture dictation***

Describe a scene to pupils. The first time, they just listen. The second time, they draw a picture. Pupils compare/check their pictures in groups.

> **Key:** (Possible answer)*There is a big field with a forest behind it. There's a tall tree in the field. Under the tree, two children (a girl and a boy) are sitting on a blanket. They are eating their picnic. Their parents are walking in the field near the forest. Next to the field there is a river. Some ducks are swimming in the river. A dog is swimming in the river too.*

Page 56

- **Consolidation activity: *Fill the gaps***

Write the second part of the audio script for Pupil's Book Activity 1 on the board (from 'Later' to the end). Miss out the new adjectives (as shown below). Pupils work in pairs to remember which word goes where. Play the **Audio**. Pupils listen and check. They write the text in their notebooks.

Simon's _____ and _____. He wants to eat.
Suzy's _____ and _____. She wants a drink.
Grandpa Star is catching a big, _____ fish. He's very _____.
Grandma Star's near the cows in the field. She's very _____.
She's drawing a baby cow. It's got _____ legs and it's very _____.
Stella isn't happy because her drawing's _____.
Mr Star's listening to the radio. His music is very _____.
Oh, yes! And finally, Mrs Star. She's sleeping because she's very _____.

- **Extension activity: *What's the situation?***

Elicit other situations and responses to add to the list in Activity Book Activity 2 (heavy bags – help; got a temperature – call the doctor; can't find a ruler – give you mine; end of the lesson – clean the board; lots of books – carry them). Write them on the board. Pupils work in pairs. They choose one of the situations (or another, with your approval). They practise miming it, e.g. one mimes carrying the heavy bags, and the other comes up and mimes taking them from the pupil's hands. This is all done in silence. Pupils take turns to perform their mimes. The rest of the class guess the situation and the suggestion.

Page 57

- **Consolidation activity: *Mime game***

Materials: The adjectives from this and the previous lesson written on small slips of paper, one for each pupil

Put the slips of paper with the adjectives on face down on your desk. In turn, pupils come to the front, take an adjective and mime it for the class to guess.

Page 58

- **Consolidation activity:** ***Rhyme orchestra***

Divide the class into four groups. Assign one sentence half from the Pupil's Book Activity 1 rhyme to each group. They take turns to say their lines. Conduct them like an orchestra, saying, e.g. *loud, quiet, fast, slow.*

- **Extension activity:** ***Writing rhymes***

Elicit other words pupils know with the /r/ sound and write them on the board. In pairs, pupils choose some of the /r/ words and use them to write their own rhymes. They read them out to the class. If you have time, pupils can illustrate their rhymes.

Page 59

- **Extension activity:** ***Role play***

Make groups of three. Elicit from pupils who the three characters in the story are (Lock, Key, Mrs Potts). Do the role play as for the page 9 Extension activity.

Page 60

- **Consolidation activity:** ***Word sort***

Write the following words in random order on the board: *tall buildings, many shops, pollution, animals, lots of trees, not many people.* In groups, pupils sort the words according to city or country. Each group adds one more word or phrase to each category.

- **Extension activity:** ***Murals***

In pairs, pupils design two murals – one to represent life in the city, and the other to represent life in the countryside.

Page 61

- **Consolidation activity:** ***Name game***

Form teams and ask them to stand in line at the board. Say a word (e.g. *chair*) or a name (e.g. *Australia*). The first pupil in each line writes it on the board. They should capitalise the names of people and places, but not the other words they hear. Teams get a point for correct capitalisation. Continue with the next player in line until everyone has had at least one turn. The team with the most points at the end wins.

Review Units 5 and 6

Page 62

- **Consolidation activity:** ***Sing a song***

Sing one of the songs or do one of the chants from Units 5 and 6 with the class.

Page 63

- **Consolidation activity:** ***Play a game***

Play one of the team games from Units 5 and 6 with the class. Let pupils choose which one.

Unit 7

Page 64

- **Extension activity:** ***Animal categories***

Draw three columns on the board and write an animal class at the top of each one: *mammals, birds, fish.* Write an example for each class underneath, using one from the animals in Activity Book Activity 1. Check understanding of *mammals*, etc. and elicit an example for mammal. Pupils work in pairs. They copy the columns into their notebooks and try to put the animals from Activity Book Activity 1 into the right categories. They can ask their friends for help. They can also add other animals they know. Check with the class and write the animals in the columns on the board.

Key: mammals: bat, bear, dolphin, kangaroo, panda, whale; birds: parrot; fish: shark

Page 65

- **Consolidation activity:** ***Whisper and draw***

Use the animal words to play Whisper and draw, as for the page 21 Consolidation activity, but pupils draw instead of write.

- **Extension activity:** ***Animal profiles***

Put pupils into groups according to the animals they wrote about for Activity Book Activity 2. If you have single pupils (the only one who wrote about, e.g. a giraffe), they can join another group. Play a game. Make statements. Pupils react accordingly in their groups, e.g. *Stand up if your animal can fly. Put your hands on your head if your animal can swim. Turn around if your animal is grey.* Use statements that pupils didn't use in their texts to make it more fun and challenging.

Page 66

- **Consolidation activity:** ***Sentences***

Write the adjectives from the Warmer on one side of the board. On the other side, elicit and write the names of classroom objects, e.g. *bag, desk, window, pencil, chair, book, ruler, eraser.*

Pupils work in pairs. They think of sentences, using the comparative adjectives and the objects. If possible, they use real objects to demonstrate. Go around the room eliciting the sentences. The class decides if they're correct. Pupils don't write their sentences. This is an oral activity. Check for correct pronunciation of *than.*

- **Extension activity:** ***Picture dictation***

Describe two (or more) simple pictures to pupils. They listen the first time. The second time they draw the pictures. They check their pictures in pairs. Elicit information about the pictures back from pupils to give them practice of the comparative forms. Possible descriptions: *1 There are two monkeys. One monkey is taller and fatter than the other monkey. The smaller monkey is brown. 2 There is a shark and a whale. The shark is longer than the whale and its teeth are bigger. The whale is fatter than the shark.*

Page 67

- **Extension activity 1:** ***Our song***

Elicit some more ideas for verses of the **Song** from pupils, e.g. *swimming – dolphin, flying – mountain.* Pupils work in groups and write the verse of the **Song**. Groups take turns to perform their verses for the class. Groups write their verse in their notebooks and illustrate it.

- **Extension activity 2:** ***Finding out***

Write the following questions on the board. Change or add your own questions as appropriate. Find out:

1 Who is taller?
2 Who is older?
3 Whose hair is longer?
4 Whose bag is heavier?
5 Whose pencil case is bigger?
6 Whose fingers are longer?

Pupils work in pairs. They compare (stand back to back), ask (birthdays), measure (hair), etc. to find out the answers. Pupils write the results in their notebooks, e.g. *Jenny is taller than me. Jenny's hair is longer than my hair.* Provide model sentences on the board if necessary. Elicit some of the results from pupils.

Page 68

- **Consolidation activity:** ***Letter race***

Materials: Four large pieces of paper or card, each with one of the spelling patterns from the lesson

Stick the four letter cards on the walls around the room. Call out a word from the **Video** with one of the four spelling patterns. Pupils say the word and the sound and run to the correct letter card.

With little or no space to run to the cards, ask pupils to point to the correct card instead.

Page 69

- **Extension activity 1: *Role play***

Put pupils into pairs. Elicit who the two characters in the story are (Lock, Key). Do the role play as for the page 9 Extension activity.

- **Extension activity 2: *Animal quiz***

Divide the class into nine groups. Demonstrate the activity first for the whole class. Choose a wild animal which is not from this unit, e.g. *tiger*. With the help of pupils, build up a description on the board, e.g. *I'm thinking of an animal. It's bigger than a dog, but smaller than an elephant. It's got four legs and a tail. It's orange and black.* Whisper to each group the name of one of the wild animals from this unit. Give the groups numbers and remember which number is writing about which animal. Pupils write a description of their animal on a piece of paper, following the model on the board. They put their group number at the top. Collect the pieces of paper and display them around the room. In their groups, pupils move around the room and guess each animal, writing the number and the animal on a piece of paper. Groups swap answer sheets with other groups. Check with the class by reading out each description and eliciting the answer (not from the group who wrote it). The group with the most correct answers is the winner.

Page 70

- **Consolidation activity: *Guessing game***

Put pupils in groups of three or four. One person in each group chooses one of the animals from the lesson. They can choose to draw, mime or describe the animal for the others to guess. Pupils swap roles so that everyone has a turn.

- **Extension activity: *Butterfly art***

Materials: Black card (one sheet per pupil), orange paper, scissors, glue

Make monarch butterflies with pupils. They fold a small sheet of black card in half. Help them draw and cut out wings so that the paper unfolds to be a simple butterfly shape. They then cut out pieces of orange paper to make the butterfly's orange markings. Ask *Have monarch butterflies got camouflage?* (no, their bright colours show that they're poisonous to birds). Make sure pupils write their names on their butterflies. Display the butterflies around the room.

Page 71

- **Consolidation activity: *Ball toss***

Materials: A small ball

Point to one of the adjectives on the board, e.g. *soft*, and make a sentence with it, e.g. *Cats are soft.* Throw a small ball to a pupil and point to an adjective on the board. The pupil with the ball makes a sentence with that adjective. Other pupils can help if necessary. Then the pupil throws the ball to another pupil. Point to a new word for the next pupil to make a sentence. Continue in the same way with several pupils.

- **Extension activity: *Word sort***

Brainstorm other adjectives pupils know and write them on the board. Put pupils into small groups. They sort the adjectives into categories, e.g. positive or negative, colours, size, emotions.

Unit 8

Page 72

- **Consolidation activity: *Sort the words***

Write the following words at random across the board: *cloud, cloudy, hot, cold, sun, sunny, rain, rainbow, snow, snowy, wet, wind, windy.* Make two columns. Write *hot* at the top of one and *wind* at the top of the other. Elicit another example for each column (adjectives in the first column / nouns in the second). Pupils work in pairs. They copy the columns into their notebooks and then complete them. They check in pairs. Check with the class. Elicit sentences, using the words to check pupils understand the difference.

Key: adjectives: (hot), cloudy, cold, sunny, snowy, wet, windy; nouns: (wind), cloud, sun, rain, rainbow, snow

Page 73

- **Consolidation activity 1: *Our weather***

Pupils copy the weather symbols from Pupil's Book Activity 1 into their notebooks and write sentences underneath, e.g. *It's snowing. / There's a rainbow.* They then write a sentence to describe what the weather is like now, e.g. *Today it's raining and very windy.* They can draw a picture if there is time.

- **Consolidation activity 2: *Matching game***

If you didn't do Photocopiable activity 8, hand out the six weather symbols to each pupil (see *Teacher Resources*). They cut them out, colour them and mark each card so that they know which are theirs. Pupils work in groups of four. They place all their cards face down on the table and mix them up. They take turns to turn over two cards and say what the weather is, e.g. *It's windy. It's cloudy.* If it's a match, the pupil takes the two cards. If not, the pupil turns them face down again and the next player has a turn. The player with the most pairs of cards in their group at the end of the game is the winner.

Page 74

- **Extension activity 1: *How many sentences?***

Teach/Review *wasn't/weren't* using the Grammar reference section of the Pupil's Book (see page 87). Put pupils into pairs. Give the sentence sections to each pair. Set a time limit. Pupils make as many sentences as they can using the words. They write each sentence they make in their notebooks. Pairs swap notebooks. Elicit the sentences and write them on the board. Pairs correct each other's work. The pair(s) with the most correct sentences is/are the winner(s).

- **Extension activity 2: *Secret messages***

Write the secret message from Activity Book Activity 6 on the board. Elicit ideas for other messages from pupils, using the same model. Pupils work individually. They use the same code as in the Activity Book to write their own message to their friends. Pupils swap messages and decode them.

Page 75

- **Consolidation activity 1: *Weather snakes***

Pupils work in pairs. They make weather snakes (word snakes of weather words and associated clothes). They swap weather snakes with another pair and find each other's words. Elicit the words from the class to find out how many words they used all together.

- **Consolidation activity 2: *Living language***

Materials: Questions and statements from different parts of the lesson using *was/were/wasn't/weren't*. Cut each sentence into single words. Include the question mark on a separate piece of paper, e.g. *Where // were // you // on // Sunday // evening // ?*

Invite groups of pupils to come to the front of the class. You need the same number of pupils as there are words in one of your questions/sentences. Give each pupil a part of the question/ sentence. They arrange themselves in the order of the question/ sentence. They say it to the class and the class confirms if it's right or not. Repeat. Pupils can work in groups. They write questions or sentences which they cut up and give to another group to arrange in order in the same way.

Page 76

- **Consolidation activity: *Guessing game***

Play a word game to review words from the unit and from *Kid's Box 3*. In pairs, pupils choose a word they learnt in this or a previous unit. Start the game. Write dashes on the board in place of the letters of your word. Draw a stick person at the top of eight steps which lead down to the water and a shark's mouth. Pairs guess letters. Write them in if they are in the word. If not, write them on the board and move the person one step down for each incorrect guess. The pair of pupils who guess correctly repeat the game with their word.

- **Extension activity: *Chain game***

Say to pupils *It's sunny so I packed a T-shirt.* Ask a pupil to continue by repeating your sentence and adding an extra item of clothing. The item of clothing should be suitable for the weather, e.g. *It's sunny so I packed a T-shirt and shorts.* Divide the class into four groups. One group start with *It's sunny*, another group with *It's rainy*, another group with *It's cloudy* and the final group with *It's snowing*. Groups play together. After a few minutes, give each group a different weather word to start with.

Page 77

- **Extension activity 1: *Role play***

Make groups of four. Elicit from pupils who the four characters in the story are (Lock, Key, Robin Motors, police officer). Do the role play as for the page 9 Extension activity.

- **Extension activity 2: *What was the weather like?***

Materials: Weather flashcards, Photocopiable activity 8, sticky tack

Elicit the weather words from pupils using the flashcards. Pupils take out the materials from Photocopiable activity 8. If you haven't used this activity before, hand out a copy of Photocopiable activity 8 to each pupil (see *Teacher Resources*). They colour the weather symbols at the bottom of the page and cut them out. Hand out the sticky tack. Pupils work in pairs. It's best if they put a bag upright between them so they can't see each other's picture. Pupil A secretly sticks the weather symbols where they want on the picture. Pupil B asks questions about the weather using *was*, e.g. *What was the weather like on your holiday in the mountains?* and sticks the appropriate weather symbols on his/her picture according to Pupil A's replies. When they have finished, they compare pictures. They take the weather symbols off and repeat, with Pupil B sticking the symbols and Pupil A asking. If time, pupils stick the symbols back on their picture and write sentences describing the weather, using *was*, e.g. *In the mountains it was cold and snowy.*

Page 78

- **Extension activity: *Musical instruments***

Allow pupils to investigate realia that can be used to make sounds, such as beads in a can, beans, sand, glasses and spoons, rubber bands. Encourage pupils to think of ways to imitate nature sounds with the items.

Page 79

- **Consolidation activity 1: *Board slap***

Write the names of all the instruments that have come up in this and the previous lesson at random across the board. Play Board slap as for the page 5 Consolidation activity 1 Find the number.

- **Consolidation activity 2: *Date, time or place?***

Write *Date, time or place?* on the board. Point out the date, time and place in the invitation. Tell pupils you are going to write some information on the board, e.g. *after school*. Pupils call out whether it is a date, time or place (time). Repeat with several other examples.

Review Units 7 and 8

Page 80

- **Consolidation activity: *Sing a song***

Sing one of the songs or do one of the chants from Units 7 and 8 with the class.

Page 81

- **Consolidation activity: *Play a game***

Play one of the team games from Units 7 and 8 with the class. Let pupils choose which one.

Values

Page 82

- **Extension activity: *Have one of mine***

Materials: Two pieces of paper per pupil

Hand out two pieces of paper to each pupil. Tell pupils to draw a toy they know the word for in English. They need to draw the same toy on both pieces of paper (e.g. two robots). Draw two pictures of a toy yourself. Call a volunteer to the front of the class with his/her pictures. Show the class your pictures, look disappointed and say, e.g. *I've got two cars.* Encourage the pupil to show his/her pictures and make a similar sentence (e.g. *I've got two robots*). Say *I haven't got a robot.* Elicit *Don't worry. I've got two* or *Have one of mine.* Say *Thank you!* Swap pictures with the volunteer, so you each have two different toys.

Pupils work in small groups to compare their pictures, swap and share in the same way. Monitor and encourage them to use language from the lesson (e.g. *Do you want my doll? That's a great idea. / Yes, please.*)

Page 83

- **Extension activity 1: *Act it out***

Play the **Audio** for Pupil's Book Activity 1 for pupils to act out in pairs.

- **Extension activity 2: *Make a poster***

Materials: A large piece of paper for each group

Write the title *Love your city* on the board. Brainstorm ways to keep your town/city clean and beautiful and write notes on the board. Pupils work in groups of three or four. They write rules using the notes on the board and ideas of their own. They can use the sentences in Pupil's Book Activity 2 as a model. Monitor, help with language and check the sentences. Hand each group a large piece of paper. They write the heading *Love your city* and copy their rules onto the paper. They can add pictures and signs to make a poster. Display the posters around the school/classroom.

Page 84

- **Extension activity: *Act it out***

Play the **Audio** for Pupil's Book Activity 1 for pupils to act out in pairs and threes.

- **Consolidation activity: *What do you say?***

Materials: Pieces of paper, each with a different phrase on from the following list: *Don't touch the ball. / Well done! / What's the matter? / Shall I help you get on the horse? / It's not OK to be angry. / Don't be angry.*

Shake hands with a confident pupil as if you have just finished playing a match together and say *You win. Well done!* Encourage the pupil to respond *Thank you*. Repeat with a different pupil, this time saying *You're really good at tennis* (the pupil responds *Thank you. You're good at tennis too.*). Mime being in pain and say *Ow!* to elicit *What's the matter? / Can I help you?*

Give a pupil a piece of paper with a phrase on. He/She stands at the front of the class and says a sentence or does a mime to get the rest of the class to say what is on the paper (e.g. if the paper says *Don't touch the ball!* the pupil mimes picking up a football and then looking as if he/she has done something wrong). Pupils put up their hands to guess. When a pupil says the correct sentence, he/she stands up and takes the next piece of paper.

Page 85

- **Extension activity 1: *Act it out***

Play the **Audio** for Pupil's Book Activity 1 for pupils to act out in pairs.

- **Extension activity 2: *Class poster***

Write the title *Help the world* on the board. Brainstorm suggestions for helping the environment and write them on the board as sentences, e.g. *Walk to school. Turn off the lights when you leave a room. Take bags when you go shopping. Catch a bus.* Pupils work in pairs or small groups. Assign a sentence from the board to each pair/group. They design a sign or a picture to illustrate their sentence. Monitor and ask about / help with ideas. Pupils write the sentence below their picture as a caption. Put all the signs/pictures together and display them on a class poster. You could ask different pupils to make a large letter each to make the title *Help the world* for the poster.

Exams folder

Page 88

- **Extension activity: *Mime and guess***

In groups, pupils mime an activity. Other members of the group guess. The person who guesses first, mimes the next activity. (Ensure every group member has had a turn miming by the end of the allotted time.)

Page 89

- **Extension activity: *False descriptions***

In pairs, pupils choose a picture in their Pupil's Book. They take turns to make up false descriptions and reject their partner's statement, e.g. with the picture on page 7:

Pupil A: Vicky's in a pink car.
Pupil B: No, she isn't. She's in a red car!
Pupil A: Max is flying a plane.
Pupil B: No, he isn't. He's flying a kite!

Page 90

- **Extension activity: *Chain game***

Play a colour memory chain game. Say a sentence with *I like* + colour + object, e.g. *I like blue ice cream.* Invite a pupil to say your sentence and add another object in a different colour, e.g. *I like blue ice cream and orange pandas.* The next pupil adds another item, e.g. *I like blue ice cream, orange pandas and green clouds.*

Pupils continue the game in small groups.

Extra support Pupils can write a list of the colours and tick them off as they are used.

Page 91

- **Extension activity: *Matching game***

Materials: Sheets of card in two different colours (one sheet of each colour per group)

In groups, pupils make a matching Pelmanism game. Give each group two sheets of different coloured card (ideally one is white for picture drawing). Pupils cut each card into six squares. They think of six words they will write the definition for. They draw a picture on a white card square and write the corresponding definition on a coloured card square.

Groups swap their cards with another group. They spread out the pictures on one side of their desk and the words on the other, face down. Pupils take turns to turn over a picture and a word. If they match, they win the set. If there is no match, they replace the cards in the same position. The winner is the pupil with the most sets.

Page 92

- **Extension activity: *What's the word?***

In groups, pupils find five words from their books, and write them on separate pieces of paper. On the back of the paper, they write the definition for the word. Then pupils form new groups, each including one person from the original group. In their new groups, one pupil reads out a definition and the first person in the group to say the correct word keeps the paper. Continue until all the definitions have been read. The winner is the pupil who has the most pieces of paper at the end.

Page 93

- **Extension activity: *Sentence puzzles***

Materials: Ten short factual sentences written on card, cut up into individual words and placed in envelopes numbered 1 to 10

Write ten short factual sentences on card (e.g. *Dolphins are smaller than whales.*) in large text. Each sentence should start with a capital letter and end with a full stop.

Cut up each sentence into words and place them in envelopes numbered 1 to 10.

Pupils work in groups of three. They write the numbers *1–10* down the left side of a piece of paper. One pupil from each group asks you for a numbered envelope (*Can I have number three, please?*). The group orders the words into a sentence and then writes the sentence next to the corresponding number on their paper. The group places the words back in the envelope, returns the envelope and asks for another one.

Extra challenge Pupils can race to write all ten sentences correctly.

Page 94

- **Extension activity: *Comparing bedrooms***

In pairs, pupils describe their bedroom. They try to find four similarities and four differences between their rooms.

Page 95

- **Extension activity: *Story-telling***

Pupils talk in pairs about the story they created during Activity 2.

Acknowledgments

The authors and publishers acknowledge the following sources of copyright material and are grateful for the permissions granted. While every effort has been made, it has not always been possible to identify the sources of all the material used, or to trace all copyright holders. If any omissions are brought to our notice, we will be happy to include the appropriate acknowledgments on reprinting and in the next update to the digital edition, as applicable.

Screenshots

Screenshots taken from Kid's Box 3rd Edition Pupil's book and Activity book Level 3.

Key: p = page

Photography

All the photos are sourced from Getty Images.

p7: gorodenkoff /iStock/Getty Images Plus. **p14:** DGL images/iStock/Getty Images Plus; Shironosov/iStock/Getty Images Plus; **p17:** Wavebreakmedia/iStock/Getty Images Plus.

The following photos are from other sources:

p19: the Authors (Caroline Nixon and Michael Tomlinson) and Liane Grainger.

Illustration

Blooberry Design (source Pronk Media Inc.), Pronk Media Inc.

Design and Typeset

Blooberry Design.

Freelance Author

Hilary Ratcliff.